NINETEENTH CENTURY STUDIES

Nineteenth Century Studies

COLERIDGE TO MATTHEW ARNOLD

BASIL WILLEY

HARPER TORCHBOOKS ♦ The Academy Library
HARPER & ROW, PUBLISHERS
NEW YORK

NINETEENTH CENTURY STUDIES

Printed in the United States of America.

All rights reserved.

This book was originally published in 1949 by Columbia University Press, New York, and by Chatto and Windus, Ltd., London. It is here reprinted by arrangement.

First HARPER TORCHBOOK edition published 1966 by
Harper & Row, Publishers, Incorporated
49 East 33rd Street
New York, New York 10016.

This book is sold subject to the condition that it shall not, by way of trade, be lent, re-sold, hired out, or otherwise disposed of without the publisher's consent, in any form of binding or cover other than that in which it is published.

Contents

Preface   *Page* vii

Chapter I. SAMUEL TAYLOR COLERIDGE

    I. Introductory   1
    II. The Early Coleridge   4
    III. Imagination and Fancy   10
    IV. Reason and Understanding   27
    V. Religion and Morality   31
    VI. The Interpretation of Scripture   38
    VII. The Constitution of Church and State   44

Chapter II. THOMAS ARNOLD

    I. The 'Eminent Victorian'   51
    II. The Idea of a Christian Society   52
    III. Arnold and the Oxford Movement   60
    IV. Religion and Education   63
    V. Scriptural Interpretation   64
    VI. Arnold and the Lake District   69

Chapter III. NEWMAN AND THE OXFORD MOVEMENT   73

Chapter IV. THOMAS CARLYLE

    I. Introductory   102
    II. Carlyle's Religion   105
    III. Carlyle's Moral and Political Ideas   126

Chapter V. A NOTE ON BENTHAM'S *DEONTOLOGY*   132

Chapter VI. JOHN STUART MILL

    I. The *Autobiography*   141

CONTENTS

Chapter VI. II. Logic: 'Ethology' and Sociology — *Page* 149
   III. The *Principles of Political Economy* — 158
   IV. *On Liberty* — 163
   V. *Utilitarianism* — 170
   VI. *Three Essays on Religion* — 176

Chapter VII. AUGUSTE COMTE
   I. The *Philosophie Positive* — 187
   II. The *Politique Positive* and 'The Religion of Humanity' — 194

Chapter VIII. GEORGE ELIOT: HENNELL, STRAUSS AND FEUERBACH
   I. Introductory — 204
   II. Hennell's *Inquiry* — 207
   III. Strauss's *Life of Jesus* — 220
   IV. Feuerbach's *Essence of Christianity* — 227

Chapter IX. GEORGE ELIOT, CONCLUSION — 237

Chapter X. MATTHEW ARNOLD
   I. Introductory — 251
   II. *Culture and Anarchy* — 254
   III. Arnold's Religious Writings — 263

INDEX — 285

Preface

IN choosing a title for this book I have purposely avoided the word 'Background'—partly because I am tired of it, but still more because the book itself makes no pretence to any sort of completeness. It comprises a group of inter-connected studies in certain nineteenth century writers who have interested me during the past eight years (some of them for much longer). I hope, indeed, that the book may be found to have some unity: I offer it mainly as a preliminary enquiry into the history of religious and moral ideas in the nineteenth century. The subject proved too vast to be treated in one volume, but I hope, in a projected sequel, to fill in some of the gaps and bring the story down to the end of the century.

My grateful acknowledgments are due to The British Academy for permission to incorporate, in the chapter on Coleridge, the substance of my Warton Lecture (*Coleridge on Imagination and Fancy*, 1946).

B. W.

PEMBROKE COLLEGE, CAMBRIDGE
1948

CHAPTER I

SAMUEL TAYLOR COLERIDGE

1. Introductory

IN two former treatises, dealing respectively with the seventeenth and eighteenth centuries, the argument led up to Wordsworth; I begin the present studies with Coleridge.

Writing in 1838, soon after the deaths of Bentham and Coleridge, J. S. Mill described these two writers as 'the two great seminal minds of England in their age', and claimed that 'there is hardly to be found in England an individual of any importance in the world of mind who . . . did not first learn to think from one of these two'.[1] In another essay (1840) Mill tried to indicate the quality of their influence: 'By Bentham', he wrote, 'beyond all others, men have been led to ask themselves in regard to any ancient or received opinion, Is it true? and by Coleridge, What is the meaning of it?'[2] In Bentham the spirit of the eighteenth century lived on; taking his stand, like any Brobdingnagian sage or visitor from China, 'outside the received opinion', he 'surveyed it as an entire stranger to it'. Coleridge, on the other hand, may be regarded as the leading English representative of the European reaction against the eighteenth century; in him the nineteenth century awakens to all that was undreamed of in the philosophy of its predecessor. 'The Germano-Coleridgean doctrine' (if I may quote Mill once again)

> 'expresses the revolt of the human mind against the philosophy of the eighteenth century. It is ontological, because that was experimental; conservative, because that was innovative; religious, because so much of that was infidel; concrete and historical, because that was abstract and metaphysical; poetical, because that was matter-of-fact and prosaic.'[3]

---
[1] *Dissertations and Discussions* (1867), vol. i, p. 330.   [2] *Ibid.*, p. 394.
[3] *Ibid.*, p. 403.

There was at this time a new spirit afloat, a sense that there were spiritual needs, and unseen realities, which had been unrecognized in the religious, ethical, political and aesthetic teachings of the immediate past. The new demand was for an interpretation of the whole range of human experience which should be richer, more deeply satisfying, than the old, dry, superficial rationalism. That Mill himself, whose mind had been cast in an eighteenth century mould, should have seen the one-sidedness of the tradition in which he had been nurtured, and recognized in Coleridge the necessary correctives, is a remarkable testimony both to his own openmindedness and to the importance of Coleridge's influence. If Mill, the successor of Hartley, Bentham, Ricardo and James Mill, felt the spell of Coleridge, it is no wonder that other, more kindred, spirits should have paid homage to him. Julius Hare, for example, in his edition of Sterling's *Remains*, wrote:

> 'At that time [*c*. 1829] it was beginning to be acknowledged by more than a few that Coleridge is the true sovereign of modern English thought. The *Aids to Reflection* had recently been published, and were doing the work for which they are so admirably fitted; that book, to which many, as has been said..."owe even their own selves". Few felt this obligation more deeply than Sterling. "To Coleridge (he wrote to me in 1836) I owe *education*. He taught me to believe that an empirical philosophy is none, that Faith is the highest Reason."' [1]

Thomas Arnold, who prefixed to one of his volumes of sermons a motto from Coleridge's *Literary Remains*,[2] often refers to him with reverence (e.g. 'a very great man indeed, whose equal I know not where to find in England'). Newman, surveying the causes of the Tractarian Movement, speaks of 'the reaction from the dry and superficial character of the religious teaching and the literature of the last generation and century', and 'the need for something deeper and more attractive'; amongst those who had contributed to the 'spiritual awakening of spiritual wants' he counts Scott,

[1] Sterling, *Essays and Tales*, ed. by J. C. Hare (1848), vol. i, p. xiv.
[2] Cf. below, p. 61.

SAMUEL TAYLOR COLERIDGE

Coleridge, Southey and Wordsworth.[1] Of Carlyle's celebrated estimate I speak in a later chapter (see pp. 108 ff.); references and acknowledgments are to be found in James Martineau, F. A. J. Hort, Charles Kingsley and many other writers. The last testimony I shall here quote is that of Coleridge's most eminent theological disciple, Frederick Denison Maurice, and I quote it at some length because it deals with matters specially germane to the ensuing discussion. The passage occurs in the Dedication of his book *The Kingdom of Christ*[2] to Derwent Coleridge; Maurice explains that his theme is the idea of a Church Universal founded on the very nature of God himself. How can all systems, sects and schools of thought contribute their quota to one which is larger and deeper than any one of them?

> 'In preparing for the consideration of this great subject I have felt, with many others, that Mr Coleridge's help has been invaluable to us. Nearly every thoughtful writer of the day would have taught us, that the highest truths are those which lie beyond the limits of Experience, that the essential principles of the Reason are those which cannot be proved by syllogisms, that the evidence for them is the impossibility of admitting that which does fall under the law of experience, unless we recognize them as its foundation; nay, the impossibility of believing that we ourselves are, or that anything is, except upon these terms. The atheism of Hume has driven men to these blessed discoveries, and though it was your father's honour that he asserted them to an age and a nation which had not yet discovered the need of them, he certainly did not pretend, and no one should pretend, that he was the first reviver or expositor of them. But the application of these principles to *Theology*, I believe, we owe mainly to him. The power of perceiving that by the very law of the Reason the Knowledge of God must be *given* to it; that the moment it attempts to create its Maker, it denies itself . . . I must acknowledge that I received from him.'

Though I have extracted this particular passage because of its relevance to what follows, I would add that the Dedication

---

[1] Cf. *Apologia* (Everyman ed.), p. 104, and *The State of Religious Parties*, in *British Critic*, April 1839, vol. xxv, p. 395.
[2] 1842 ed., p. xxv.

also contains much valuable criticism on other aspects of Coleridge's work. Of the *Biographia Literaria*, for instance, Maurice remarks that it can greatly help any young reader who is puzzled by the problems of literary criticism, who is haunted 'by a sense of the connexion between his own life and the books he reads' or disturbed by dogmas about the worth or worthlessness of particular poems, or by attempts to set up 'laws' of art. The young reader will find in the *Biographia Literaria* no system, but something better—a thinker who is 'feeling his way' out of Associationism into an acknowledgment of that with which things are associated, and a critic who can enter into the spirit of an author without assuming to be his judge. In the history of Coleridge's mind Maurice sees an epitome of the history of his age. Coleridge is, indeed, representative of his own generation in that he himself, in his own personal development, evolved from the eighteenth century to the nineteenth century standpoint. We must remember that Coleridge had originally been a materialist and a necessitarian of the school of Hartley, and a Unitarian of the school of Priestley. I do not propose to speak in any detail of his earlier phases; a few rough strokes must suffice to sketch the outline of his growth up to the time of his maturity.

II. The Early Coleridge

The seminal principle, the original impulse, which was in him from childhood, was a sense of the Whole as a living unity, a sense of God in all and all in God, a faith in a divine spiritual activity as the ground of all existence. This faith never really left him, though it was obscured for a while by other influences, and modified in successive stages by his contacts with other minds. His great dread was lest, losing his wholeness of vision, he should be constrained to view the universe merely as an assemblage of parts, 'an immense heap of *little* things'. 'My mind feels as if it ached to behold and know something *great*, something *one* and *indivisible*.' From the winter evening when, as a boy of eight years old, he had listened entranced to his father's discourse about the night sky, and from the time of his childish reading of fairy-tales, 'my mind had been habituated *to the Vast*, and I never regarded *my senses* in any way as the criteria of my belief'. Those who have been '*rationally* educated', he said, seemed 'to want a sense which I possess'.[1]

Nevertheless we find him, as an undergraduate at Cambridge, professing 'advanced' philosophical and republican views, of the very kind which he afterwards repudiated. His rooms at Jesus College were a veritable left-wing cell of those days. He was, for instance, an ardent supporter of Mr Frend, a don who was deprived of his fellowship and banished from the university for his Arianism. 'I am a complete necessitarian', he writes to Southey (Dec. 11, 1794), 'and understand the subject as well almost as Hartley himself, but I go farther than Hartley, and believe the corporeality of *thought*, namely, that it is motion.' He meets Holcroft; he dines with Godwin—to whom (as to Priestley and Kosciusko) he addresses a sonnet:

> 'Nor will I not thy holy guidance bless
> And hymn thee, Godwin! with an ardent lay;
> For that thy voice, in Passion's stormy day,
> When wild I roam'd the bleak Heath of Distress,
> Bade the bright form of Justice meet my way,—
> And told me that her name was Happiness.'

Following Godwin's lead, he teaches at this time that vice is the effect of error, and the product of circumstances—amongst which must be numbered monarchy and 'that leprous stain, nobility'. But better times are coming; France will deliver us: 'France! whose crimes and miseries posterity will impute to us. France! to whom posterity will impute their virtues and happiness.' For about a year from the time of his visit to Oxford and introduction to Southey, in June 1794, political interests predominate in his letters. The tone of his mind can be illustrated from the letter to Southey which begins: 'S. T. Coleridge to R. Southey, Health and Republicanism to be!' and continues:

[1] *Letters* (ed. E. H. Coleridge, 1895), vol. i, p. 16.

'It is *wrong*, Southey! for a little girl with a half-famished sickly baby in her arms to put her head in at the window of an inn—"Pray give me a bit of bread and meat!" from a party dining on lamb, green peas and salad. Why? Because it is *impertinent* and *obtrusive*! "I am a gentleman! and wherefore the clamorous voice of woe intrude upon mine ear?" My companion is a man of cultivated, though not vigorous understanding; his feelings are all on the side of humanity; yet such are the unfeeling remarks, which the lingering remains of aristocracy occasionally prompt.'[1]

He appends some lines from a poem entitled *Perspiration, A Travelling Eclogue*, of which the following are a sample:

'The dust flies smothering, as on clatt'ring wheel
Loath'd aristocracy careers along.'

In the same letter we have the first mention of 'Pantisocracy', which, as is well known, was a scheme intended to realize the principles of *Political Justice* without delay. It was, indeed, a variant of Plato's plan for the immediate establishment of the just State. The philosophic rulers, it will be remembered, 'regarding justice as the greatest and most necessary of things', were to begin by sending out into the country all who were over ten years of age, and by taking possession of their children, who would be unaffected by the habits of their parents: these they would train in the principles of justice. 'Yes', says Glaucon; 'I think, Socrates, that you have very well described how, if ever, such a constitution might come into being.' The Pantisocrats, on the other hand, as denizens of a vast modern nation-state, had no alternative but to remove *themselves* from it, and found their own Republic on the banks of the Susquehannah. The best general account of their intentions is given by Thomas Poole, in a letter dated Sept. 22, 1794: 'Twelve gentlemen of good education and liberal principles', he says, 'are to embark with twelve ladies in April next', and fix their abode 'in a delightful part of the new back settlements'. The labour of each man, for two or three hours a day, would suffice to support the colony, and the produce would be common property. There was to be a good library, and the ample

[1] *Ibid.*, p. 72.

leisure was to be devoted to study, discussion and the education of the children. The women were not only to look after the infants, but also to cultivate their own minds. It was undecided 'whether the marriage contract shall be dissolved if agreeable to one or both parties'. There was, however, to be complete freedom of political and religious opinion. Each gentleman provides £125 at the start.[1]

Of the gradual fading of the Pantisocratic dream it is needless to speak here. Southey, who was only twenty when Coleridge had first met him, had begun to grow up, and a sense of real things began to come strongly upon him, especially when prospects of advancement at home offered themselves. Coleridge, whose 'sense of real things' had never been strong, but who had sacrificed to the dream some very real things (Mary Evans in particular), found himself deserted. The cottage at Clevedon, and his own twelfth part of the Pantisocratic sisterhood, were all that remained.

Before passing on to later milestones in his development we should observe that the enthusiasms of this period were largely froth upon his mind's surface; the deeper currents of his nature ran steadily forwards all the while, and were even then not wholly concealed. True, he urges Southey not to enter the Church, but it is 'for God's sake'; true, he is horrified at the news that Mrs Fricker is to accompany the party: 'we shall have her teaching the infants *Christianity*'—but he adds, 'I mean that mongrel whelp that goes under its name'. In a letter to his brother George (Nov. 6, 1794) he defends himself against the charges of being a 'democrat' and an 'infidel'. He sees clearly that the present state of things is not the best and highest of which mankind is capable, but if 'you ask me what the friend of universal equality should do', he answers 'Talk not politics. *Preach the Gospel.* Yea, my brother! [in spite of my supposed infidelity] I have at all times in all places defended the Holy One of Nazareth against the learning of the historian, the libertinism of the wit, and (his worst enemy) the mystery of the bigot!' The history of Coleridge's attitude to Godwinism may serve to illustrate my point. We have seen how he addressed Godwin

[1] See Mrs Sandford, *Thomas Poole and His Friends* (1888), vol. i, p. 97.

in December 1794; already, however, he had hinted characteristically at a defect in him: all necessary ethical knowledge is, indeed, embodied in the Godwinian 'Justice', but abstract assent to all this is not enough; 'the *heart* should have *fed* upon the *truth*'. In the *Conciones ad Populum* (Feb. 1795) there is still much Godwinian language, much discourse of universal benevolence, of illumination, of necessitarianism and of the identity of vice and ignorance. But Coleridge adds that Godwin is suited only to the few, while what is needed by the poor is (once again) to have the Gospel preached to them:

> 'He would appear to me to have adopted the best as well as the most benevolent mode of diffusing truth who, uniting the zeal of the methodist with the views of the philosopher, should be *personally* among the poor, and teach them their *duties*, in order that he may render them susceptible of their *rights*.'

'Prudential reasonings' will be powerless with the poor; '*religion* appears to offer the only means efficient'.

> 'Let us beware of that proud philosophy, which affects to inculcate philanthropy, while it denounces every home-born feeling, by which it is produced and nurtured.... The intensity of private attachments encourages, not prevents, universal benevolence.'[1]

I conclude with two extracts from *The Watchman*, which mark the latter stages of his emancipation from Godwin (they were written at the very time when Wordsworth was composing *The Borderers* at Racedown). In the first he is addressing a self-styled 'Patriot':

> 'You have studied Mr Godwin's Essay on Political Justice; but to think filial affection folly, gratitude a crime, marriage injustice, and the promiscuous intercourse of the sexes right and wise, may class you among the despisers of vulgar prejudices, but cannot increase the probability that you are a Patriot.' [To become a real Patriot] 'your *heart* must believe, that the good of the whole is the greatest possible good of each individual'.[2]

[1] *Essays on His Own Times* (ed. S. Coleridge, 1850), vol. i, pp. 16-25.
[2] *Ibid.*, p. 135.

In the second he is replying to a critic of the foregoing:

> 'I do consider Mr Godwin's principles as vicious; and his book as a pandar to sensuality. Once I thought otherwise—nay, even addressed a complimentary sonnet to the author, in the *Morning Chronicle*, of which I confess with much moral and poetical contrition, that the lines and the subject were equally bad. I have since *studied* his work, ... and am not quite convinced with yourself and Mr Godwin that mind will be omnipotent over matter, that a plough will go into the field and perform its labour without the presence of the agriculturist, that man may be immortal in this life, and that death is an act of the will!!!' [1]

In February 1797 Coleridge wrote (to Thelwall) 'thank Heaven! I abominate Godwinism!' He had met Wordsworth, and read *The Borderers*, and the friendship between the two men had begun upon a common impulse of reaction against that uncongenial philosophy.

We may now largely drop the chronological account, and, admitting no further impediment, proceed to consider the results of that marriage of true minds. Coleridge had been passing through Hartley to Berkeley and Spinoza; he now meets that which can move him to the depths; a true and new poet. One more reference to his *Letters* may here suffice to indicate the mood of Alfoxden, from which sprang most of his best poetry, and most of his best thinking about Imagination and Fancy. Writing to his brother George (April 1798), he now dissociates himself from French politics, ethics, metaphysics and 'theology'. The Lord was not in the wind, the earthquake or the fire; he now awaits, 'with a subdued and patient thought', the still small voice. He has snapped his 'squeaking baby-trumpet of sedition', and withdrawn from the consideration of immediate causes to meditate upon the 'causae causarum'. His aims now are

> 'in poetry, to elevate the imagination and set the affections in right tune by the beauty of the inanimate impregnated as with a living soul by the presence of life—in prose, to the seeking with patience and a slow, very slow mind, "Quid sumus, et quidnam victuri

[1] *Ibid.*, p. 164.

gignimus"—what our faculties are and what they are capable of becoming. I love fields and woods and mountains with almost a visionary fondness. And because I have found benevolence and quietness growing within me as this fondness has increased, therefore I should wish to be the means of implanting it in others, and to destroy the bad passions not by combating them but by keeping them in inaction.'[1]

There follow some lines of Wordsworth's, of which a later version is to be found in *The Excursion* (Book iv, 1207):

> 'Not useless do I deem
> These shadowy sympathies with things that hold
> An inarticulate Language; for the Man—
> Once taught to love such objects as excite
> No morbid passions, no disquietude,
> No vengeance, and no hatred—needs must feel
> The joy of that pure principle of love
> So deeply, that, unsatisfied with aught
> Less pure and exquisite, he cannot choose
> But seek for objects of a kindred love
> In fellow-nature and a kindred joy.
> Accordingly he by degrees perceives
> His feelings of aversion softened down;
> A holy tenderness pervade his frame!
> His sanity of reason not impair'd,
> Say, rather, that his thoughts now flowing clear
> From a clear fountain flowing, he looks round,
> He seeks for good; and finds the good he seeks.'

He is regulating his mind so as to prevent 'the passions from turning reason into a hired advocate'—a clear allusion to the anti-Godwinian theme of *The Borderers*.

III. Imagination and Fancy

One chief outcome of Coleridge's enquiry into 'what our faculties are, and what they are capable of becoming', was his distinction between Imagination and Fancy. I propose now to examine what Coleridge meant by this, and why he thought it so important.

[1] *Letters*, vol. i, p. 243.

SAMUEL TAYLOR COLERIDGE

A recent critic has referred to the distinction as 'celebrated but useless'. 'Celebrated' we know it to be; its 'usefulness', however, cannot be determined without raising some important questions. Are we interested in enquiring into the nature of poetry, and the ways in which it comes to be written? Do we wish to think seriously of poetry as in some sense an approach to truth? Has it any significant relationship with life in general? What place can we give it in our scheme of values? And if we decide that poetry can make a vital contribution to the good life, how can we determine which are the best kinds of poetry? It seems to me that Coleridge's distinction can be 'useful', not by furnishing us with final or explicit answers to such questions, but by deepening and enriching our understanding of their meaning. It is natural and right that questions like these should occasionally be asked, and it would be surprising if the greatest of our poet-critics had no light to throw upon them.

We can best begin by reminding ourselves of the passage in the *Biographia Literaria*, chapter iv, where Coleridge describes the birth of his own idea. It came to him, we find, as a direct result of his discovery of Wordsworth's poetry; here was a new poet, speaking with a superiority of accent which linked him with the great poets of a former age. To what was that superiority due? What was it that lifted Wordsworth above the eighteenth century level, and placed him with Shakespeare or Milton? Already, while an undergraduate at Cambridge, Coleridge had been greatly impressed by the *Descriptive Sketches*: 'seldom, if ever', he writes, 'was the emergence of an original poetic genius above the literary horizon more evidently announced'. But two years later came a more memorable experience:

> 'I was in my twenty-fourth year, when I had the happiness of knowing Mr Wordsworth personally, and while memory lasts, I shall hardly forget the sudden effect produced on my mind, by his recitation of a manuscript poem [afterwards incorporated in *Guilt and Sorrow*].'

What struck Coleridge in this poem was not so much the 'freedom from false taste'; it was

> 'the union of deep feeling with profound thought: the fine balance of truth in observing, with the imaginative faculty in modifying the objects observed; and above all the original gift of spreading the tone, the *atmosphere*, and with it the depth and height of the ideal world around forms, incidents, and situations, of which, for the common view, custom had bedimmed all the lustre, had dried up the sparkle and the dewdrops.'

This peculiar excellence, he goes on to tell us, 'I no sooner felt than I sought to understand'—a phrase which (we may note in passing) epitomizes Coleridge's distinctive quality as a critic: he first feels keenly, and then tries to understand what he has felt.

> 'Repeated meditations led me first to suspect (and a more intimate analysis of the human faculties... matured my conjecture into full conviction) that fancy and imagination were two distinct and widely different faculties, instead of being, according to the general belief, either two names with one meaning, or, at furthest, the lower and higher degree of one and the same power.'

It is well known that when Coleridge felt himself confronted by an important duty he instinctively shrank from it, or postponed its performance to a more auspicious occasion. Hence his endless digressions and asides, both in writing and in conversation, and hence his habit of scattering his most pregnant remarks in marginalia or footnotes, where he could say the vital thing *tanquam aliud agendo*. Unfortunately this desynonymizing of Fancy and Imagination seemed to him a supremely important task, and he accordingly shies off at a tangent whenever he approaches it. We have therefore to be content with hints and glimpses, and must piece together his meaning from several scattered passages. All he vouchsafes here is that Milton had a 'highly *imaginative*' and Cowley a 'very *fanciful*' mind; that the distinction is analogous to that between *delirium* and *mania*; and that it can be illustrated by contrasting Otway's line

SAMUEL TAYLOR COLERIDGE

'Lutes, lobsters, seas of milk and ships of amber'[1]

with Shakespeare's

'What! have his daughters brought him to this pass?'

These interesting suggestions are here left undeveloped, but they foreshadow the fuller account in chapter xiii and in the Shakespeare Lectures. In delirium the mind pours forth its contents incoherently, that is, with no unifying principle to order its sequences save the law of association; in mania, the mind, obsessed by a fixed idea, sees and interprets all things in relation to that idea, and so has (though in a morbid form) a co-ordinating power. If we translate disease into health, delirium becomes Fancy, and mania Imagination: Fancy assembling and juxtaposing images without fusing them; Imagination moulding them into a new whole in the heat of a predominant passion.

We may now turn to chapter xiii, where Coleridge, face to face at last with his central problem, and alarmed by his own chapter heading: 'On the imagination, or esemplastic power', slips lizard-like into a thicket of learned excerpts, and vanishes from sight, leaving in our hands his tail only—a letter from himself to himself about his forthcoming masterpiece. But the tail is not without a sharp point—the last two paragraphs, and these we must now inspect. First, what of the distinction here introduced between the two kinds of Imagination, the Primary and the Secondary? I fear that some readers are misled by the oracular sublimity of Coleridge's definition of the former: 'The primary Imagination', he declares (in oft-quoted words),

> 'I hold to be the living Power and prime Agent of all human Perception, and as a repetition in the finite mind of the eternal act of creation in the infinite I AM.'

This is not to be dismissed as metaphysical babble; a weight of thought, indeed a whole philosophy, lies beneath each phrase. Coleridge is here summarizing the great struggle and victory of his life—his triumph over the old

---

[1] Coleridge misquotes Otway, who actually wrote:
'Lutes, laurels, seas of milk and ships of amber.'

tradition of Locke and Hartley, which had assumed that the mind in perception was wholly passive, 'a lazy looker-on on an external world'. We should here recall the letter to Poole, written in March 1801, in which Coleridge announces the overthrow of 'the doctrine of association as taught by Hartley, and with it all the irreligious metaphysics of modern infidels'. The mind, he now teaches, works actively in the mere act of perception; it knows its objects not by passive reception, but by its own energy and under its own necessary forms; indeed, it knows not mere objects as such, but itself in the objects:

> 'If the mind be not *passive*, if it be indeed made in God's Image, and that, too, in the sublimest sense, the *Image of the Creator*, there is ground for suspicion that any system built on the passiveness of the mind must be false, as a system.' [1]

In speaking thus of the Primary Imagination, then, Coleridge is affirming that the mind is essentially and inveterately creative: 'we receive but what we give', and in the commonest everyday acts of perception we are making our own world. We make it, indeed, not *ex nihilo*, but out of the influxes proceeding from Nature, or as Coleridge preferred to say, 'the infinite I AM'. Whatever we perceive is what we have made in response to these stimuli; perception is an activity of the mind, not a merely mechanical registering of impressions. However (and this is now the point to be emphasized), it is the Secondary Imagination, not the Primary, which he proceeds to contrast with Fancy; it is the Secondary Imagination which is at work in the making of poetry. For how does it operate?

> 'It dissolves, diffuses, dissipates, in order to recreate . . . it struggles to idealize and to unify. It is essentially *vital*, even as all objects (*as* objects) are essentially fixed and dead.'

Here speaks the seer, the poet and the romantic; not content with the automatic 'poetry' which we all create, and which we call the world of everyday appearances, he would transcend this for a vision more intense, more true, than is afforded

[1] *Letters*, vol. i, p. 352.

by the light of common day. The daily routine world may be the product of a faculty essentially creative—indeed, in opposition to Locke and Hartley, Coleridge asserts that it is —yet in itself it is cold and inanimate, filled only with 'the many shapes of joyless daylight'. As Sidney had expressed it in his *Apologie*, Nature's world is brazen, 'the poets only deliver a golden'. To retain the Midas-touch, to be constantly in possession of the transforming power, this for Coleridge meant life, and joy, and triumph; to lose it meant failure and spiritual death, the reduction of existence to a state of somnambulism; in which we languish amidst

> 'The repetitions wearisome of sense
> Where soul is dead, and feeling hath no place.'
> [Wordsworth, *Excursion*, iv, 620.]

Coleridge knew all too well the misery of this condition; it was the mood of dejection which he describes in the Ode of that title, where, like Wordsworth (but without the Wordsworthian compensation), he laments the passing of the visionary gleam:

> 'And would we aught behold, of higher worth,
> Than that inanimate cold world allowed
> To the poor loveless ever-anxious crowd,
> Ah! from the soul itself must issue forth
> A light, a glory, a fair luminous cloud
> Enveloping the Earth. . . .'

If we ask, then, what it is which the Secondary Imagination must 'dissolve, diffuse, and dissipate', the answer is given here: it is the 'inanimate cold world' of the Primary Imagination; all that is allowed to the daily, prosaic consciousness of average humanity, and to poets themselves when power deserts them. I shall say a word more on this topic later, but I would suggest here, in passing, that this desire (as Wordsworth expresses it)

> 'for something loftier, more adorned,
> Than is the common aspect, daily garb
> Of human Life'   [*Prelude*, v, 575.]

is no mere romantic escapism, though it may sometimes

take that form; it is the originating impulse of poets at all times (including our own time), and not merely of poets, but of seers and saints and scientists as well—of all whose task it is to fight the habit of

> 'Viewing all objects unremittingly
> In disconnection dead and spiritless.'
> [*Excursion*, iv, 961.]

The Imagination, then (we may now drop the word 'secondary'), is the mind in its highest state of creative insight and alertness; its acts are acts of growth, and display themselves in breaking down the hard commonplaceness which so easily besets us, and in remoulding this stubborn raw material into new and living wholes. And now, what of Fancy? These are Coleridge's well-known words:

> 'Fancy, on the contrary, has no other counters to play with, but fixities and definites. The Fancy is indeed no other than a mode of Memory emancipated from the order of time and space. . . . But equally with the ordinary memory the Fancy must receive all its materials ready made from the law of association.'

In so far as it involves acts of selection and of arrangement ('that empirical phenomenon of the will, which we express by the word Choice'), Fancy is on a higher level than mere perception or mere memory. But it is below Imagination in that, instead of making all things new, it merely constructs patterns out of *ready-made* materials, 'fixities and definites'. It juxtaposes images, but does not *fuse* them into unity; its products are like mechanical mixtures (as of salt with iron filings), in which the ingredients, though close together, remain the same as when apart; whereas those of Imagination are like chemical compounds (say, of sodium and chlorine), in which the ingredients lose their separate identities in a new substance, composed of them indeed, but differing from them both. We may fitly use, as an illustration, the two passages quoted by Coleridge himself from *Venus and Adonis*, on which Dr I. A. Richards has ably commented in his *Coleridge on the Imagination*. The first, illustrating Fancy, is:

SAMUEL TAYLOR COLERIDGE

> 'Full gently now she takes him by the hand,
> A lily prison'd in a gaol of snow,
> Or ivory in an alabaster band;
> So white a friend engirts so white a foe.'

On this Dr Richards observes that the activity of putting together these images is, as Coleridge has said, that of choice, 'an empirical phenomenon of the will'; it is 'an exercise of selection from amongst objects already supplied by association, a selection made for purposes which are not then and therein being shaped, but have been already fixed'. 'Lily' and 'snow', 'ivory' and 'alabaster', are drawn out from the storehouse of memory and juxtaposed, but they remain themselves, not passing into each other, nor becoming one with the hands of Venus and Adonis with which they are compared. We may note here another remark of Coleridge on Fancy: its images, he says, 'have no connexion, natural or moral, but are yoked together by the poet by means of some accidental coincidence' (*Table Talk*, June 23, 1834). Many of the conceits of the Metaphysical poets, and of some modern poets, could be classified in this way as fanciful: for instance Donne's comparison of his mistress's hair with his own spinal cord, or Herbert's comparison of his sins with rocks in the stream of the Redeemer's blood. Two other examples, one serious and one frivolous, may serve to clarify the point:

> (a) 'So, when the Sun in bed,
>   Curtain'd with cloudy red,
>   Pillows his chin upon an Orient wave.'
>   [Milton, *Ode, On the Morning of Christ's Nativity*]
>
> (b) 'And, like a lobster boiled, the morn
>   From black to red began to turn.'
>   [Butler's *Hudibras*]

The juxtapositions of 'chin' and 'pillow' with 'Sun' and 'Orient wave', and of the boiling lobster with dawn, are products of the faculty which, in another phrase of Coleridge's, brings together 'images dissimilar in the main by some one point or more of likeness'. In neither example is there any plastic stress shaping the images into one; the poets are not *realizing* a situation nor compelling us to do so.

Coleridge's second Shakespearean example, illustrating Imagination, is this:

> 'Look! how a bright star shooteth from the sky,
> So glides he in the night from Venus' eye.'

His comment is:

> 'How many images and feelings are here brought together without effort and without discord—the beauty of Adonis—the rapidity of his flight—the yearning yet helplessness of the enamoured gazer—and a shadowy ideal character thrown over the whole.'

This is 'imaginative', according to Coleridge, because Shakespeare is here seen in the act of realizing, making real to himself and to us, the departure of Adonis from Venus; the fall of the shooting star and the flight of Adonis become one in a flash of creative vision, and are henceforth inseparable. Or take a well-known line from *The Merchant of Venice*:

> 'How sweet the moonlight sleeps upon this bank!'

In saying that the moonlight 'sleeps', Shakespeare has said an imaginative thing; the more one dwells upon the metaphor, the more intimate become the links between sleep and moonlight—silence, the prone position of sleeper and moonlit bank, tranquillity, unconsciousness, a trance-like or enchanted state: Shakespeare has seen that all these (and more) are qualities which sleep and moonlight have in common, and in a single word he has made them permanently one. Here is a final pair of illustrations, taken this time from Keats:

(Fancy)
> 'When Cynthia smiles upon a summer's night,
> And peers among the cloudlets jet and white,
> As though she were reclining in a bed
> Of bean blossoms, in heaven freshly shed.'
> [*To Charles Cowden Clarke*]

(Imagination)
> '... the moon, lifting her silver rim
> Above a cloud, and with a gradual swim
> Coming into the blue with all her light.'
> [*I stood tiptoe* ...]

I suggest that the first passage is fanciful, because in spite of the *curiosa felicitas* of the comparison (it is based upon accurate observation), moonlit cloudlets do not really fuse with bean blossoms, chequered though they both are. The black-and-white is their only link; the warmth and scent of the beanfield and all its suggestions of summer daytime and luxury are unwanted here, whereas in Imagination all the essential qualities of the images are made to interpenetrate. In the second passage I think this actually happens; the keyword is 'swim', which is emphasized by its position at the end of the line. Here everything connected with the movement of a swimmer is apt and relevant to the moon: slow, smooth, steady, purposive motion, and motion in a blue, liquid medium (the night sky is well realized as a sea, with clouds as islands). It is significant that when Keats is treating the moon thus imaginatively he does not need to call her Cynthia.

The Imagination was concerned not merely in the creation of living metaphor (as in the examples quoted above); as the coadunating, shaping power its function was to see all things as one, and the one in all things. It was typically displayed in 'the balance or reconcilement of opposite or discordant qualities'. What discordant qualities? Here are some given by Coleridge: 'a sense of novelty and freshness with old and familiar objects'; 'a more than usual state of emotion with more than usual order'; 'to make the external internal, the internal external, to make nature thought, and thought nature'; 'sameness with difference'; 'truth in observing with the imaginative faculty in modifying the object observed'; 'reducing multitude to unity' or 'succession to an instant'. These are all modes of the fundamental imaginative activity: dissolving in order to re-create, struggling to idealize and to unify 'dead' objects. Objects, taken as such, are fixed and dead, but it is the uncreative mind which fixes and kills them. They need not be so taken; when imaginatively seen they can be vitalized with an energy which comes indeed from within the mind, but which is also, mysteriously, their *own* life so revealed. The cold world of objects will not seem alive unless the poet takes the initiative.

'Extremes meet' was a favourite maxim with Coleridge; indeed, he saw in the interpenetration of opposites the very meaning and inmost process of existence. Life itself, abstractly considered, consists in the tension between polar opposites, the One becoming the Many, and the Many being resolved into the One. 'Subject' and 'Object' coalesce in Knowing; and in Art, Nature becomes Thought and Thought Nature.

> 'Every power in nature and in spirit must evolve an opposite, as the sole means and condition of its manifestation: and all opposition is a tendency to re-union. . . . The identity of thesis and antithesis is the substance of all being. . . . It is the object of mechanical, atomistic philosophy to confound synthesis with synartesis, or rather with mere juxtaposition of corpuscles separated by invisible interspaces.'[1]

Coleridge must needs postulate a Faculty: Imagination (or Reason, as we shall see later), whose special function it is to see parts as a whole, and the whole in the parts. It is not surprising, then, to find that, as a critic, Coleridge conceives himself to be engaged in uniting opposites in a new synthesis, or, as he puts it, 'acting the arbitrator between the old school and the new school'.[2] He wished to preserve what was valuable in the 'classical' tradition, while infusing into it the new life and passion of his own age. In that concluding passage of the *Biographia Literaria* (ch. xiv) from which I have already quoted phrases, 'classical' and 'romantic' are reconciled and transcended: Coleridge welcomes the passion and the life, but he will have it expressing itself in a greater, not a less, degree of organization—'a more than usual state of emotion' *with* 'more than usual order', 'the individual' *with* 'the representative', 'judgment ever awake and steady self-possession' *with* 'enthusiasm and feeling profound or vehement'.

The fusion of subject and object in the act of imagination may be attained in a number of ways, though all may be reduced to the 'balance or reconcilement of opposite or discordant qualities'. For instance, while Shakespeare 'darts

---

[1] *The Friend* (Bohn ed.), pp. 57-8, n. [2] *Letters*, vol. i, p. 387.

himself forth, and passes into all the forms of human character and passion', Milton 'attracts all forms and things into himself, into the unity of his own ideal. All things and modes of action shape themselves anew in the being of Milton; while Shakespeare becomes all things, yet for ever remaining himself' (*Biog. Lit.*, ch. xv). In both poets, though in opposite ways, the external becomes internal, and the internal external. Again, both Coleridge and Wordsworth make use of the antithesis of 'sameness with difference', or 'similitude with dissimilitude', in their theories of metrical language—language which is at once 'the same' as, yet other than, the language of 'speech'. Coleridge applies the principle in his psychological account of the origin of metre; here, the 'balance of antagonists' lies between *passion*, which demands a heightened mode of utterance, and *will*, which seeks to master and 'hold in check the workings of passion'. Out of this interpenetration of passion and will springs that organization, that 'ordonnance' of language which we call metre. But he applies it still more widely to the whole relation between subject-matter and treatment, where the synthesis is to be sought in 'the balance of truth in observing with the imaginative faculty in modifying the object observed'. This 'balance', first noted by Coleridge as the distinctive mark of Wordsworth's poetry (see above, p. 12), is the topic of several celebrated passages in the *Preface to Lyrical Ballads* and in the *Biographia Literaria*, where the aim of both poets is said to be to combine the truth of Nature with the modifying colours of the Imagination. Moonlight or sunset over a 'known and familiar landscape' proved an apt symbol for the imaginative act as they conceived it; hence, perhaps, the prevalence of the moon in their poetry of 1798. Everyone knows Coleridge's statement of Wordsworth's purpose, a statement which deepens the principle of sameness-and-difference into the notion of awakened insight into the life of common things:

> 'to give the charm of novelty to things of every day, and to excite a feeling analogous to the supernatural, by awakening the mind's attention from the lethargy of custom, and directing it to the loveli-

ness and the wonders of the world before us; an inexhaustible treasure, but for which, in consequence of the film of familiarity and selfish solicitude, we have eyes, yet see not, ears that hear not, and hearts that neither feel nor understand'.[1]

The 'colouring' without the 'truth of Nature' could yield nothing but fanciful kaleidoscope-patterns; 'Nature' alone, on the other hand, would be inanimate and cold. The authentic miracle occurred only when mind and matter, Imagination and observation, fused together to produce that which was neither the one nor the other, but both at once: a living compound, not a mechanical mixture. It is noteworthy that 'the sense of novelty and freshness with old and familiar objects' could be achieved especially by carrying on 'the feelings of childhood into the powers of manhood', by combining 'the child's sense of wonder and novelty with the appearances, which every day for perhaps forty years had rendered familiar'. The power to do this, Coleridge believes, is 'the character and privilege of genius, and one of the marks which distinguish genius from talents'.[2] How distinctive this view is of Coleridge's period may be gauged by imagining what, say, Ben Jonson, Dryden, Boileau or Dr Johnson would have thought of it.

The specific function of the 'esemplastic' or 'coadunating' faculty—the one-making or 'shaping' power—is the fusion of the many into one: its energy is eminently seen, as Coleridge puts it, in the reducing of multitude to unity or succession to an instant. And this in turn is a form of the fusion of subject and object, since the usual mode of its operation is the subordination of the multitude of 'things' to a predominant mood in the poet. Examples of these aspects of Imagination could be collected from any of the major poets: e.g. (multitude to unity)

> 'As when far off at sea a fleet descried
> Hangs in the clouds, by equinoctial winds
> Close sailing from Bengala' ...
> [*Paradise Lost*, i, 636.]

[1] *Biog. Lit.*, ch. xiv, Shawcross ed., vol. ii (1907), p. 6.
[2] *Ibid.*, vol. i, p. 59.

SAMUEL TAYLOR COLERIDGE

or
> 'the visible scene
> Would enter unawares into his mind
> With all its solemn imagery, its rocks,
> Its woods, and that uncertain heaven received
> Into the bosom of the steady lake'.
> [Wordsworth, *There Was a Boy*, 21.]

or (succession to an instant)
> 'The fierce confederate storm
> Of sorrow barricadoed ever more
> Within the walls of cities'.
> [*Excursion, Prospectus*, 78.]

or (both at once)
> 'And all that mighty heart is lying still.'
> [*Sonnet on Westminster Bridge*]

All these extracts probably illustrate also the subordination of multiplicity to the poet's mood; this is perhaps more clearly seen in

> 'The moving waters at their priestlike task
> Of pure ablution round earth's human shores'.
> [Keats, *Bright Star*]

or in
> 'April is the cruellest month, breeding
> Lilacs out of the dead land....'
> [*The Waste Land*]

But every reader must test Coleridge for himself; whoever will do so attentively, will generally find his understanding of the creative process deepened and clarified.

To grasp the significance of Fancy in this wider context, we must remember that in Coleridge's view the mental habits of the previous century had resulted in the exclusion of Imagination from poetry. Since Milton, poets had on the whole ceased to maintain the creative interchange between mind and object, and had been content to use ready-made material created in earlier, more imaginative times, or at best to say supremely well what had been greatly imagined by others, but less perfectly uttered. As we have seen, the

23

essence of the Imagination was that it involved the poet's whole soul in a creative act; Fancy merely used the results of previous activity. This, for Coleridge, was the only kind of poetic activity possible in the eighteenth century climate; it had taken the form of selecting images from older poets—from the ancients, from Milton, and later from Celtic, Norse or mediaeval sources. 'The Gothic' was at first fancifully used rather than imaginatively, but it helped, in virtue of its unfamiliarity, to evoke new imaginative life. It encouraged the poet (in a phrase of Mrs Radcliffe) 'to send forward a transforming eye into the distant obscurity'. If we remind ourselves of the age in which Coleridge lived, we shall not wonder that notions of life, growth and *transformation* were in the ascendant. In the first half of the eighteenth century life was conducted, on the whole, within a framework which was accepted as fixed and final. Fixities and definites were the order of the day: in society, the appointed hierarchy; in religion, the establishment; in Nature, the admirable order with its Chain of Being and its gravitational nexus which was mirrored in humanity by 'self-love and social'; in art, the rules and the proprieties. The aim of politics, religion and philosophy was not to transform, but to demonstrate and confirm existing perfection; the aim of poetry was to decorate. But with the onset of the revolutionary age all this was altered; the fixities yielded to flux, mechanics to life and organism, order to process, and the imaginative mouldings of the poets reflected on the ideal plane the great social changes which were proceeding on the material level. Life, and growth, and consciousness—those very mysteries which had never fitted comfortably into the mechanical scheme, now came into their own. Poets could feel, as seldom before, and hardly since, that they were allies of the ascendant forces, the leaders and legislators of mankind, instead of being elegant triflers or refugees from reality:

> 'O pleasant exercise of hope and joy!
> For mighty were the auxiliars which then stood
> Upon our side, us who were strong in love!'

Within the life-span of Wordsworth and Coleridge most of

this transforming energy of love and hope was deflected by events from political into imaginative and ideal channels; the soul comforted itself for political disillusionment by exulting in its own 'mighty and almost divine powers' (Wordsworth, 1815 *Preface*). Nothing, it seemed, could be more important than exertions of such powers, nothing more satisfying than their results—so satisfying, that they could only be expressed in terms of 'Truth'. For the human mind, for better or worse, does call by the name of Truth whatever deeply satisfies, as well as that which, on the practical level, is found to *work*. But—and this is where Fancy comes in again—not all such transformations were found to satisfy; there were those which merely amused or titillated, as well as those which seemed meaningful. The first were fanciful, the second imaginative. The business of the Imagination was not to generate chimaeras and fictions—the *imaginary*—but to 'disimprison the soul of fact'. 'What the imagination seizes as beauty must be Truth', says Keats. Why must it? One can only reply in such terms as Wordsworth's, that when the mind of man is 'wedded to the universe', and works 'subservient strictly to external things', the creation 'which they with blended might accomplish' does, in fact and in experience, produce a sense of something seen, something truly realized. Of course, there will be a metaphysical way of putting this, and naturally we find it in Coleridge: the world is really alive, and not dead; the life we project into it meets a life which is already there, and there is a mysterious link between man and Nature, whereby man, in moulding Nature, can be *unfolding* Nature in the direction of its own striving. 'Dare I add', says he, 'that genius must act on the feeling that body is but a striving to become mind—that it is mind in its essence!' [1] But whatever the metaphysical validity of what is seen by the visionary light, it remains important for us that the soul should be able to project upon the world 'the light, the glory, the fair luminous cloud'. It is only in dejection that the world seems cold and inanimate; if it can be transfigured (and the poets know that it can), then why say that the cold world is the real, the true world? Meanwhile, when

[1] *On Poesy or Art*, in Shawcross, *op. cit.*, vol. ii, p. 258.

joy and vision fail, there is always the metaphysical consolation that perhaps Nature is not *naturata* after all—not really fixed and dead, that it is *naturans*, alive and growing, and ready to yield its secret to the eye that brings with it the means of seeing.

I cannot therefore agree with those who call the Fancy-Imagination distinction 'celebrated but useless'. It seems to me to point, not only to an observable difference between kinds of poetry, but to a profound distinction in our ways of responding to experience. In our own time the task of poets has become harder than ever; they must resist and subdue a world far colder and more hostile than Coleridge's. But some of them are doing it, even if each poem must be 'a fresh start and a fresh kind of failure'; and we can still use Coleridge's theory to distinguish between those who are genuinely performing this task and those who are merely using bygone modes to produce what is superficially or academically pleasing. Let us say, in conclusion, that no poetic output demonstrates the distinction more strikingly than Coleridge's own. The difference between his 'great three' poems and most of his other verse is so extraordinary that it can only be called a difference in kind, and only accounted for on the supposition that in them he was using faculties and powers which lay dormant at other times. Professor Lowes has demonstrated that in the 'great three' poems the images stored in Coleridge's mind had undergone alchemical change by being plunged in the deep well of his subconsciousness, whereas elsewhere they are merely produced by a deliberate choice of the will, and rhetorically juxtaposed. Today we talk familiarly about the subconscious, and think we are speaking more scientifically than our predecessors who discoursed about 'the soul'. But the difference remains valid, however we describe it or account for it, between poetry which is merely made or contrived in the top layer of the consciousness and that which springs from the energy of the poet's whole being, and in us (the readers) 'calls the whole soul into activity, with the subordination of the faculties to each other according to their several worth and dignity'.

iv. Reason and Understanding

This distinction between kinds of poetry has become so familiar that we may forget that we owe the perception of it to Coleridge. But we must now ask, why did Coleridge think it so important? It was important for him because, as Wordsworth said, 'to him the unity of all had been revealed'; he was of that rare class of minds which cannot contemplate any one thing without becoming aware of its relation to everything else. For Coleridge, any important thought or distinction in one field must have its counterpart in another, and in every other. The Fancy-Imagination antithesis is not merely the product of literary sensitiveness in Coleridge, though it may have taken its origin from this; it is also a vital stage in his life-and-death struggle against the mechanical materialism of the eighteenth century. He needed the distinction, that is, not merely to show why one line of Shakespeare is superior to another, or why Milton and Wordsworth are superior to Cowley or Gray, but also because it was essential to his campaign against what he called the 'philosophy of death'. Coleridge became convinced that the tradition of Descartes and Locke had 'untenanted Creation of its God', and substituted

> 'a universe of death
> For that which moves with light and life informed,
> Actual, divine, and true.'

Speaking of the modern scientific and commercial spirit, he says: 'We have purchased a few brilliant inventions at the loss of all communion with life and the spirit of nature.' This protest of the imaginative consciousness against the scientific 'neutralization of nature'—a protest which is one of the deepest meanings of Romanticism—has been vehemently repeated by the arch-Romantic of our own century, D. H. Lawrence: 'Give me the mystery!' he cries, 'and let the world live again for me!' Or,

> 'The universe is dead for us, and how is it to come alive again?
> "Knowledge" has killed the sun, making it a ball of gas with spots;

"Knowledge" has killed the moon—it is a dead little earth fretted with extinct craters as with smallpox; the machine has killed the earth for us. . . . How, out of all this, are we to get back the grand orbs of the soul's heavens, that fill us with unspeakable joy? How are we to get back Apollo, and Attis, Demeter, Persephone, and the halls of Dis? We've got to get them back, for they are the world our soul, our greater consciousness, lives in. The world of reason and science . . . this is the dry and sterile little world the abstracted mind inhabits . . . the two ways of knowing, for man, are knowing in terms of apartness, which is mental, rational, scientific, and knowing in terms of togetherness, which is religious and poetic.'[1]

This 'knowing in terms of togetherness' is very much what Coleridge claimed for Imagination in poetry, and for Reason in religion and ethics. 'The modern mind', he wrote in *The Statesman's Manual*, 'has become infected with the contagion of its mechanic philosophy.' With the words of Lawrence in our minds, let us turn to Coleridge's diagnosis of the spiritual maladies of England since the Glorious Revolution. It appears in phrases like these (taken from *The Friend*): 'Mechanical philosophy'; 'a system of natural rights instead of social and hereditary privileges'; 'Imagination excluded from poesy'; 'The wealth of nations substituted for the well-being of nations and of man'; or these (from *The Constitution of Church and State*): 'The guess-work of general consequences substituted for moral and political philosophy'; 'The true historical feeling, the immortal life of the nation, generation linked to generation by faith, freedom, heraldry, and ancestral fame, languishing and giving place to the superstitions of wealth and newspaper reputation'. Lawrence's 'two ways of knowing' appear in Coleridge under the designation of Reason and Understanding, a distinction as central in his religious and ethical thought as that of Imagination and Fancy in his literary theory. Indeed, it is the same distinction transposed into another key, Reason being to Understanding what Imagination is to Fancy. It is important to grasp the meaning of the Reason-Understanding distinction and its relation to Imagination-Fancy; nothing

---

[1] *A Propos of Lady Chatterley's Lover* (1930), p. 54.

better illustrates the unity and scope of Coleridge's thought than this: that with him a literary distinction cannot remain that and nothing more, but must pass into an antithesis of two contrasted world-views. He gives meanings of his own to 'Reason' and 'Understanding', which are not those of ordinary parlance: Reason is 'the organ of the supersensuous'; Understanding is the faculty by which we generalize and arrange the phenomena of perception. Reason is 'the knowledge of the laws of the whole considered as one'; Understanding is 'the science of phenomena'. Reason seeks ultimate ends; Understanding studies means. Reason is 'the source and substance of truths above sense'; Understanding is the faculty which judges 'according to sense'. Reason is the eye of the spirit, the faculty whereby spiritual reality is spiritually discerned; Understanding is the mind of the flesh. Understanding has a wide and legitimate field of activity: it is necessarily used for measurement, analysis, classification and all the other processes of natural science, and it controls our lives on the practical routine level. It begins to err when it encroaches on the spheres where Reason alone is valid, that is, when it pretends to erect its limited theories into absolute laws, mistaking a technique of experiment or a method of classification for an exhaustive account of reality. And this, for Coleridge, was precisely what had happened in the eighteenth century: with what results? Materialism, determinism, atheism, utilitarianism, the 'godless revolution', 'moral science exploded as mystic jargon', the 'mysteries of religion cut and squared for the comprehension of the understanding', 'imagination excluded from poesy' (it is noticeable that this last phrase occurs not in isolation, but as an item in the general polemic). He sums up in a passage strikingly similar in meaning (though not in vocabulary) to the passage I quoted from Lawrence:

> 'The groundwork therefore of all true philosophy is the full apprehension of the difference between the contemplation of reason, namely that intuition of things which arises when we possess ourselves as one with the whole . . . and that which presents itself when . . . we think of ourselves as separated beings, and place nature

in antithesis to the mind, as object to subject, thing to thought, death to life.'[1]

This last is 'abstract knowledge', the product of the 'mere reflective faculty'; it is useful for the practical exigencies of daily living, but in itself it is 'the translation of a living word into a dead language'.

Coleridge's central preoccupation was with the antithesis between a living whole or organism on the one hand and a mechanical juxtaposition of parts on the other. The eighteenth century had reduced the universe to an assemblage of parts, the mind of man to an aggregate of sense-impressions, and poetry to a judicious arrangement of ready-made images culled from the memory. Coleridge cared so intensely about the distinction between the mechanical and spiritual world-views that he habitually used the images of 'death' and 'life' to express it; the struggle he was engaged upon was indeed, for him, a matter of life and death. He hoped that Wordsworth, in his projected philosophical poem, would teach the world

> '... the necessity of a general revolution in the modes of developing and disciplining the human mind by the substitution of life and intelligence ... for the philosophy of mechanism, which, in everything that is most worthy of the human intellect, strikes *Death*, and cheats itself by mistaking clear images for distinct conceptions, and which idly demands conceptions where intuitions alone are possible or adequate to the majesty of the Truth.'[2]

In all this Coleridge is using the certainties of Plato, of Christianity and of German idealism (together with his own profoundest intuitions) as weapons against the eighteenth century tradition, just as the Cambridge Platonists had used Platonism and Christianity against Hobbes. Lawrence, in our century, could only appeal to the blood, the solar plexus and the dark gods of paganism. To Coleridge it seemed that the most important of all truths were precisely those which could not, like those of mathematics, be demonstrated by the Understanding: the existence of God, the freedom of the

---

[1] *The Friend* (Bohn ed.), p. 366. [2] *Letters*, vol. ii, p. 649.

will and the autonomous power of the soul. It is the conscience, not the intellect, which commands us to attribute reality to these truths, because without them our moral life would be unmeaning. In setting up Reason and Imagination above the mind of the flesh, Coleridge was seeking to protect the region of spiritual experience against all attacks from the mere Understanding, that is, against the *Zeitgeist*. Is there a living God, in whom all things live and move and *have* their being (not *had*)? Is Nature a living organism? Is there a bond between Nature and the soul of man? Is the soul of man active and creative, not a link in the chain of causation? To all these questions Coleridge answered passionately 'Yes!' We have not said the last word about Coleridge's theory of the Imagination, until we have said that for him it was inseparable from the defence of religion. The question about the Imagination was of supreme importance, because it was a part of the question about God.

v. Religion and Morality

I would now remind my readers of the remarks of F. D. Maurice (quoted above, p. 3) about the debt of nineteenth century Christianity to Coleridge. He claimed that his generation had learnt from Coleridge to apply to theology the principles that 'the highest truths are those which lie beyond the limits of experience', and that 'the essential principles of the Reason are those which cannot be proved by syllogisms'. Von Hügel has said that 'a certain superhumanness is of the very essence of all full religion'; Coleridge helped to teach his century wherein the genuine superhumanness of Christianity really lay. Moreover, he taught this before the main attacks of the higher criticism and of science were launched, so that when the crisis came (in the middle of the century in England) the defensive positions were already laid down. If, throughout the century of biblical criticism and scientific agnosticism, Christianity held its ground, contrary to the expectations of many; if it did this by discarding its pseudo-foundations in historical, prophetic, natural or miraculous 'evidences', and by discovering a firmer foundation in the specific religious experience, in man's need for a God who comes to meet and to redeem him; if this is so (and I believe that it is), then the debt of modern theology to Coleridge is very considerable. His instinct was always, as Mill said, to ask of a received opinion 'What does it *mean*?'; applying this to religious faith he found that it 'meant' a great deal more than either the scoffers or the unillumined apologists supposed it to mean. 'Our most holy religion', Hume had ironically said, 'is founded on *Faith*, not on reason', and for him that meant that it had no real foundation at all. Coleridge was in a position to use Hume's argument against himself: founded upon Faith? yes! founded, then, upon our central experience as moral beings, upon all in us that responds to value—to truth, beauty, goodness and the sense of duty—and not merely to logical demonstration; founded, too, upon modes of knowing higher than the understanding or mind of the flesh, in a word, upon 'Reason' in his sense of the term. As poet and as seer, Coleridge knew (as other poets and seers have known) that for any full insight the head and the heart must act together. Keats could never be sure of any truth after merely hearing an abstract demonstration: axioms must be 'proved upon the pulses', or in Coleridgean phrase, the 'heart must have fed upon' the truth before it can be possessed. 'My opinion is this', he wrote (soon after his 'victory' over Locke and Hartley):

> 'that deep thinking is attainable only by a man of deep feeling, and that all truth is a species of revelation.'

At a time when religion was supposed to be capable of proof by 'evidences', and therefore of disproof by other evidences; when it was too often associated with a reactionary clinging to the existing order in society, or with an ill-guided evangelical zeal; at a time, too, when conspicuous intellects—Byron, Bentham, Shelley, the Mills—were known to think it all humbug and opium: at that very time Coleridge was showing that religion was a higher and more philosophical thing than had been dreamed of by either its enemies or its so-called friends. How did he do this? by a conjoint appeal to the head and the heart, to philosophical first principles and to the inward witness of the human spirit.

In the *Treatise on Method* (his preface to the *Encyclopaedia Metropolitana*) Coleridge classifies the various subjects of study according to the 'faculty' concerned in each. Thus, he assigns to 'Reason', the 'Pure Sciences': the Formal, which are concerned solely with the laws of the mind itself—Grammar, Logic, Mathematics—and the 'Real', which comprise Metaphysics, Morals and Theology. The Pure Sciences 'represent pure acts of the mind, and those only'; the Real Sciences are concerned with the true nature and existence of the world, with the guiding principles within us, and with the nature of the 'Great Cause of all'. On the other hand, the Mixed and Applied Sciences—Mechanics, Electricity, Physics, Chemistry, Biology—belong to the sphere of the Understanding. Here the mind, instead of framing its own necessary laws, is submitting itself to the shows of things for the purposes of classifying and controlling them. Understanding, the head disjoined from the heart, the 'mere reflective faculty', can only analyse and abstract; it cannot build the parts, so separated, back into a whole; this is the function of Reason, wherein head and heart, light and warmth, are working in unison. If we make the 'unenlivened generalizing understanding' the measure of Nature or of Deity, we get all the disastrous results seen in the previous century, culminating in 'mysteries of religion . . . cut and squared for the comprehension of the understanding, or else torn asunder from reason altogether'.[1]

Theology and Ethics, then, belong to the sphere of Reason, not of Understanding. Reason discerns the necessary laws and postulates of the moral life, for Reason includes the Conscience or moral sense ('practical Reason') which is the chief witness of spiritual realities. By means of this distinction Coleridge is able on the one hand to attack the so-called 'rationalists' (a word which, he thinks, has been debased in meaning) and also to refer approvingly to the 'rational theologians' of the seventeenth century. Their 'Reason' was Reason indeed, for it was a faculty inde-

[1] *Aids to Reflection* (Bohn ed.), p. 199.

pendent of sense, and linked with the Will; the eighteenth century *raison* had invaded regions beyond its competence. 'Wherever' (he writes in *Aids to Reflection*)

> 'Wherever the forms of reasoning appropriate only to the *natural* world are applied to spiritual realities, it may be truly said, that the more strictly logical the reasoning is in all its parts, the more irrational it is as a whole.'[1]

The postulates of ethics belong to the category of the 'supersensuous'; they are autonomous, and in assuming them the mind is directed solely by the laws of its own being, and not by external considerations of any kind. We now approach the most Kantian part of Coleridge's teaching: what are these postulates of the moral life? They are God, the Freedom of the Will, the authority of Conscience, the need for a Will harmonized with the intuitions of Reason, the Immortality of the Soul, and (Coleridge adds) the fact of Original Sin. 'My metaphysics', he says, 'are merely the referring of the mind to its own consciousness for truths indispensable to its own happiness.'[2] Conscience demands these postulates as necessary preconditions of the good life; they are thus Ideas 'that derive their origin and substance from the Moral Being, and to the reception of which as true objectively (that is, as corresponding to a reality out of the human mind) we are determined by a *practical* interest exclusively'.[3] The Understanding can discern merely a mechanical universe, and can only lead us in the last resort to negations: denial of God and of the freedom of the will, that is, denial of the fundamentals of the moral life. But if spiritual realities are spiritually discerned, if, that is, the primary evidence for them is supplied by our moral experience and not by empirical reasoning, then we can defy the infidels to do their worst:

> 'The Law of Conscience, and not the Canons of discursive Reasoning, must decide in such cases. At least, the latter have no validity, which the single veto of the former is not sufficient to nullify. The most pious conclusion is here the most legitimate.'[4]

[1] *Ibid.*, p. 168. [2] *The Friend*, p. 67. [3] *Aids*, p. 108. [4] *Ibid.*, pp. 108-9.

Or again:

> 'Conscience unconditionally *commands* us to attribute *Reality* and actual *Existence* to those Ideas, and those only, without which the conscience itself would be baseless and contradictory.'[1]

These ideas, or postulates, differ from those of mathematics in this respect, that those of mathematics no man *can* deny, while those of morality no *good* man *will* deny; belief in them is inseparable from an act of the will.

In chapter x of the *Biographia Literaria* Coleridge describes his Nether Stowey musings upon the foundations of religion and morals, and traces some of the stages by which he arrived at his mature convictions. For a long time, he says, 'my head was with Spinoza, though my whole heart remained with Paul and John'. 'Yet', he goes on,

> 'Yet there had dawned upon me, even before I had met with the Critique of the Pure Reason, a certain guiding light. If the mere intellect could make no certain discovery of a holy and intelligent first cause, it might yet supply a demonstration, that no legitimate argument could be drawn from the intellect *against* its truth. And what is this more than St Paul's assertion, that by wisdom (more properly translated by the powers of reasoning) no man ever arrived at the knowledge of God? . . . I became convinced that religion, as both the corner-stone and the key-stone of morality, must have a *moral* origin; so far at least, that the evidence of its doctrines could not, like the truths of abstract science, be wholly independent of the will. It were therefore to be expected, that its *fundamental* truth would be such as MIGHT be denied; though only by the fool, and even by the fool from the madness of the heart alone!'[2]

Faith, in other words, involves an element of venture, almost of wager; it means embarking with no more than an assurance of things hoped for, and 'believing where we cannot prove'. No man was ever argued into faith; it must be embraced at first upon 'insufficient' evidence, on evidence (that is) which would be insufficient for rational demonstration, but which grows sufficient when it is lived out into practice. Indeed, if faith could be mentally received, instead of being

---

[1] *The Friend*, p. 70.   [2] *Biog. Lit.* (Shawcross), vol. i, pp. 134-5.

worked for and wrought out, it would lose its *raison d'être*; like Imagination, it must half create its own objects. 'To credit ordinary and visible objects is not faith, but persuasion.' Coleridge puts it thus:

> 'It [the existence of God] could not be intellectually more evident without becoming morally less effective; without counteracting its own end by sacrificing the *life* of faith to the cold mechanism of a worthless because compulsory assent.'[1]

He defines Faith as 'the personal realization of the reason by its union with the will' (*The Friend*, p. 306), or, in greater elaboration:

> 'Faith subsists in the *synthesis* of the Reason and the individual Will. By virtue of the latter, therefore, it must be an energy, and, inasmuch as it relates to the whole moral man, it must be exerted in each and all of his constituents or incidents, faculties and tendencies; —it must be a total, not a partial—a continuous, not a desultory or occasional—energy.'[2]

No religious teacher can, like a mathematician, render it impossible to disbelieve; his message must be an injunction, an imperative: *crede ut intelligas!* do His will if you would know of the doctrine! Life itself, as Coleridge taught, is a tension between opposite forces, and the life of faith subsists in a tension between two poles of experience: between the head, which finds no sufficient evidence, and the heart, which bids us trust the larger hope. Coleridge notes, in this connexion, the 'oracular' or 'apodeictic' tone of the Bible; nowhere in that volume is there any attempt to demonstrate the truths of religion: we are enjoined to 'be still, and *know* that I am God'. Faith, in words of Charles Wesley's of which Coleridge would have approved (though for 'reason' he would read 'understanding') 'lends its realizing light':

> 'The things unknown to feeble sense,
> Unseen by reason's glimmering ray,
> With strong, commanding evidence
> Their heavenly origin display.'

The usual 'rationalistic' objection to this line of argument

---

[1] *Ibid.*, pp. 135-6.   [2] *Essay on Faith* (in *Aids*, p. 349).

is that merely believing a thing does not make it really so; I may delude myself into accepting any fiction by wishing hard enough. God may be very desirable or even necessary, but does that guarantee His existence? This objection is valid over the whole region of our practical, terrestrial lives; I must not believe that peace, or prosperity, or fine weather, or success, are coming, or that the stars are with me, merely because I wish for these things. But belief in God happens to be quite different from beliefs of this kind; it is more like the inspired guess of a Newton, which, *when tried out*, proves to be true. 'Trying out' religious belief is not an easy or grateful task; it means trusting our insight first (believing first that He is, as the writer to the Hebrews puts it), and then living it out daily and yearly, sustaining without complaint the loss of our separate, everyday selves. Only those who have made this venture have the right to speak of the grounds of faith; the 'rationalistic' argument collapses because it takes no account of the evidence of saintliness.

The importance of the 'Will' becomes so great, on this view, that Coleridge must separate it from 'Nature'; this he does, in opposition to the materialists and necessitarians, by affirming that the Will is not a link in the chain of cause and effect, but a self-determining entity not wholly subject, like Nature, to causation, nor conditioned by time and space. Its function is to accept and execute the will of God as discerned by the conscience or Reason, and the 'freedom' of a finite being consists in its becoming one with the will of God. Morality is thus concerned with our inward impulses, not with outward acts. Coleridge condemns Paley and the Utilitarians for making 'consequences' the criterion of the right or wrong of particular actions. If we base ethics on what is external, particularly if we base them on utility, on consequences of actions, we are submitting to a 'heteronomy', subjecting Reason to Understanding, the spirit to the flesh. The Utilitarian criterion is unstable, varying according to the foresight of the individual making the calculation. We are justified, not by works (consequences), nor by outward acts, but by faith (that is, by the submission of the Will to Reason and the will of God), and by the 'inward and absolute ground of our actions'. 'That which God sees, that alone justifies.' This does not mean undervaluing good works, but seeing them as the result of good principles, not as the whole of morality. 'Good works may exist without saving principles . . . but saving principles never did, and never can, exist without good works.'[1] Our actions must be performed from Faith as their centre, not from self-love or even universal benevolence. It is possible that 'an enlightened self-interest would recommend the same course of conduct as the sense of duty would do'; supposing then that 'actions diverging from self-love as their centre should be precisely the same as those produced from the Christian principle', where would be the difference? He replies '*in the agents themselves*'.[2] The religious principle, he concludes, is the 'one sure anchorage, without which our organic life is but a state of somnambulism'; it is 'the sole solution of the riddle of the world'. The Understanding may suggest motives and calculate consequences, but religion '*produces* the motives' and '*involves* the consequences'. Christianity, as Coleridge interprets it, demands, not the mere light of the Understanding ('light without heat') nor mere feeling ('warmth without light') but the union of light and warmth, head and heart, in the act of Faith.

vi. The Interpretation of Scripture

Coleridge's distinctive service to nineteenth century religion can be well illustrated from his *Letters on the Inspiration of the Scriptures*, published posthumously (1840) as *Confessions of an Inquiring Spirit*. The Bible being the religion of Protestants, it was inevitable that in England, when the results of half a century of German criticism became known, and when Lyell, Darwin and the rest added their quota to the disturbance, the storm should have centred upon this very question. It was therefore of great importance that an Englishman, in touch with German thought yet essentially orthodox, should already, before the storm broke in earnest,

---

[1] *The Friend*, pp. 217-19.   [2] *Ibid.*, p. 301 (my italics).

have demonstrated the true invulnerability of the Bible. In order to do this he had first to show that its alleged invulnerability was an idol and a superstition, and secondly that the way to deal with criticism was not to offer blind resistance but to deepen one's understanding. As Hooker had said, 'no untruth can possibly avail the patrons and defenders long', and in so far as the Bibliolaters (a term of Coleridge's own coining) were committed to an impossible 'fundamentalism' they were betraying their own cause. During the first thirty years of the nineteenth century in England a barren and reactionary bibliolatry was prevalent. Little was known of what was going on abroad, and from that little, which seemed the index of so much that was horrifying, our divines recoiled into a more determined insularity. Van Mildert, in his Bampton Lectures (1814), said that acceptance of any biblical 'criticism' indicated moral defectiveness, unsoundness of faith and disloyalty to the Church. The view most generally accepted (save by a few isolated spirits like Alexander Geddes, Connop Thirlwall and—surprisingly perhaps —Pusey) was that the Bible was a theological text-book and rule of faith composed by Almighty God, and dictated by Him verbatim to the inspired writers. Being inspired in this way 'from cover to cover', every statement and sentiment it contained, whether historical, scientific, moral or prophetic, and whether expressed in a prosaic or a figurative manner, must be accepted as the undoubted word of God. It is difficult indeed now to recapture, by an effort of historical imagination, the outlook of a period in which it could be supposed that religion must stand or fall by a misapprehension so colossal as this. All the more gratitude is due from us, then, if we have attained to wiser insights, to those who in the nineteenth century faced obloquy and condemnation to remove the misapprehension. Professor Leonard Hodgson has well expressed our debt to them in the following passage:

> 'When in the nineteenth century that way of accepting the Bible was challenged by the progress of scientific and historical enquiries, the challenge had to be met, and the only honest way in which the Church could meet it was by encouraging its theologians them-

selves to subject the Bible to the most rigorous criticism. This had to be done, and we today owe a debt of gratitude to those of our forefathers who had faith enough to do it. . . . We should think of those scholars as men upon whom the circumstances of their time laid the intolerable strain of finding that what they had taken to be the foundation of their faith was full of quicksands, as men who had faith and courage enough to dig and sift until they secured the solid ground on which they could and we can stand. For the time being this digging and sifting was a whole time job. If they could not be expounding the Bible as the Word of God, that was because they were occupied in making it possible for us to do so.' [1]

Coleridge was not himself one of the diggers and sifters, though when in Germany he had read Eichhorn's *Introduction to the Old Testament*, Lessing's *Tracts* and fragments of Reimarus. Nor were his *Letters on Inspiration* written in reply to any specific challenge from the side of scientific and historical criticism. But in demonstrating that Christianity could and must be disengaged from the millstone of fundamentalism he was in effect producing a blue-print for all possible future defences of the faith. Bibliolatry was exposing religion then, as it had done during the eighteenth century, to infidel attacks which would have been perfectly justified if faith had really rested on such foundations. Coleridge's literary and spiritual insight placed him upon a point of vantage from which he could overlook the nineteenth century country in front of him, and reply in advance to all that the *Zeitgeist* would thereafter bring forward. The standpoint of the *Letters* transcends the level of the later Science-and-Religion controversies, none of which need have arisen had his ground been firmly occupied from the beginning.

The key-note of his argument is struck in this phrase:

'*Evidences* of Christianity! I am weary of the word. Make a man feel the *want* of it; rouse him, if you can, to the self-knowledge of his *need* of it; and you may safely trust it to its own Evidence.' [2]

Faith, for Coleridge, like Imagination in poetry, must be an

---

[1] *Biblical Theology and the Sovereignty of God* (Cambridge, 1947), pp. 16-17.
[2] In *Aids to Reflection* (Bohn ed.), p. 272.

energy of the whole being, not a mechanical acceptance of an *opus operatum*; and the Bible, its outward support and continual enlivener, must be approached as a receptacle of living truths, and not as a dead letter. The first step in spiritual experience is neither the search for intellectual certainty nor submission to authority; it is, quite simply, to *hunger and thirst* after righteousness, to be aware 'of a deep sense of infirmity and manifold imperfection', and to feel accordingly 'the want, the necessity of religious support'. Let anyone who knows this take up the Bible and 'read it for the first time' as he would read 'any other work'; he will find in it 'copious sources of truth, and power, and purifying impulses'; words for his inmost thoughts, songs for his joy, utterances for his hidden griefs, pleadings for his shame and feebleness.

> 'In short whatever *finds* me, bears witness for itself that it has proceeded from a Holy Spirit.'[1]

And in the Bible there is more that 'finds' him, and at greater depths of his being, than in all other books put together. But the doctrine of verbal inspiration is a stumbling-block to one who feels that 'the Bible and Christianity are their own sufficient evidence'; moreover, it exposes the believer to the 'cold and captious' questioner who will ask 'what, then, of the Book of Esther? verses 6-20 of Psalm cix, or the last verse of Psalm cxxxvii?' This is the mischief of fundamentalism, that it 'petrifies' the whole body of sacred literature, and 'turns at once into a colossal Memnon's head, a hollow passage for a voice', that which is in truth a living, breathing organism. The 'heart-awakening utterances' of Deborah, or of the sweet psalmist of Israel, lose their power over us if we regard the speakers as mere automata of a superhuman—'O bear with me if I say—Ventriloquist'. Another inconvenience of the doctrine is that it forces grave and pious men into pitiful subterfuges for the removal of 'discrepancies' in the sacred narratives—discrepancies which are quite analogous to those found 'in

[1] *Ibid.*, p. 295.

all other known and trusted histories', and which at any rate their infallible Author (on the fundamentalist view) had not seen fit to harmonize. In this way the 'ordinary criteria of full or defective evidence in historical documents', applicable to the biblical text as to any other, are subverted, and counsel hopelessly darkened. Other evils are the literal rendering of figurative passages, and the uncritical acceptance of 'the hydrography and natural philosophy of the Patriarchal ages'. 'My Brother!' exclaims Coleridge (and how much later misunderstanding might have been spared if his words had been heeded)—'My Brother! What has all this to do with the truth and the worth of Christianity?' Meanwhile, don't be 'an Infidel on the score of what other men think fit to include in their Christianity'. The Bible contains, but does not constitute, the Christian religion; we must not say that whatever the Bible contains is the Christian religion, but that the truth revealed through Christ, truth whose divine authority is proved by its fitness to our nature and needs, is communicated by it. Coleridge, in a passage of torrential eloquence, disposes of the view that once we admit human imperfections in Scripture, its whole authority goes by the board. The Bible is the Word of God, not because it is in all parts unquestionable, but because for all who seek truth with humble spirits it is an unquestionable guide. And this incomparable Volume, in which the hungry have found food and the thirsty a living spring; this foundation-stone of our civilization for a thousand years; this 'organ and instrument of all the gifts, powers and tendencies by which the individual is privileged to rise above himself'—shall it lose its value because 'in the framework and outer case of this instrument a few parts may be discovered of less costly materials and meaner workmanship'? Because David 'cruelly tortured the inhabitants of Rabbah' and sometimes invoked 'the bitterest curses on his enemies', are we not to believe in God's redemption of the world through Christ? Because Abijah slew 500,000 of Jeroboam's 800,000, must we believe that the injunction to love our enemies cannot proceed from the Holy Spirit? If in the biblical writers 'all imperfection of knowledge, all participation in the mistakes and limits of their several ages had been excluded, how could these Writings be or become the history and example, the echo and more lustrous image of the work and warfare of the sanctifying Principle in us?'

'If, after all this', Coleridge concludes, 'and in spite of all this,

'some captious litigator should lay hold of a text here or there— St. Paul's *cloak left at Troas with Carpus*, or a verse from the Canticles, and ask: "Of what spiritual use is this?"—the answer is ready:—It proves to us that nothing can be so trifling as not to supply an evil heart with a pretext for unbelief.'

The modern Christian will find Coleridge in one respect too uncritical: all passages of Scripture 'in which the words are by the sacred historian declared to have been the Word of the Lord supernaturally communicated, I receive as such'— though he adds, indeed, 'with a degree of confidence proportioned to the confidence required of me by the writer himself, and to the claims he himself makes on my belief'. But the strength of Coleridge lies in his application to religion of his central teaching, that life consists in the interpenetration of opposites, the subjective human needs coalescing here with the Logos, the Word which is the Light of men. Starting from the experience of his own weakness and the need for deliverance, the probationer finds in the Bible 'an objectiveness, a confirming outwardness, and all the main characters of reality, reflected therefrom on the spirit'. There is

'A balance, an ennobling interchange,
Of action from within and from without';

'as much of Reality, as much of objective truth, as the Scriptures communicate to the subjective experiences of the Believer, so much of present life, of living and effective import, do these experiences give to the letter of these Scriptures.' As, in speculation, the enemy is the philosophy which turns Nature into a dead mechanism, so, in religion, it is the doctrine which petrifies the living word into a dead letter, and reduces the life of faith to a torpid routine, or extinguishes it altogether.

vii. The Constitution of Church and State

It is only for convenience that one attempts to separate the various sides of Coleridge's thought, and to discuss successively his literary, philosophical, religious or political views. To him all alike were meaningless in disconnexion from that living core of energy which in poetry is imagination, and in life itself is religion. Coleridge's mind was never 'made up', in the sense of being closed into a system; it was, like the fundamental postulate of his philosophy, an active principle, 'an open thoroughfare for all thoughts, not a select party'. His knowledge was 'growledge', and like Plato he invites us to share with him the pains and pleasures of growing. Thus, in spite of appearances, it is unwise to think of him as 'changing his mind'. When we recall his early republican ardours, his sonnets to Godwin and Priestley, and his Pantisocracy, and then contemplate him as the sage of Highgate, denouncing Jacobinism and the godless Revolution, exploding the 'rights of man', defending inequalities of rank and property and opposing the Reform Bill, we may feel that we are witnessing one more illustration of the Tory reaction of that age. But if Coleridge's mind changes, it changes only as (to use a favourite image of his) the larva changes through chrysalis to perfect insect; his change is the working out of an inward principle of development which was inherent from the start. And this seminal principle, I have suggested, was always a sense of the Whole as a living unity, rooted and grounded in God. In coming finally, then, to his mature political views, it will be no surprise to find that his politics are religious, and his religion political. For this very reason he was able to survey the whole human scene from an elevation above the reach of his English contemporaries, and to subject it to a critique more searching and comprehensive (though fitfully conducted) than any it could receive from the Utilitarians or Evangelicals, or indeed had received since the seventeenth century. He was the first of the nineteenth century 'prophets', and if not (because of his incomplete achievement) actually the greatest, yet potentially so, for he combined with the prophetic animus the philosophic vision of the schoolman.

In *The Constitution of Church and State*[1] Coleridge offers a reasoned defence of the 'Ideas' of both, that is, of both State and Church considered as fulfilling their proper historical functions. By 'Idea' he means, not the conception of a thing abstracted from its particular form at any given time, but that which is 'given by the knowledge of its ultimate aim'. An 'Idea' may be true without ever having been a historical 'fact', or without being fully realized in day-to-day living. An illustration of the first is the 'social contract', which, though unhistorical, derives its validity from the 'ever-originating social contract' implied in the continuance of society at all. Similarly the Ideas of God, freedom, will, good, true, beautiful, 'regulate' our practical lives; they are 'truth-powers of the reason', even though the understanding may reject them, and even though they may never be lived-out into full actuality. 'Ideas', he says, 'correspond to substantial beings, to objects the actual subsistence of which is implied in their idea, though only by the idea revealable'; they are 'spiritual realities that can only be spiritually discerned'. What, then, are the 'Ideas', in this sense, of State and Church? The Idea of a State consists in the balance or equilibrium of two main antagonist or opposite interests: *permanence* and *progression*. 'Permanence' is represented by the landed interest, comprised under the 'Major Barons' (House of Lords) and the 'Minor Barons' or 'Franklins' (House of Commons); 'Progression' by the 'Burgesses', or the mercantile, manufacturing, distributive and professional classes (the most numerous body in the House of Commons). Parliament, as Mr Brinton says, 'represents not the people in the sense of an aggregate of individuals, but the interests, the group-loyalties, into which the people are really divided, and in which alone they have a political life'.[2] The Constitution was never historically framed with the intention of

---

[1] Published 1829.
[2] Crane Brinton, *Political Ideas of the English Romanticists*, pp. 77-8.

securing this balance, yet the balance was the Idea towards which its evolution has tended. Coleridge does not make the mistake of confusing the ideal with the actual, and of basing a reactionary conservatism upon an acceptance of the *status quo*. He sees clearly wherein the existing balance falls short of a true equilibrium; he sees, for example, that, as things are, the 'landed' interest has too much preponderance over the monied, and that we give 'to the real or imagined interests of the comparatively few the imposing name of the interest of the whole'. Wherever there is life and energy, the health of the body politic demands organized powers to express them. But the deeper malady of the modern State lies in a more disastrous unbalance: the failure of the Third Estate to counter-balance the other two, and to supply the pre-conditions of any good life. The Idea of this Estate is that of a National Church, whose concern is with the ground, the necessary antecedent condition of the other Estates, namely *cultivation*, 'the harmonious development of those qualities and faculties that characterize our humanity'. 'We must be men in order to be citizens.' This 'National Church', Coleridge explains, does not mean the Christian Church as such nor the Church as by law established. In 'Idea' it is a third organ of the State, in which is vested a portion of the national wealth ('Nationalty') for spiritual and cultural ends. This 'Nationalty' is intended to support 'The Clerisy', that is, all the clerkly persons whose functions are spiritual and educational: the learned (a small class devoted to advanced academic teaching and enquiry) and a numerous body of clergymen and teachers so distributed as to leave no corner of the country 'without a resident guide, guardian and instructor'. The Church of England, though falling short of the Idea, does at least maintain, as a nucleus of culture, a scholar and a gentleman in every parish of the land. Coleridge's 'National Church', then, is a comprehensive (and perhaps rather ill-chosen) term covering all those educational and cultural influences for the maintenance of which the State must set aside adequate funds. Now that State services of all kinds, and especially State education, have come into existence, part of Coleridge's pleading loses its importance, though he need lose none of the credit for being so far ahead of his time. But there is admonishment for us still, perhaps more than ever, in his emphatic reminder that there is an Idea to be reached, and a civilization to be cherished, 'without which the nation could be neither permanent nor progressive'. Most of what he says in chapter vii (called 'Regrets and Apprehensions') is applicable now. In a passage anticipating *Culture and Anarchy*, Coleridge has just rehearsed the catalogue of 'inventions, discoveries, public improvements, docks, railways, canals and the like' for which that age was justly famous. 'We live', he exclaims, 'under the dynasty of the understanding: and this is its golden age.' But the understanding, as we have seen, deals with *means*: 'with these the age, this favoured land, teems. . . . But the ultimate ends? Where shall I seek for information concerning these?' He passes on (anticipating, this time, *Past and Present*, and much besides) to deplore that all this 'progress' has merely produced a 'wealth-machine' on the one hand, and pauperism on the other; that the national welfare—the weal and happiness of the people—has not advanced with the increase of 'circumstantial prosperity'; that education is soon to be severed from all religion, and reduced to 'instruction' in mechanic arts; that the 'Church' is no longer an Estate, but has become a Sect.

Coleridge distinguished the 'National Church' from the 'Christian Church' in this way:

> 'In relation to the national Church, Christianity, or the Church of Christ, is a blessed accident. . . . Let not the religious reader be offended with this phrase [he adds in a footnote]. I mean only that Christianity is an aid and instrument which no State or realm could have produced out of its own elements, which no State had a right to expect. It was, most awfully, a GOD-SEND!'[1]

It is distinguished by four main characters: (i) it is not a kingdom of this world, nor an estate of any realm, but 'the appointed opposite of them all collectively—the sustaining, correcting, befriending opposite of the world; the compensating counterforce to the inherent and inevitable evils and

[1] *Op. cit.* (1852 ed.), pp. 65-6.

defects of the State'. This aspect of Christianity Coleridge has developed most cogently in the *Lay Sermon* of 1817, where he traces our present distresses to one main cause: the over-balance of the commercial spirit in the absence or weakness of the proper 'counter-weights'. He has mentioned, amongst these counter-weights, 'the ancient feeling of rank and ancestry', and the pursuit of philosophic truth as understood, not by the modern physical and psychological empiricists, but by the ancients and the schoolmen. Then he comes to the third and most important: Religion, and gives us a piece of sociological analysis of a kind hardly to be met with before him. Amongst a religious and respectable bourgeoisie like ours, might we not expect to find 'Christianity tempering commercial avidity, and sprinkling its holy damps on the passion of accumulation'? But alas! many of these 'zealous religionists' (he mentions the Quakers as typical), though patrons of Sunday Schools, though alms-givers, and though often distributors of edifying tracts (as a side-line while travelling for orders), are avaricious to the marrow. Does religion of this kind 'exert any efficient force of control over the commercial spirit'? No! the Christian Mammonists are heavily-laden camels trying vainly to pass through the needle's eye. Modern religion has unfortunately parted company with the 'bookish theology' which had the power to divert the mind from worldly ends; by professing, as it too often does, to hunger after righteousness alone (in the sense of 'respectability'), and by taking the whole sphere of spiritual truth 'for granted', it has left the mind vacant for temporal preoccupations, and its adherents thus commonly become shrewd business men. (ii) The second distinguishing character of the Christian Church is that it is neither a secret community, nor the inward Kingdom 'which cometh not with observation', but a visible, militant institution. (iii) Thirdly, the two former characters are reconciled, and can co-exist, in virtue of the absence of any visible head or sovereign or any local centre of unity. The Church is no 'state' in rivalry with 'The State'; it counteracts, not the world's institutions, but only the evils which may arise from them; and Caesar, receiving always what is Caesar's, recognizes, in Christians, subjects distinguished 'by the more exemplary performance of their duties as citizens'. (iv) Lastly, it is 'universal'—that is neither Anglican, Gallican, Roman nor Greek, but simply the Catholic Church under Christ. Coleridge, in spite of his reverence for the religion and the religious philosophy of the Middle Ages, condemns the Roman Catholic Church as neither national nor universal.

It was this distinctive blend of religion with politics and education which made Coleridge's teaching so influential, first with Thomas Arnold for whom (as we shall see later) the Church *was* the State viewed in its spiritual aspect, and who wished to include all Christian denominations within the 'established' Church; and later, with F. D. Maurice and the Christian Socialists, who, starting from the Idea of the Kingdom of God as real, believed it to be the Church's duty to actualize it, to make that Kingdom come on earth as it is in heaven. We began this chapter with Mill, and we may fitly end it with him. The eighteenth century philosophers, as Mill said, thought that perfection could be easily achieved by sweeping away the heritage of the past—by abolishing priests and kings, and all the loyalties traditionally associated with them, and leaving the individual free to follow Nature and Reason and The Main Chance. Coleridge, aware how complex a growth society is, and how dependent upon other forces and influences than the naked reason, urged that by the 'soul' alone can nations be great and free. In place of the Utilitarian *laissez-faire*, the free competition of all individuals for worldly wealth, he puts forward a conception of the State as the condition in which all can realize the good life, and their own best selves. The State is indeed a spiritual organism, or—in the phrase of Burke, who had already seen it in the same light—a partnership in perfection, a community of the noble living and the noble dead. The condition of Europe in the early nineteenth century fell so far short of these ideals that it was bound, Mill says,

'to call forth two sorts of men—the one demanding the extinction of the institutions and creeds which had hitherto existed; the other that they be made a reality: the one pressing the new doctrines to their utmost consequences; the other reasserting the best meaning and purposes of the old. The first type attained its greatest height in Bentham; the last in Coleridge.'[1]

[1] *Dissertations and Discussions* (1867 ed.), vol. i, p. 436.

CHAPTER II

THOMAS ARNOLD

1. The 'Eminent Victorian'

AFTER reading Sir J. T. Coleridge on Keble, Matthew Arnold wrote to his mother:

'my one feeling when I close the book is of papa's immense superiority to all the set, mainly because, owing to his historic sense, he was so wonderfully, for his nation, time, and profession, European, and thus so got himself out of the narrow medium in which, after all, his friends lived.'[1]

This might be discounted as filial piety in the author of *Rugby Chapel*, yet today it seems nearer the mark than the mocking ironies of Lytton Strachey. At this distance the Eminent Victorians begin rather to appear to us like the peaks of a mountain-range, hitherto obscured by foreground objects, but now visible in its true proportions, impressive in its altitude and its noble outlines. Strachey wrote at the time when it was exciting and comforting to debunk the nineteenth century; the post-war generation of the 'twenties, at once emancipated and disillusioned, found compensation for its own aimlessness in mocking at the earnestness, the high tone, the 'moral thoughtfulness', of its grandparents. Arnold, and Arnold's Rugby, were easy targets for the anti-Victorian sniper. By the devices of bathos and the subtle misuse of quotation Lytton Strachey produced a skilful and very readable piece of falsification. Arnold's doubts about the Trinity are juxtaposed with his difficulty in early rising; his appearance, expressive of 'energy, earnestness, and the best intentions', is robbed of its dignity by an aside about his short legs; his views on the inspiration of Scripture are represented as confined to such petty matters as the parentage of Abijah's mother; his sermons in Chapel are deflated as

[1] *Letters*, vol. ii, p. 5 (Feb. 20, 1869).

explanations of 'the general principles both of his own conduct and that of the Almighty'; his reforms at Rugby are exhibited as the origin of the public-school cult of good form and athletics. In this way, and by using as a leitmotiv the 'puzzled' expression of Arnold's face in the well-known portrait, Strachey leaves us with an Arnold who is a high-minded but blundering and conventional prig.

The impression Arnold is likely to make upon any candid reader who now considers his life and work is very different. If, after the first World War, we were all debunking the nineteenth century, after the second we are deferring to it, and even yearning nostalgically after it: *tendentesque manus ripae ulterioris amore*. In our own unpleasant century we are mostly displaced persons, and many feel tempted to take flight into the nineteenth as into a promised land, and settle there like illegal immigrants for the rest of their lives. In that distant mountain country, all that we now lack seems present in abundance: not only peace, prosperity, plenty and freedom, but faith, purpose and buoyancy. Leading men, of whom Arnold was a type, were then conscious of a destiny and a duty, whose fulfilment, whether conceived as an obligation to God or to one's fellow-creatures, would make life significant and satisfying. This unquestioning sense that life has momentous meaning, and the 'unhasting, unresting diligence' in the effort to realize it, gives to the great men of the last century a quality which inevitably overawes the present generation—a generation which has so largely lost its sense of direction and of any distinct moral summons, and yet is anxious to recover both.

ii. The Idea of a Christian Society

I do not propose to speak here, except incidentally, of Arnold as the great Headmaster who changed the face of education all through the public schools of England, but to consider his place in that development of religious and moral ideas which is the main theme of this book. No account of Arnold will do him justice which fails to recognize the depth and intensity of his religious convictions; his life was indeed, as a disciple said, 'rooted in God'. Earnestness, zest and 'moral thoughtfulness' were the leading traits of his character, and he had an extraordinary power of communicating these qualities to others. 'Every pupil was made to feel', says the same informant, 'that there was work for him to do —that his happiness as well as his duty lay in doing that work well. Hence an indescribable zest was communicated to a young man's feeling about life; ... and a deep respect and ardent attachment sprang up towards him who had taught him thus to value life and his own self, and his work and mission in this world.'[1] When we have said of him that he had that continual consciousness of God's reality of which he noted the insufficiency in himself and others, we have already said what should dispose us to a respectful approach. But this statement by itself is insufficient; we must go on to say that his whole life echoed that exclamation of Whichcote's: 'Give me a religion that doth attain real effects.' Christianity he regarded as 'the sovereign science of life in all its branches'.[2] 'The "*Idea*" of my life', he wrote to Mr Justice Coleridge,

> 'to which I think every thought of my mind more or less tends, is the perfecting the "idea" of the Edward the Sixth Reformers—the constructing a truly national and Christian Church, and a truly national and Christian system of education.'[3]

Arnold was deeply influenced by Coleridge, above all by his *Constitution of Church and State*; in him, the Coleridgean 'Ideas' become a programme of action. Arnold's special greatness consists largely in this: that he had not only the desire, but the actual ability, to make ideas real; it was noted by his pupils that he made history and the ancient classics *live* for them. The leading principle of his whole life's effort was to realize the idea of a Christian Society, in microcosm at Rugby, and at large in the nation. 'The idea of a Christian school', as Stanley says, 'was to him the natural result, so to speak, of the very idea of a school in itself; exactly as the idea of a Christian State seemed to him to be involved in the

---

[1] B. Price, quoted in Stanley's *Life of Arnold* (1898 ed.), vol. i, p. 37.
[2] *Ibid.*, p. 295.   [3] *Ibid.*, vol. ii (Nov. 18, 1835), p. 12.

very idea of a State itself.'[1] For him the worst apostasy, the source of all woes, was the separation of things secular from things spiritual: this meant, on the one hand, the handing over of all temporal concerns to the devil or to the operation of natural laws, and on the other, the retreat of religion into priestly inutilities. The first was the sin of the Evangelicals and Puritans. The second, that of the 'Oxford Malignants'. Like the Cambridge Platonists, he stands as a middle-man between High Church and Puritan; his place is in the succession which descends from Hooker, through the Platonists to Coleridge, and leads on through F. D. Maurice to William Temple. 'The true and grand idea of a Church' is that it should be 'a society for the purpose of making men like Christ,—earth like heaven,—the Kingdoms of the world the Kingdom of Christ'; instead, 'men look upon it as "an institution for religious instruction and religious worship"',

> 'thus robbing it of its life and universality, making it an affair of clergy, not of people—of preaching and ceremonies, not of living—of Sundays and synagogues, instead of one of all days and all places, houses, streets, towns and country.'[2]

The *end* of the Church is 'the putting down of moral evil'; its *nature*, 'a living society of all Christians'. He was equally opposed both to the Jacobinical-Evangelical view of the State as existing only for physical ends, and to the priestly view of the Church as a separate society governed by a divinely appointed hierarchy; it was above all the perversion of the Church into a sacerdotal caste which hindered the coming of the Kingdom. The Nation (and in miniature the School) was in his view the true sphere for the realization of Christianity, and this could never be achieved as long as there were great areas of human activity—war and peace, economics, education—which were regarded as secular or profane, and thus as exempted from the spiritual critique. His favourite idea, the idea which gave unity and meaning to all sides of his work, was to introduce 'the highest principles of action into regions comparatively uncongenial to their reception'.[3] Of these

[1] *Ibid.*, vol. i, p. 95. [2] *Ibid.*, vol. ii, p. 13. [3] *Ibid.*, vol. i, p. 86.

'regions', that which Arnold knew best was the nature of boyhood, and no one realized more clearly than he how 'uncongenial' this was apt to be to the reception of the 'highest principles'. Though he hoped to make Rugby 'a place of Christian education', he never expected to do more than begin to form Christian men, 'for Christian boys I can scarcely hope to make; I mean', he adds,

> 'that from the natural imperfect state of boyhood, they are not susceptible of Christian principles in their full development upon their practice, and I suspect that a low standard of morality in many respects must be tolerated amongst them, as it was on a larger scale in what I consider the boyhood of the human race.'[1]

It was because he realized how 'uncongenial' also were the regions of secular politics and the social order, that he wished to rally all Christians into one great national society for Christianizing our whole social, political and economic organism. The alarms and disturbances of the Reform Bill period, and all the prevalent miseries, inequalities and injustices, seemed to him to be due to the failure of the national Church to check the national sins. 'I cannot understand', he wrote,

> 'what is the good of a national Church if it be not to Christianize the nation, and introduce the principles of Christianity into men's social and civil relations, and expose the wickedness of that spirit which maintains the game laws, and in agriculture and trade seems to think that there is no such sin as covetousness, and that if a man is not dishonest, he has nothing to do but make all the profit of his capital that he can.'[2]

From at least as early as 1827 Arnold had conceived the idea of a *magnum opus* on Christian Politics or Church and State; he never completed this, but we have his leading ideas in the *Principles of Church Reform* (1833), in the *Fragment on the Church* (published 1844) with its Appendices, and in his Sermons and letters. These ideas were fully formed before the Oxford Movement began, though his later pronounce-

[1] *Ibid.*, vol. i, p. 75.   [2] *Ibid.*, p. 243.

ments were often influenced by his opposition to the spirit of Tractarianism. The point on which he first attained to clear certainty was that the Christian view of the true end of man has a direct bearing on 'our views of national wealth, and the whole question of political economy'. Where Church and State are properly united according to the true idea of each, 'the Gospel is directly brought into contact with political institutions, and has to purify these as well as private individuals; the clergy are directly called upon to Christianize the nation, not only to inculcate the private virtues of the Gospel'. This duty the Church of England has neglected; on the unchristian principles of statecraft, on the unchristian order of society, on war, on the slave trade, its pronouncements have been equivocal. The purpose of the Gospel is righteousness, not 'imputed' merely, but actual and operative: 'the restoration of our moral nature from its state of corrupt principles and practice, and the raising it into a capacity of enjoying everlasting communion with God'.[1] To represent Christianity as an 'awful mystery' is to separate it from living issues; it is this above all which has provoked the German rationalist reaction. With that iteration which became a still more marked mannerism in his son Matthew, Arnold insists that the Church is a society 'for the putting down of moral evil', 'for the moral improvement of mankind'; edification, devotion, consolation and the like are important objects, but they are means, not ends in themselves. The 'social character' of religion has been lost sight of, and the ministry has been corrupted into a priesthood, almost monopolizing 'the active functions of the whole body'. And if the Church has failed through this sacerdotal aloofness, it has failed no less through a misconception of the nature of Christian doctrine; the predominant character of Christian doctrine has been supposed to be 'truth', whereas it is, in fact, 'efficacy for moral good'; its inmost *raison d'être* is the transformation of men and society, not the declaration of certain propositions. Christian doctrine is made up of 'precept' and 'exemplary facts', and it is an error to exclude precept from it, consigning this to a lower

[1] *Fragments on Church and State* (1845), Appendix I, p. 11.

category as 'practical instruction'. The practical side of Christianity is, for Arnold, its very essence, and

> 'there can be no more fatal error, none certainly more entirely at variance with the Scripture model, than to acquaint the mind with the truths of religion in a theoretical form, leaving the application of them to be made afterwards.'[1]

Scripture is 'wholly relative and practical', 'as producing a certain particular moral impression on our minds,—not as declaring some positive truth in the nature of things'. It is here that the Articles differ from Scripture, for they convey Christian doctrines 'in the shape of abstract truths', instead of conveying them 'as lessons'.

But the weakness of the Church has been due also to disunity, and especially to the existence of one 'established' Church and a number of 'dissenting' Churches. The true aim of the State is identical with that of 'the Church': the highest well-being of society, moral and spiritual as well as physical; in a Christian country the State cannot but *be* the Church. Arnold would therefore comprehend the Dissenters within the 'idea' of the national Church; this proposal he works out in his *Principles of Church Reform*, a subject about which there was then (1833) much talk, most of it springing, however, in his view, from a desire for 'Church Destruction' or 'Church Robbery'. In defending the idea of an Establishment, he first elaborates Coleridge's point about the importance, in an age of *laissez-faire*, when every individual scrambles for all he can get, of having part of the national wealth 'saved out of the scramble of individual selfishness, and set apart for ever for public purposes'. In England we are 'beset on every side by the exclusiveness of private property'; the Establishment provides a counterpoise and a mitigation of this exclusiveness. Further (another Coleridgean topic), there is the advantage of having a Christian scholar and gentleman in every parish of the land, a man whose sole function is to do as much good as he can; why should anyone doubt the wisdom of this arrangement? However, the sectarian spirit unfortunately exists: it is an

[1] *Ibid.*, Appendix II, p. 34.

inevitable result of the Reformation, for different constructions were bound to be put upon the Scriptures which were acknowledged by all to be authoritative. The Roman Catholic Church avoids the difficulty by claiming infallible wisdom: a 'false claim' indeed, yet the Reformers, while demanding uniformity and conformity, 'disclaimed what alone could justify them in enforcing it—the possession of infallibility'. There followed conflict, persecution and finally 'toleration': anything, in short, rather than Christian charity and Christian union. In the 'deep calm of the first seventy years of the eighteenth century' the Church's stiffness and want of adaptability caused dissent to spread amongst the new manufacturing masses; this calm was succeeded by revolutionary agitation. What then is now to be done? Since, in Protestantism, there is no infallible authority, why not try a different system? why not 'unite in one Church different opinions and different rites and ceremonies'?[1] Arnold considers the possibility of union under three heads: doctrine, government and liturgy. There would be no difficulty in making a résumé of Christian belief in which Anglicans, Presbyterians, Methodists, Independents, Baptists and Moravians could all concur. Quakers could be conciliated by expunging from the Articles the needless justifications of war and oaths. The Unitarians present a rather tougher problem: they would have to go so far as to call Christ 'Lord' and 'God', and use prayers to Him, though we need not force them to explain what they mean by these terms. Arnold was quite sure that the tenets of Unitarianism were irreconcilable with Christianity, as his letter to a Unitarian parent[2] shows, yet he was equally certain that no 'opinions', whether orthodox or not, could as such constitute the bond of communion. Opinions about God's *moral* attributes, indeed,

> 'are of the last importance, because such as we suppose him to be morally, such we strive to become ourselves; but opinions as to his nature metaphysically may be wholly unimportant, because they are often of such a kind as to be wholly inoperative upon our spiritual

[1] *Principles of Church Reform* (1833), in *Miscellaneous Works* (1845), p. 279.
[2] Stanley's *Life*, vol. i, p. 225.

state: they neither advance us in goodness; nor obstruct our progress in it.'[1]

As for Church government, Arnold held with Hooker that the Scriptures are the sole authority for Christian truth, but not for the constitution and rules of the Church, on which Christ and the apostles left us no instructions. The original idea of the Christian Church was that the whole body of Christians should share in its concerns, the notion of a 'human priesthood' being excluded by the primary recognition of Christ as the sole priest and intercessor. 'To restore Christ's church, therefore, is to expel the antichrist of priesthood', and to restore the laity to the discharge of their proper duties.[2] At present, Church organization is far too thin and sketchy, and not democratic enough. In a parish we have only the parish clerk, the churchwardens, the overseers of the poor, the beadle and constable: 'what an organization for a religious society!' he exclaims. His proposed remedies were numerous: he would, first, revive the Order of Deacons, which would provide a much-needed link between clergy and laity, and dispel the prevailing confusion of 'church' and 'clergy'; he would repeal the laws forbidding deacons to follow a secular calling. Behind this proposal is Arnold's desire to abolish the distinction between 'spiritual' and 'secular'; for him, all things are secular, and all things spiritual. He would, moreover, modify the Articles, so that dissenting ministers might at once become ministers of the Establishment. To make the constitution of the Church more democratic, and to give the laity a greater interest in its concerns, he would have church officers in every parish, lay and clerical, to share responsibility with the parson; he would even allow election of ministers. He would, indeed, retain Episcopacy, and holds that insistence on episcopal ordination would not be unreasonable in return for his many concessions.

Lastly, on the question of public worship, Arnold's main proposal is to use the parish churches for all the varying

---

[1] *Principles* (postscript), p. 325.
[2] Cf. Introd. to *Sermons*, vol. iv (1841), p. lii.

services of the united sects: services which would be held at different times, not only on Sundays, but on weekdays as well: 'I hardly know a more melancholy sight', he says, 'than the uninterrupted loneliness in which our Churches are so often left, from one Sunday to another.'[1] The Church's constant repetitions of the same liturgy are to him an evil, and he would welcome the proposed variety—though he does not expect the denominations to attend each other's services unless they like. The aesthetic appeal of the parish church is of the highest importance, and this new use of it would ensure

> 'that some of the most perfect specimens of architecture in existence should no longer be connected, in any man's mind, with the bitterness of sectarian hostility; that none should be forced to associate, with their most solemn and dearest recollections, such utter coarseness and deformity as characterize the great proportion of the Dissenting chapels throughout England.'

High Churchmen will probably denounce him as 'latitudinarian' and 'liberal', he concludes; but the issue is nothing less than the continuance of England as a Christian country, 'and England, to a true Englishman, ought to be dearer than the peculiar forms of the Church of England'.

III. Arnold and the Oxford Movement

It is not surprising that a man who held such views, a man who disliked the Articles because they 'represent truth untruly', whereas the same truth 'becomes more Christian, just in proportion as it is less theological'—should have been utterly opposed to the Oxford Movement. He described the Tractarians as 'the very bad party', considered that they were teaching 'old error' instead of 'new truth', and professed himself unable to account for the strange infatuation of those who found Newmanism attractive. Oxford men, in his opinion, were idolaters, because they placed Church and Sacrament above Christ himself. Moreover, at a time when

[1] *Principles*, p. 305.

differences between Christian and Christian had become insignificant beside the profound and ever-growing opposition of Christian and non-Christian, 'all this stuff about the true Church' seemed to him tragically irrelevant and futile. The sort of clergyman who could anxiously doubt whether, unless appointed by genuine Apostolical succession, he could safely and assuredly administer the sacraments, appeared to Arnold to be 'substituting unrealities for realities'. His view of the Oxford Movement is well seen in the Introduction to the fourth volume of his Sermons, to which he characteristically prefixes this extract from Coleridge (*Literary Remains*, iii, 386):

> 'As far as the principle on which Archbishop Laud and his followers acted went to re-actuate his idea of the church, as a co-ordinate and living power by right of Christ's institution and express promise, I go along with them; but I soon discover that by the church they meant the clergy, the hierarchy exclusively, and then I fly off from them in a tangent.'

Arnold quotes a phrase from Newman's celebrated letter to Dr Jelf (1841) explaining the purpose of Tract xc; this is what Newman had said (I have italicized the quoted phrase):

> 'There is at the moment a great progress of the religious mind of our Church to *something deeper and truer than satisfied the last century*.... The poets and philosophers of the age have borne witness to it many years. Those great names in our literature, Sir Walter Scott, Mr Wordsworth, Mr Coleridge, though in different ways and with essential differences one from another, and perhaps from any Church system, bear witness to it.... The age is moving towards something, and most unhappily the one religious communion among us which has of late years been in practice in possession of that something is the Church of Rome. She alone, amid all the errors and evils of her practical system, has given free scope to the feelings of awe, mystery, tenderness, reverence, devotedness, and other feelings which may be especially called Catholic.'

With much of this, and especially with the quest for 'something deeper and truer than satisfied the last century', Arnold could not fail to be in full sympathy. His own strivings were in precisely that direction, and he too saw in Wordsworth, and still more in Coleridge, happy omens of the spiritual awakening of the age. In Newman's famous essay on *The State of Religious Parties* (*British Critic*, April 1839)[1] Arnold could have found little to offend, and much to encourage him. Newman's references to the European reaction against the superficial rationalism of the eighteenth century, to the shrivelling of Benthamism under a warmer and richer philosophy; his analysis of the three main forces in current European opinion: Popery (Italy), Pantheism (Germany) and Democracy (France); his demand for a *Via Media* which would lead us safely through the pitfalls of all three; his conclusion, especially, that 'though the current of the age cannot be stopped, it may be directed; and it is better that it should find its way into the Anglican port, than that it should be propelled into Popery, or drifted upon unbelief'[2] —all this was fully after Arnold's own heart. But what was Newman's 'something deeper and truer'? Reiterating the phrase in the authentic Arnoldian manner, Arnold finds that it is really, in the last resort, the doctrine of the Apostolical Succession, the doctrine that 'God's grace, and our salvation, come to us principally through the virtues of the sacraments [not through preaching]', and that 'the virtue of the sacraments depends on the apostolical succession of those who administer them'. Newman and the Newmanites, in their reaction from 'the whole period of which the last century was the close, and which began nearly with the sixteenth century', over-idealize the Middle Ages; detesting and dreading their own century, they exalt all that its time-spirit denies. In so doing they revive the mediaeval conception of the Church as a sacerdotal caste, and this to Arnold seemed tragic blindness and folly. 'When we look', he wrote a year before his death,

> 'When we look at the condition of our country; at the poverty and wretchedness of so large a part of the working classes; at the intellectual and moral evils which certainly exist among the poor,

[1] *British Critic*, vol. xxv, p. 395. [2] *Ibid.*, p. 426.

but by no means amongst the poor only; and when we witness the many partial attempts to remedy these evils—attempts benevolent indeed and wise, so far as they go, but utterly unable to strike at the heart of the mischief; can any Christian doubt that here is the work for the Church of Christ to do; that none else can do it; and that with the blessing of her Almighty Head she can.'[1]

And Newman comes forward with nothing better to offer than—the Apostolical Succession! When we consider how utterly inadequate is the present Establishment to meet the needs of the great new manufacturing towns and districts, we may well feel that our business is 'not so much to reform the Church, as to create one'.

IV. Religion and Education

It was Arnold's conviction, expressed in his Inaugural Lecture at Oxford (Dec. 1841), that 'belief in the desirableness of an act differs widely from belief in the truth of a proposition'. 'All societies of men, whether we call them states or churches, should make their bond to consist in a common object and a common practice, rather than in a common belief; in other words, their end should be good rather than truth.'[2] It is for religion to teach us wherein 'good' consists, and how to realize it in our individual lives and in society. Let us not delude ourselves, he warns the Rugby Mechanics' Institute, into supposing that the diffusion of useful knowledge is genuine 'adult education'; neither science nor literature alone can instruct the judgment—only moral and religious knowledge can do this.[3] To discuss educational aims or public reforms as if Christianity did not exist was therefore to sail without a rudder and compass. Christianity is precisely a system for propagating a certain given set of moral standards; to imagine that either intellectual belief or ceremonial practice are its essence is to miss the true proportions of things. He defines

[1] Introd. to *Sermons*, vol. iv (1841), p. lxv.
[2] *Introductory Lectures on Modern History* (1842), pp. 50-2.
[3] Lecture to the Mechanics' Institute at Rugby, *Miscellaneous Works* (1845), p. 423.

religion, indeed, as 'a system directing and influencing our conduct, principles and feelings, and professing to do this with sovereign authority and most efficacious influence'[1]; in a Christian country, therefore, a knowledge of Christianity is essential even to intellectual education. In our own time, a hundred years after Arnold, much is being thought and said about the dangers of specialized training in schools and universities, and especially about the gulf between science and 'the humanities'. In these discussions it often seems to be implied that if only the scientists could be sufficiently dosed with 'culture', and the arts students with science, all would be well. A literary don may perhaps be pardoned for thinking that since much 'literature' contains the Christian and humanist values in solution, the former kind of dosage is even more important than the latter. But in fact Arnold's point stands firm; neither science nor literature alone, nor a mechanical mixture of both, can 'instruct the judgment'. Standards derived from a superior source must be brought to bear upon 'masterpieces' if they are to be rightly appraised, and upon scientific results if we are to learn how to use and apply them without catastrophe.

v. Scriptural Interpretation

It is in his *Essay on the Right Interpretation of the Scriptures*[2] that Arnold most clearly shows that quality designated by his son as 'wonderfully European'. Arnold was one of that very small group of scholars and clergymen who, through Coleridge's writings and through independent study, were aware of German criticism, and awake to its meaning for the future of Protestantism. Already in January 1835 we find him asking Mr Justice Coleridge whether he has seen his uncle's 'Letters on Inspiration', and remarking that they are fitted to 'break ground' on a question which 'involves so great a shock to existing notions'[3]—the greatest shock, he adds, since the exposure of the falsehood of the Papal infallibility doctrine (he does not specify when he thinks that took

---
[1] Stanley's *Life*, vol. ii, p. 69.   [2] *Sermons*, vol. ii (1832).
[3] *Life*, vol. i, p. 344.

place). This shock will most certainly come, but it will end, he characteristically affirms, 'in spite of the fears and clamours of the weak and bigoted, in the higher exalting and more sure establishing of Christian truth'. Two days later he writes to Julius Hare cordially supporting the latter's proposal for a Theological Review; such a Review should, amongst other things, 'make some beginnings of Biblical Criticism, which, as far as relates to the Old Testament, is in England almost non-existent'. What Wolf and Niebuhr have done for Greece and Rome 'seems sadly wanted for Judaea'[1]—that is, the fixing of the dates and real origins of the Old Testament books. What gave Arnold courage and confidence in facing this issue was that deepest of all his convictions, that

> 'Christian unity and the perfection of Christ's Church are independent of theological Articles of opinion; consisting in *a certain moral state and moral and religious affections*, which have existed in good Christians of all ages and all communions, along with an infinitely-varying proportion of truth and error.'[2]

The same conviction enabled him at once to transcend Protestant bibliolatry, and to see the absurdity of that Protestant prejudice which talks of 'Popery as the great Apostasy', and looks for Christ's Church 'only amongst the remnant of the Vaudois'—though he finds it equally absurd 'to look to what is called the Primitive Church or the Fathers for pure models of faith in the sense of opinion or of government'. How, then, should a modern educated man approach his Bible? If he reads it in the old Protestant way, as if it were 'all composed at one time, and addressed to persons similarly situated', he will be perplexed with apparent obscurities, contradictions and immoralities. To guide him through these perplexities Arnold proffers two main conceptions: one, that revelation was 'progressive'; the other, that 'questions of criticism' are quite separate from 'questions of religion'. Revelation was progressive—that is to say, God did not think proper 'to raise mankind at once to its highest state of moral perfection', nor therefore did He reveal His purposes

[1] *Ibid.*, p. 351. [2] *Ibid.*, p. 345 (my italics).

from the outset in a fixed, universal or final form. In any such communication 'between a Being of infinite knowledge, and one of finite', 'accommodation' was inevitable; the commands issued, and the training applied, must be appropriate to each stage of human development. Arnold accordingly lays down his first main principle of interpretation: that

> 'a command given to one man, or one generation of men, is, and can be, binding upon other men and other generations, only so far forth, as the circumstances in which both are placed are similar.'[1]

As in the education of our own children, acts are commanded or forbidden in the childhood of mankind which would be inappropriate at a later and more advanced stage of moral development. We have already seen that Arnold did not consider Rugby 'new boys' to be 'susceptible of Christian principles in their full development', and the same must be true of the boyhood of the human race. The slaughter of the Amalekites enjoined upon Saul, for instance, shocks and appals us, but what would be its moral quality to a chieftain in Saul's age and situation? It would be a command enjoining self-denial: destruction for God instead of exploitation for Saul's own enrichment. We know now that God abhors such acts as the sacrifice of Isaac, but Abraham did not, and the renunciation of what is dearest still remains a necessity of spiritual discipline. Arnold's method leads us virtually to this: that we must distinguish between the original meanings of such passages—their meanings to the patriarchs or to the narrators of their story—and the meanings which they yield when taken as types of Christian truths to be revealed later. The same principle (as Professor Hodges has recently suggested) may be applied to 'prophecy'; the promise of Israel's ultimate triumph, at first interpreted in terms of worldly dominion, was only gradually and painfully seen to be fulfilled through a reversal of earthly hopes, and Christ becomes the antetype of Isaiah's 'suffering servant'. We may concede to 'criticism' that the Old Testament writers were neither 'predicting', nor wrapping up advanced insights in dark parables; nevertheless the Messianic 'prophecies', for ex-

[1] *Sermons*, vol. ii (1832), p. 431.

ample, were indeed 'about Christ' in the sense that what was there mirrored in a glass darkly was in him seen face to face.

On the topic of miracles Arnold's voice becomes more uncertain; I think the subject puzzled and distressed him. He professes to be unable to understand the general argument against all miracles, except on the ground of atheism. Once we reach even the deistical position, once a supernatural reality is admitted, it becomes illogical to deny the possibility of supernatural interventions. If the *a priori* possibility of miracles be admitted, then all will be dependent upon the truth of one miracle: the Resurrection; if *that* is true, we may reject all others without rejecting the Gospel. Arnold evidently does not feel ready to take this line, but he sees that his doctrine of progressive revelation can be applied to the interpretation of miracles. The Old Testament miracles might be disproved, and yet the core of their meaning might remain; they might mean that Israel was conscious of a divine leading, and could only express this consciousness through supernatural imagery. We in the nineteenth century, says Arnold, can dispense with miracles; the lower forms in God's school could not. Does this mean, however, that the miracles 'actually happened', or that the Israelites needed to believe that they had? Arnold's own belief in the divine guidance of the Jews 'inclines' him to accept them literally, though his own principles certainly allowed him greater latitude.

Arnold rises to his best level of insight, however, when he is applying his distinction between 'questions of criticism' and 'questions of religion'. Here his most deeply felt certainty, the conviction that the true basis of religion was moral and spiritual, served him well, and gave him a firm foothold. We hear a great deal, he says, of historical, critical and scientific 'objections' to the Bible, and it seems to be supposed that the Christian faith depends upon their solution, whereas it is really quite unconcerned with them. Even if we jettison the 'inspiration' of the historical records, the 'truths' therein mediated remain unaffected. He protests against the *fear* with which religious people regard critical enquiry; such fear turns 'critical' into 'religious' issues and forces the critics to become impugners of orthodoxy. It is quite true that the critical spirit is often identified with coldness and irreverence; that scholars often discuss God in the abstract, with no feeling of personal relation to Him: 'the Bible has presented itself to their minds more frequently in connexion with their studies than with their practice'. The study of Hebrew is neglected in England, and the student is thus thrown into the arms of the Germans. The remedy is, not to shrink in terror from such studies, but to pursue them more deeply, and in full awareness that they *are* critical studies, and neither devotional exercises nor subversive attacks. 'We know', he writes,

> 'the vehemence with which some of the conclusions of *geology* . . . have been resisted, *as if these, too, interfered with our belief in revelation.*'[1]

But a true believer's faith is 'too deeply rooted to need the paltry aid of ignorance and fear'. What is 'revealed' in Scripture is the will of God and the duty of man, and it is with these that religion is concerned. Historical or geological theories do not, in themselves, belong to the sphere of faith; all that may be demanded of them is that they shall correctly read God's thoughts after Him. Are they true? the believer will ask: then, if so, they cannot conflict with revelation; if they seem to conflict, it is because we have failed, as Israel so often failed, to grasp the deeper meaning of God's message.

> 'With neither the unbeliever's prejudice on one side, nor on the other the prejudice of a faith not duly aware of its own immovable foundations, and approaching therefore, with secret fear, to the examination of questions really powerless to affect it, he will seek truth only, sure that whatever it may be, it must turn to the glory of God.'[2]

Of these 'immovable foundations' Arnold gave a succinct account in two letters to Lady Egerton[3] on 'the conversion of a person with atheistical opinions'; it is an account in the

---

[1] *Ibid.*, p. 482 (my italics).   [2] *Ibid.*, p. 484.
[3] *Life*, vol. i, pp. 271 and 274.

spirit of Coleridge, and almost certainly influenced by him. *Intellectually*, the difficulties of faith are no greater than those of unbelief; *morally*, faith wins every time, for it is a necessary condition of health for the soul. We must not expect or demand that there shall be *no* difficulties; faith, however, determines us to 'embrace that side which leads to moral and practical perfection'. The unbeliever

> 'makes the greatest moral sacrifice to obtain partial satisfaction to his intellect: a believer insures the greatest moral perfection, *with partial satisfaction to his intellect also; entire satisfaction to the intellect is, and can be, attained by neither.*' [1]

vi. Arnold and the Lake District

> '*Be thankful, thou; for if unholy deeds
> Ravage the world, tranquillity is here!*'
>
> [Wordsworth]

So Thomas Arnold might have written of Fox How; so, in other language, he constantly did. For his life was not all 'unhasting, unresting diligence' [2]; like nearly all the Christian (and other) Pilgrims of the nineteenth century, he turned periodically for solace to Beulah and the Delectable Mountains. Near the banks of the Rothay, and in close neighbourhood to Wordsworth at Rydal Mount, Arnold built his holiday home; and there, in that incomparable valley, he (and his family long after him) found rest and regeneration. I speak deliberately of this in a book devoted mainly to other themes, for I think that the whole course of English thought and letters in the nineteenth century would have been different if this island had not contained the mountain paradise of Westmorland and Cumberland. The Lake District was part of its religious creed; as Mr Aldous Huxley has said, for good Wordsworthians a tour through Westmorland was 'as good as a visit to Jerusalem'. The Alps, indeed, offered their rarer ecstasies to the leisured and the adventurous, but the Lakeland mountains, linking heaven with home, spoke more healingly and intimately to the heart

---

[1] *Ibid*. (my italics).   [2] Carlyle's phrase about him.

Throughout that 'iron time of doubts, disputes, distractions, fears', they remained, for the dweller on the darkling plain, a silent and constant symbol of possible sublimity. Amidst the shaking of creeds and the crumbling of foundations, 'Nature' had already, in the previous century, attracted to itself much religious feeling, but it was in the nineteenth century that this particular geographical region became part of the national mythology. Doubtless Wordsworth had much to do with this, but I suspect that even without him the clear streams, the exquisite grass and flowers, the bog-scented air, the silence and the solitude of the district would have supplied their tonic and anodyne to the townsman and the inhabitant of Doubting Castle. For an England becoming steadily smokier and more hideous, and becoming less and less assured of its spiritual foundations and direction, it was (as it still is) of momentous importance that there should remain a region owing nothing to human contrivance and undesecrated by human hand, which could symbolize permanence, grandeur and joy, and convey

> 'Authentic tidings of invisible things;
> Of ebb and flow, and ever-during power;
> And central peace, subsisting at the heart
> Of endless agitation.' [1]

Arnold's passion for Fox How was all the more intense because the lines had not fallen to him in pleasant places; he speaks of the 'unsurpassable dulness of Rugby', and gazes with 'humorous despair' across the fields and hedgerows east of the town, reflecting that 'there is nothing fine between us and the Ural mountains'. Sensitive, like a true son of his century, to every nuance of landscape, he feels the spell of Oxfordshire, and concludes from this that Warwickshire, like Cambridgeshire and most of the eastern counties, is genuinely 'uninteresting', and has not merely suffered in comparison with Westmorland. But Westmorland delighted him not merely because of its beauty, freedom and repose, not merely because of its running streams—'the most beautiful object in nature'—or its wild flowers, which affected him

[1] *Excursion*, bk. iv, 1144.

like music. He valued it also as a retreat from the crudities of school life, and from the sad preoccupations of his working days. When he was at Fox How, the problems of Church and State, rich and poor, faith and reason, and

> 'what we feel of sorrow and despair
> From ruin and from change, and all the grief
> That passing shows of Being leave behind,
> Appeared an idle dream, that could not live
> Where meditation was.'

And so, even in the 'cool, flowery lap of earth', his unsleeping conscience felt the nettle danger; was it, perhaps, ignoble ease that he found in Easedale, 'most delicious of vales'? He looks at the mountains which shut in the valley, and thinks he could be content never to wander beyond them any more, and to take rest in a place he loves so dearly. But then he feels ashamed of the wish; Fox How is 'a home so peaceful and delightful that it would not be right to make it one's constant portion'.[1] Christians must seek not yet repose, and even natural beauty may become a temptation, luring the pilgrim into enchanted gardens and bowers of Acrasia. 'Really, in these most troublous times, it seems more than is allowable to be living, as we are here, in a place of so much rest and beauty.'[2] And yet his normal life was such a 'perpetual turmoil' that surely it could not be amiss to retire at rare intervals to the mount of transfiguration, and stand there with the Lord? Mountain joy can be sacred, not profane; from the days of Moses and the Psalmist to the time of Christ himself and onwards, great things have been when men and mountains met.

> 'I often used to think of the solemn comparison in the Psalm, "the hills stand round about Jerusalem; even so standeth the Lord about his people". The girdling in of the mountains round the valley of our home is as apt an image as any earthly thing can be of the encircling of the everlasting arms, keeping off evil and showering all good.'[3]

No, the truly fatal lure was not the mountains, but the beckoning shadow of the High Church reaction, tempting

---

[1] *Life*, vol. ii, p. 90. [2] *Ibid.*, p. 166. [3] *Ibid.*, p. 43.

us into the mediaeval maze—'like that phantom which Minerva sent to Hector to tempt him to his fate, by making him think that Deiphobus was at hand to help him'.[1] From the hills comes real help:

> 'Early had he learned
> To reverence the volume that displays
> The mystery, the life that cannot die;
> But in the mountains did he *feel* his faith.
> All things, responsive to the writing, there
> Breathed immortality, revolving life,
> And greatness still revolving; infinite:
> There littleness was not; the least of things
> Seemed infinite; and there his spirit shaped
> Her prospects, nor did he believe,—he *saw*.'[2]

Besides, these joys, and this communion, were not tasted in selfish isolation: they were shared with his family and many friends, and above all with Rugby boys.

> 'I find Westmorland very convenient in giving me an opportunity of having some of the Sixth Form with me in the holidays; not to read, of course, but to refresh their health when they get knocked up by the work, and *to show them mountains and dales, a great point in education*, and a great desideratum to those who only know the central or southern counties of England.'[3]

Arnold's sudden death, at the age of forty-seven, sent a wave of sorrow and consternation throughout the whole country. Newman had once asked with affected incredulity 'Is *he* a Christian?' But when he died, not only his devoted pupils and disciples, but men of all creeds and parties, recognized that a great spirit had departed from their midst.

[1] *Ibid.*, vol. i, p. 334.   [2] *Excursion*, bk. i, 223.
[3] *Life*, vol. i, p. 334 (my italics).

CHAPTER III

NEWMAN AND THE OXFORD MOVEMENT

'Forty years ago, when I was an undergraduate at Oxford, voices were in the air there which haunt my memory still. Happy the man who in that susceptible season of youth hears such voices! they are a possession to him for ever. No such voices as those which we heard in our youth at Oxford are sounding there now. Oxford has more criticism now, more knowledge, more light; but such voices as those of our youth it has no longer. The name of Cardinal Newman is a great name to the imagination still; his genius and his style are still things of power. But he is over eighty years of age; he is in the Oratory at Birmingham; he has adopted, for the doubts and difficulties which beset men's minds today, a solution which, to speak frankly, is impossible. Forty years ago he was in the very prime of life; he was close at hand to us at Oxford; he was preaching in St. Mary's pulpit every Sunday; he seemed about to renew what was for us the most national and natural institution in the world, the Church of England. Who could resist the charm of that spiritual apparition, gliding in the dim afternoon light through the aisles of St. Mary's, rising into the pulpit, and then, in the most entrancing of voices, breaking the silence with words and thoughts which were a religious music—subtle, sweet, mournful?'

SO spoke Matthew Arnold in 1883, introducing his American discourse on Emerson; such, in general, has been the prevailing estimate of Newman in England, and no one has stated it more memorably. In that passage of cadenced prose, so akin in spirit and tone to Newman's own manner, Arnold has given us a Newman who, like the dreaming spires and moonlit gardens of Oxford, has become a symbol of lost youth and lost causes. 'Somewhere or other I have spoken of those "last enchantments of the Middle Age" which Oxford sheds around us, and here they were!' The story of the Oxford Movement has been often told, and it is no part of my intention to repeat it here.

But our account of the nineteenth century, though pretending to no exhaustiveness, would be out of proportion without some attention to its significance. I propose, therefore, to enquire briefly how far Newman's thought and work belong to the main line of nineteenth century development. I shall suggest that he was no mere spell-binder, beckoning his hearers with mysterious gestures into an enchanted garden of the spirit, but a seer through whose prophesyings some of the deepened insights of the age found utterance: insights none the less 'advanced' because of their 'reactionary' colouring.

What was it that gave to the 'Movement Party' in its early years its joyous, exuberant energy, its militant self-confidence, its sense of leadership? This kind of *élan*, so clearly marked in the early stages of the Oxford Movement, and echoing throughout Newman's many retrospects of its history, is usually only given to a party which knows and feels that it holds the clue to a contemporary problem, and can minister to the special needs of its time; it is not the 'note' of a merely romantic or antiquarian craze. Something must have been rotten in the state of Protestantism for a Catholic movement started by a few academic clergymen to have attracted so much attention, and to have become known so soon 'to the police in Italy, and the backwoodsmen of America'.[1] The movement was, in fact, a part of that great deepening of seriousness, that impulse to come to grips with history, with the unseen, and with the fundamentals of the general human plight, which showed itself also as the French Revolution, as Romanticism and as Evangelicalism. That other and older Oxford Movement, the Methodist, had begun with the same glow and warming of the heart, but occurring in the eighteenth century it had had other tasks to perform, and could melt the spiritual ice-pack by reaffirming the old Protestant certainties. Tractarianism, if only because it followed the revolutionary and romantic upheavals, was bound to be more scholastic, dogmatic and ecclesiastical—in a word, more 'Catholic'. To un-protes-

[1] Newman, *Difficulties Felt by Anglicans in Catholic Teaching* (4th ed. 1850), p. 86.

tantize the English Church was a project so wildly paradoxical, so flatly opposed to ingrained national prejudice, that at any previous time since the Reformation it could not have been entertained without risk of bloodshed. The significant thing about the period we are now considering is that then, in a country where Popery had so long been abhorred and tabooed, it began to be possible to listen to popish arguments—at first perhaps with a guilty joy as in tasting forbidden fruit, and then with exhilaration in finding the fruit medicinal after all. Newman habitually speaks of the movement as spontaneous in its origin, not contrived; it was 'in the air', it was a 'spirit afloat', a 'spiritual awakening of spiritual wants'. 'There has been for some years', he wrote in 1839, 'a growing tendency towards the character of mind and feeling of which Catholic doctrines are the just expression'; opinions long obscured begin to be revived, and captivate by their seeming novelty, but still more by the 'touching beauty, loftiness of idea, and earnestness of character which they evidence or require'.[1] Scott, Southey, Coleridge and Wordsworth have all contributed something towards this climatic change, though they are to be counted rather as 'indications of what was secretly going on in the minds of men, than as causes of it'. When a historical situation has for long enough been undermined and riddled, it only needs the unimaginable touch of time and of genius to send it toppling; such, in a sense, was the condition of Protestantism in the England of Newman's prime. So he could write 'the spirit of Luther is dead; but Hildebrand and Loyola are still alive'; so he could say, in one of his first sermons: 'I do not shrink from uttering my firm conviction that it would be a gain to the country were it vastly more superstitious, more bigoted, more gloomy, more fierce in its religion than at present it shows itself to be.' Slowly, as the mists of controversy and illusion begin to clear, the forms of the two real spiritual antagonists come into view, and are discerned to be those of Catholicism and Rationalism. The battle is on, and it lies between these two; all alleged intermediaries—all evangelicalisms, Erastian establishments, liberalisms or lati-

[1] Essay: *State of Religious Parties*, in *British Critic*, April 1839, vol. xxv, pp. 395 ff.

tudinarianisms are things of straw, without life or cohesion. When these real opposites meet, 'then, indeed, will be the stern encounter, when two real and living principles, simple, entire, and consistent, one in the Church, the other out of it, at length rush upon each other, contending not for names and words, or half views, but for elementary notions and distinctive moral characters'.[1]

Newman always remembered and kept July 14, the day of Keble's Assize Sermon of 1833, as the starting-point of the Tractarian Movement. That Sermon was a protest against interference by a secularized Parliament in matters spiritual, and the movement has accordingly been regarded as political in its origin. As Hurrell Froude pointed out, the House of Commons in Hooker's time had been a Synod of the laity of the Church of England, and for that reason alone could Hooker tolerate its interference in spiritual concerns. But now, after the Reform Bill and the repeal of the Test and Corporation Acts, the true situation of the Church became apparent; its liturgy, its articles and its status could be altered, as its Bishops would be appointed, at the will of a parliamentary majority which might be non-Anglican or even non-Christian. So, in one sense, the original impulse of the movement might be expressed in Froude's exclamation: 'let us give up a *national* Church and have a *real* one'. Or again, Newman himself has said that its object was 'to withstand the liberalism of the day'. But the movement was only political and anti-liberal because it was primarily spiritual; its deepest concern was with the invisible world, not with politics or the obsolete; its driving power, a hunger and thirst after righteousness, an effort towards true sanctity. Newman's influence over his Oxford hearers was due to no ritual practices or popish affectations—he wore a black gown, and used no incense and no eastward position: it was due to 'the wonderful charm of his mysterious and almost unknown personality'.[2] When men passed him on an Oxford pavement, and whispered 'Look, that's Newman!', it was with reverence towards a 'spiritual apparition'—for Newman had the air of one whose converse has been in heaven, as

---

[1] *Ibid.*, p. 419. [2] The phrase is Dean Stanley's.

indeed it had. He was opposed to Erastianism, then, and he was opposed to liberalism, because both these things struck at the spiritual life: Erastianism by enslaving its divine guardian, and liberalism by destroying its dogmatic foundation. Looking back in later years upon the past, he names, as the party's 'great and deadly foe, their scorn and their laughing-stock', 'that imbecile, inconsistent thing called Protestantism'. It was Protestantism which, by rejecting Papal authority, had subjected the Church to the State; it was Protestantism which, by exalting Scripture and 'private judgment', had opened the way to schism and sect, and finally to infidelity; it was Protestantism which, by decrying asceticism and good works, and by rejecting so much of the ritual, symbolism and practice that Catholicism had held conducive to holiness, had lowered the whole devotional life of the Church in England, and left it exposed and defenceless in its hour of greatest need. Above all, by watering down the doctrines of the Eucharist and of baptismal regeneration, by minimizing the authority of the priesthood, by turning the Bishops into civil servants, and by dismissing as 'Romish' so many essential means of grace, it had left Christianity unprotected against those forces of unbelief which, as the nineteenth century drew on, were assembling for the destruction of all religion whatsoever. To the Tractarians Protestantism seemed weak and rotten not merely because it was aesthetically meagre, but because it was worldly and unspiritual, and because it had no centre of spiritual authority. Even its palmary efforts after holiness—its Methodism and Evangelicalism—were houses built upon sand: the sands of inward assurance and of private judgment. The Tractarians needed no Tübingen critics to teach them that the Bible, and the Bible alone, could not be the rule of faith; it was enough for them to know that the authority of Scripture rested upon the authority of the Church, and that the Bible existed to prove dogmas, not to supply or constitute them.

The strength of Tractarianism lay, then, in its diagnosis of the age as blighted by the upas-tree of worldliness, and of contemporary Protestantism as incapable of rescuing it from spiritual decay and death. The original plan of the Oxford men, long before it was borne in upon Newman that 'the Church of Rome will be found right after all'[1], was to un-Protestantize the Church of England without Romanizing it. 'We are Catholics without the Popery, and Church-of-England men without the Protestantism', wrote Hurrell Froude in 1835.[2] 'The Reformation was a limb badly set—it must be broken again in order to be righted.'[3] 'The spirit of lawlessness came in with the Reformation, and Liberalism is its offspring.'[4] The ancient religion 'had well nigh faded away out of the land, through the political changes of the last 150 years, and it must be restored. It would be in fact a second Reformation:—a better reformation, for it would be a return not to the sixteenth century but to the seventeenth.'[5] Compare the Church of England now, in its decorous torpor, with the Church of the first centuries A.D. in all the 'joyous swing of her advance'! It is not the old Reformation that can save her now, or restore her jubilant militancy. Nearly all the assumptions on which English Protestantism had unthinkingly rested for two centuries could now be represented as baseless. The 'plain man's Bible'—but which plain man? and who gave the scriptural books their canonical authority? 'Justification by Faith only'—then has moral effort no intrinsic worth? has the old Christian ethical and ascetic ideal no value in the sight of God? And is not the Church of England, in fact, deficient precisely in the 'note of sanctity'? 'Must it not be owned that the Church of England saints, however good in essentials, are with a few rare exceptions deficient in the austere beauty of the Catholic $\mathring{\eta}\theta o\varsigma$?'[6] 'The State Church'—but we are united to the State as Israel was to Egypt, and 'if the State will but kick us off we may yet do in England'![7] The alleged 'purity' of the Church as opposed to 'Romish corruptions'?—but what is the 'pure' state of any living organ-

---

[1] *Apologia*, p. 121 (references are to Everyman ed.).
[2] *Remains* (1838), vol. i, p. 404.
[3] *Ibid.*, p. 433.   [4] *Apologia*, pp. 180-1.
[5] *Ibid.*, p. 63.
[6] Froude's *Remains, loc. cit.*, p. 395.
[7] *Ibid.*, p. 302.

ism: the embryo or the adult? the seed or the flower? It needed all Newman's knowledge of the early Church, and all his argumentative subtlety, to show in a lengthy work how 'corruptions' may be distinguished from genuine 'developments'. The Reformers of the sixteenth century were not the men they have been taken for; they were often time-servers and politicians rather than prophets or saints. Froude scorned Jewell for calling the Mass a 'cursed, paltrie service', for laughing at the Apostolical Succession, for denying the Lord's Supper to be a means of grace as distinct from a pledge of remembrance, and for saying that the only 'Keys of the Kingdom' are instruction and correction, and that the only way they open the Kingdom is by touching men's consciences. 'Really I hate the Reformation and the Reformers more and more, and have almost made up my mind that the rationalist spirit they set afloat is the $\psi\epsilon\upsilon\delta o\pi\rho o\phi\acute{\eta}\tau\eta s$ of the Revelation.'[1] 'I shall never call the Holy Eucharist "the Lord's Supper", nor God's Priests "ministers of the word", or the Altar "the Lord's table", etc. etc.; innocent as such phrases are in themselves, they have been dirtied.... Nor shall I even abuse the Roman Catholics *as a Church* for any thing except excommunicating us.'[2]

As long as Newman retained his Englishman's suspicion of Rome as corrupt, crafty and idolatrous—a 'stain upon my imagination', he later called it—he continued to believe in the possibility of a *Via Media*: an English Catholic Church like that of Laud, apostolic, yet free from 'the practical abuses and excesses of Rome'. If we were tied to the Reformation, then Anglicans might well be forced towards Rome, but fortunately (or should we not rather say providentially) the Church of England is not implicated in the conduct and opinions of the Reformers. It might have been so, but happily Henry VIII wanted only as much doctrinal and liturgical change as would enable him to steal church property and usurp church government; Edward VI died young, and Elizabeth liked the old ritual. All this might 'even suggest the idea of a Design to prevent the English Reformation from proceeding in any point to express con-

[1] *Ibid.*, p. 389.   [2] *Ibid.*, pp. 394-5.

tradition of Antiquity'.[1] We may thus legitimately interpret the formularies of the Church of England, 'in all essentials, conformably to the doctrine and ritual of the Church Universal'.[2] It was to prove just this that Newman wrote Tract xc (1841). The Prayer-Book might breathe the spirit of Catholicism, but the Thirty-nine Articles seemed stubbornly Protestant: were they really so? His thesis was that the Articles do not oppose Catholic teaching, and but partially oppose Roman dogma; they for the most part oppose only the 'dominant errors of Rome'. To the argument that the Articles were composed *against* Rome he replies that it was only so in a political sense; had Elizabeth 'a conscience against the Mass'? The only 'popery' then opposed was the Papal Supremacy, and the Articles were even drawn up in the hope of gaining the Papists. This Tract, this attempt to put a Catholic construction upon the Articles, was grounded, says Newman, upon the belief that 'the Articles need not be so closed as the received method of teaching closes them, and ought not to be for the sake of many persons. If we will close them, we run the risk of subjecting persons whom we should least like to lose to the temptation of joining the Church of Rome.' In truth the attempt was hopeless; the new ('reformed') bottles would not stand the old wine. The earlier Tracts had appealed to English ecclesiastical patriotism, but No. xc outraged Anglican susceptibilities, and the attacks upon it showed how far the movement had forfeited the support of average Churchmen. How hopeless was the attempt, Newman has nowhere shown more clearly than in the *Lectures on Difficulties Felt by Anglicans in Catholic Teaching*, addressed to his former associates from the further side of the Rubicon. To illustrate the antagonism of the English Bishops towards the very party which had toiled to uphold their spiritual authority, he quotes from episcopal Charges such phrases as these:

> 'It is impossible not to remark upon the subtle wile of the Adversary; it has been signally and unexpectedly exemplified in the

[1] Preface (by Newman and Keble) to Part II (1839) of Froude's *Remains*, p. xxiii.
[2] *Ibid.*, p. xxi.

present day by the revival of errors which might have been supposed buried for ever.'

'Those who sit in the Reformers' seat are traducing the Reformation.' They are 'walking about our beloved Church, polluting the sacred edifice, and leaving their slime about her altars'.[1]

Well might Newman mourn that 'it is not at all easy (humanly speaking) to wind up an Englishman to a dogmatic level'![2] It became clear that there were but two alternatives, 'the way to Rome, and the way to Atheism: Anglicanism is the halfway house on the one side, and Liberalism is the halfway house on the other'. He became more sure that England was in schism than that Roman 'additions' were not true 'developments' of the primitive Christian doctrine. Speaking later, from his post-conversion vantage-point, he could show how impossible it was for the Anglican Church to be 'wound up' to the Catholic level without denying its own nature and ceasing to be itself. The Church of England has perhaps been a bulwark against worse things, and historically it has 'diluted the virulence of Protestantism'. But it is no real Church at all; it is a mere department of Government, dependent on the civil power; its Prayer-Book is authorized by an Act of Parliament passed two centuries ago; its cathedrals are 'the spoils of Catholicism'. The Privy Council has decided (in the Gorham case) that a clergyman may hold whatever views he likes on Baptismal Regeneration; what, then, is to hinder the national will from sliding down the slippery slope into Arianism and finally Atheism? Protestants may rejoice over the Gorham judgment, but in their blindness they do not see that to weaken a *part* of the dogmatic structure is to weaken the *whole*.

'What though the ritual categorically deposes to the regeneration of the infant baptized? The Evangelical party, who in former years had the nerve to fix the charge of dishonesty on the explanations of the Thirty-nine Articles, put forward by their opponents, could all the while be cherishing in their own breasts an inter-

[1] *Difficulties*, 4th ed. (1850), pp. 97-9.   [2] *Apologia*, p. 190.

pretation of the Baptismal Service, simply contrary to its most luminous declarations.'[1]

Ah well, 'may not the free-born, self-dependent, animal mind of the Englishman choose his religion for himself?' The Establishment has life indeed, but not Catholic life; it is the life of a nation, of a state, which is irretrievably Erastian and Protestant in sentiment. But the very first principle of the movement was ecclesiastical liberty—antagonism to the Royal Supremacy, to the Establishment as such. On this principle depended, for the Tractarians, the preservation of dogma, of the sacraments, ceremonial observances, practical duty, counsels of perfection; without it, what could prevent the sacrifice or rationalization of dogma? Without it, the time could easily come when a man would fraternize with Unitarians, and 'pronounce his butler to be as able to give communion as his priest'. 'Establishment' principles 'destroyed the supernatural altogether, by making emphatically Christ's Kingdom a Kingdom of this world'. The Establishment 'keeps back those doctrines which, to the eye of faith, give real substance to religion'.[2] Are you going to be lulled into acquiescence, he asks the Anglo-Catholics, with the daily and weekly routine of comfortable unreality? No! You must secede! The Church of England has always been an imposture; now, it is a mere wreck. Don't be afraid to leave the sinking ship; in so doing, you will be weakening nothing divine. Such as the State is, will the State Church ever be. Where is its authority to be found? whose teachings unmistakably declare its doctrines? Driven from Prayer-Book and Bible, first upon the Anglican divines, and thence upon the Fathers, it seeks in vain for the authoritative principle which resides in Rome alone. The established Church *is* the nation (not in Arnold's favourable sense), and therefore you cannot use it to resist the nation, which is 'on its way to give up revealed truth'.

In much of this book of Newman's we can see an oblique self-justification; there is a tension in his mind between triumph and regret. At rare moments this resolves itself in

---

[1] *Difficulties*, p. 20.   [2] These phrases are quoted from *Difficulties*.

one of those moving and tender passages which bring us close to his inmost self, and give us a glimpse into the hiding-places of his personal power. He pauses, for example, and asks, is there then no such thing as Grace working savingly in the heart? and has not this Grace worked inwardly through the offices and devotions of the Church of England? No one, no Catholic, will deny it, and least of all Newman himself:

> 'Why should I deny to your memory what is so pleasant in mine? Cannot I too look back on many years past, and many events, in which I myself experienced what is now your confidence? Can I forget the happy life I have led all my days, with no cares, no anxieties worth remembering; without desolateness, or fever of thought, or gloom of mind, or doubt of God's love to me and providence over me? Can I forget,—I never can forget,—the day when in my youth I first bound myself to the ministry of God in that old church of St. Frideswide, the patroness of Oxford? nor how I wept abundant, and most sweet tears, when I thought what I then had become; though I looked on ordination as no sacramental rite, nor even to baptism ascribed any sacramental virtue? Can I wipe out from my memory, or wish to wipe out, those happy Sunday mornings, light or dark, year after year, when I celebrated your communion-rite, in my own church of St. Mary's; and in the pleasantness and joy of it heard nothing of the strife of tongues which surrounded its walls? When, too, shall I not feel the soothing recollection of those dear years which I spent in retirement, in preparation for my deliverance from Egypt, asking for light, and by degrees gaining it, with less of temptation in my heart, and sin on my conscience, than ever before? O my dear brethren, my Anglican friends! I easily give you credit for what I have experienced myself.' [1]

Yes, God's grace may be available to individuals everywhere, even to pagans. But is it *safe* to rely entirely even upon the felt, inward evidence of God's presence and favour? 'It is quite impossible to conclude', he says, 'that a certain opinion is true, or a religious position *safe* [my italics], simply on account of the confidence or apparent excellence of those

[1] *Difficulties*, pp. 71-2.

who adopt it.' If it were possible, then we must admit that there are finer examples of Christian character, and on that principle safer positions, to be found outside the national Church than within it—above all John Wesley, and the Methodists generally. 'Personally I do not like him [Wesley]', he adds,

> 'if it were merely for his deep self-reliance and self-conceit; still I am bound, in justice to him, to ask, and you in consistency to answer, what historical person in the Establishment, during its whole three centuries, has approximated in force and splendour of conduct and achievements to one who began by innovating on your rules, and ended by contemning your authorities?'[1]

What, too, of Elizabeth Fry? or Howard? 'Even old Bunyan' is 'more Apostolical than you'. And consider the death of Dr Arnold:

> 'Does the extreme earnestness and reality of religious feeling, exhibited in the sudden seizure and death of one who was as stern in his hatred of your opinions as admirable in his earnestness, who one evening protested against the sacramental principle, and next morning died nobly with the words of Holy Scripture in his mouth —does it give any sanction to that hatred and that protest?'[2]

The answer to that rhetorical question will not be unanimous. Newman is here maintaining a delicate position: he cannot deny the workings of grace in non-Catholics, but he has to deny that they come through the operation of non-Catholic ordinances. Now the Catholic ordinances are divinely appointed for the salvation of sinners, therefore it is precarious to rely on direct access to the divine source.

The magnetism of Newman, wrote J. A. Froude in *The Nemesis of Faith* (1849), 'took us all his own way; all, that is, who were *not Arnoldised*' [my italics]. With W. G. Ward in mind, we might add that it also attracted some who were. Arnold and Newman, indeed, may be taken to symbolize the two conflicting trends in nineteenth century religious thought: Arnold, ethical and liberal, aiming at the promo-

---

[1] *Ibid.*, p. 80. [2] *Ibid.*, p. 81.

tion of goodness by Christian gentlemen; Newman, mystical and dogmatic, aiming at the production of saints by an infallible Church. We have seen how Arnold condemned the exaltation of the sacerdotal caste, and rejected as trivial 'all this stuff about the True Church'—all, in fact, that to Newman seemed vital. Arnold accused the Tractarians of teaching old error instead of new truth, and of exalting Church and Sacrament above Christ himself; Newman would reply that error is always renewing itself, while truth is ever the same; and that we do no dishonour to Christ by holding that we can only know Him fully through the Church and the ordinances which He instituted, and through which His spirit is mediated. Arnold accepted the spirit of the age, and believed that, in so far as it was searching for truth, it could be Christianized; Newman dreaded and resisted it, believing that the spirit of enquiry was in its very nature destructive of faith in the unseen, and that, unless checked, it must inevitably lead to atheism. It was, and is, commonly said of the Tractarians that they were reactionary dreamers, out of touch with their times, caring little about the 'condition of England question', ignoring modern science and modern criticism, and in general 'substituting unrealities for realities'. F. D. Maurice, who believed that the Kingdom of Christ, though transcending this world, could and must be made to include it, commented thus on the Oxford Tracts:

> 'To me they are, for the most part, more unpleasant than I quite like to acknowledge to myself or others. Their error, I think, consists in opposing to the spirit of the present age the spirit of a former age, instead of the ever-living and acting Spirit of God, of which the spirit of each age is at once the adversary and the parody.' [1]

To Newman this distinction would have been meaningless; his concern, as he said, was not with the obsolete, but with the invisible. Truth, divinely communicated, attested and guarded, belongs to no age more than another—it must remain for ever the same; while the unregenerate nature of fallen man tends at all times towards error and denial. If Newman was unmoved by the specific challenges of his own

[1] *Life of F. D. Maurice*, by his son, vol. i, p. 217.

century, it was because he saw in them merely the reincarnation of early heresies, over which the Catholic Church had triumphed centuries ago. After he had wound his dangerous way, 'with anxious eyes and a beating heart', through the dreary mazes of Arianism, Sabellianism, Nestorianism and the rest, how could nineteenth century rationalisms alarm or even interest him, save as new sproutings from the age-old hydra of misbelief? Newman's view of history was apocalyptic, and not—like that of most of his contemporaries—progressive; he did not view it as a linear forward movement towards light and truth. Where others saw, and rejoiced in, a progress along the ringing grooves of change, he saw simply light amid the encircling gloom: the Word that was with God and was God, coming incarnate into the darkness, bringing light, grace and truth which the darkness apprehended not.

If we then, like Arnold and others, ask how it was possible for a mind so trenchant as Hurrell Froude's, so subtle, profound and imaginative as Newman's, or so sceptical and logical as Ward's, to attach, in that enlightened age, such high, such supreme importance to 'externals', 'forms' and dogmas, which the *Zeitgeist* had interpreted and rationalized away—if we ask this, the reply must be that they believed what many only professed and others denied, and were 'not afraid of inferences'.[1] Accept the view of history and of fallen humanity taken by Newman or Ward, and the inferences follow in an unbroken series. To the average Englishman and Churchman of the time—to a man like Kingsley, for example—it was so shocking to hear proclaimed, as vital truths, doctrines long regarded as exploded superstitions, so disturbing to find the charges of ignorance and inconsistency retorted upon themselves, that one explanation alone seemed possible: these Catholics were crafty priests who did not, could not, mean or believe what they said. I will not enter here upon the details of the Kingsley–Newman controversy, but the famous passage in the *Apologia* introducing the 'General Answer to Mr Kingsley'[2] is so revealing, and so pertinent to the question we have just raised, that it must be summarized at this point. Newman is dealing with the

[1] Hugh Rose's phrase about R. H. Froude. [2] Pp. 215 ff.

Protestant suspicion that the Catholic creed is 'set up in inevitable superstition and hypocrisy', and its upholders intellectually dishonest. He lifts us straight up to the highest level of spiritual vision, and from this vantage-point interprets for us the vast and tragic panorama of existence:

> 'Starting then with the being of a God (which, as I have said, is as certain to me as the certainty of my own existence . . .), I look out of myself into the world of men, and there I see a sight which fills me with unspeakable distress. The world seems simply to give the lie to that great truth, of which my whole being is so full; and the effect upon me is, in consequence, as a matter of necessity, as confusing as if it denied that I am in existence myself. If I looked into a mirror, and did not see my face, I should have the sort of feeling which actually comes upon me, when I look into this living busy world, and see no reflexion of its Creator.'

Were it not for the voice within the conscience and the heart, the spectacle of the world would make him an atheist, pantheist or polytheist; the sight is 'nothing else than the prophet's scroll, full of "lamentations, and mourning, and woe"'. To consider the world and the ways of man,

> 'the disappointments of life, the defeat of good, the success of evil, physical pain, mental anguish, the prevalence and intensity of sin, the pervading idolatries, the corruptions, the dreary hopeless irreligion, that condition of the whole race, so fearfully yet exactly described in the Apostle's words, "having no hope and without God in the world"—all this is a vision to dizzy and appal; and inflicts upon the mind a sense of profound mystery, which is absolutely beyond human solution.'

It forces us to the inference, either that there is no Creator, or that man has been 'discarded from His presence'. '*If* there be a God, *since* there is a God, the human race is implicated in some terrible aboriginal calamity.' So the doctrine of original sin becomes almost as certain as that God and the world exist.

> 'And now, supposing it were the blessed and loving will of the Creator to interfere in this anarchical condition of things'—

is it not natural to suppose that He would use abnormal means, miraculous means? What must be 'the face-to-face antagonist, by which to withstand and baffle the fierce energy of passion and the all-corroding, all-dissolving scepticism of the intellect in religious enquiries?' *Right* reason indeed, even unaided by revelation, can point to the saving truths, but reason as it acts habitually in fallen man tends 'towards a simple unbelief in matters of religion'. Today, outside the Catholic Church, things are tending with acceleration towards atheism:

> 'What a scene, what a prospect, does the whole of Europe present at this day! and not only Europe, but every government and every civilization through the world, which is under the influence of the European mind! Lovers of their country and of their race, religious men, external to the Catholic Church, have attempted various expedients to arrest fierce wilful human nature in its onward course, and to bring it into subjection. The necessity of some form of religion for the interests of humanity, has been generally acknowledged: but where was the concrete representative of things invisible, which would have the force and the toughness to be a breakwater against the deluge?'

Religious 'establishments' served their turn in Protestant countries, but now their crevices are 'admitting the enemy'; education, the hope of world-peace, the optimisms of the Great Exhibition era—all have failed to check the onrush. Even of the Bible the same must be said; it 'does not answer a purpose, for which it was never intended'; no book, however divine, can by itself 'make a stand against the wild living intellect of man'.

Newman now proceeds to the last inference in this chain of impassioned argument: if the Creator has made provision for 'retaining in the world a knowledge of Himself, so definite and distinct as to be proof against the energy of human scepticism'—supposing that this is so (and we cannot suppose otherwise), would it be surprising

> 'if He should think fit to introduce a power into the world, invested with the prerogative of infallibility in religious matters'? . . . and, when I find that this is the very claim of the Catholic Church, not

only do I feel no difficulty in admitting the idea, but there is a fitness in it, which recommends it to my mind. And thus I am brought to speak of the Church's infallibility, as a provision, adapted by the mercy of the Creator, to preserve religion in the world, and to restrain that freedom of thought, which of course in itself is one of the greatest of our natural gifts, and to rescue it from its own suicidal excesses . . . a working instrument, in the course of human affairs, for smiting hard and throwing back the immense energy of the aggressive intellect.'

The force and momentum of Newman's rhetoric are spoilt by this compression, but I have given enough, I hope (and less would hardly have sufficed), to convey something of the sweep and coherence of his vision. Few, I think, after deeply pondering this passage, would be inclined to dismiss Newman as a reactionary dreamer, out of touch with his time; if he lacked interest in what was specifically of the nineteenth century, it was because he was a spectator of all time and all existence. What concerns him is not the local and the transient, but the perennial plight of fallen man. The solution which he proposed seemed to many, as it did to Arnold, 'frankly impossible'; indeed, to the average Englishman, for whom Catholicism had long been an object of scorn and fear (associated with Guy Fawkes and hocus-pocus), it seemed preposterous. Yet in so far as Catholicism meant really believing what others only professed, and really using means of grace which others had abandoned or used as mechanical routine: in so far as it meant a return and a recall to spiritual first principles, it could again, as of old, form the advance-column in the holy war against the principalities and powers. The current of the Reformation had run its course, and its spent energies were losing themselves in the flats and shallows of worldliness and unbelief; could it be that Rome had been right all along? The question could never have been asked if Protestantism had not become moribund, and if Catholicism had not been exhibited, in the saintliness and visionary power of Newman and his associates, as a source —perhaps the only source?—of spiritual power, and as a discipline—perhaps the true one?—for the wayward will of humanity. No Protestant historian need deny that Catholicism, as Newman presented it, was both intellectually more coherent and imaginatively more alluring than what Protestantism had largely become; nor need he deny that unbelief could then be more effectually opposed by inflexible dogmatism than by the softened and blunted weapons of the Reformation. Protestantism, indeed, proved capable of new life, but it needed for its rejuvenation the challenges of Catholic asceticism and of scientific enquiry; it needed, too, a deepened understanding of the grounds of faith and the nature of religious experience. It is because Newman contributed so largely to the deepening of that understanding that we may claim for him a place, not amongst the reactionaries or obscurantists, but amongst the light-bearers of the nineteenth century.

The Oxford Movement, as A. P. Stanley pointed out, may have owed some of 'its exclusive peculiarities to an intense revolt against every kind of latitude', but it also derived 'some of its most persuasive elements, not from those points in which it differs, but from those points in which it agrees, with the liberal and historical impulse which long preceded it'.[1] There is, in particular, a remarkable consonance between the teachings of Coleridge and of Newman about Faith and Reason—an affinity so real that many have regarded Newman as Coleridge's disciple. This can hardly be, since Newman records that in 1835, when he had already 'taken up all his distinctive positions', he read parts of Coleridge for the first time. But he significantly adds, 'I am surprised how much I thought mine, is to be found there'.[2] We have seen that for Coleridge Faith meant a commitment of the will to the insights of Reason, an acting-out of confidence in the reality of 'things hoped for', and that in his view it sprang from our whole experience as moral and spiritual beings, not from the intellect in isolation. Coleridge, accepting Hume's view of faith but inverting its sense,

---

[1] A. P. Stanley, *The Oxford School*, in *Edinburgh Review*, April 1881, vol. cliii, p. 309.

[2] See H. F. Davis, *Was Newman a Disciple of Coleridge?* in *Dublin Review*, Oct. 1945, p. 171.

had shown that faith was indeed incapable of rational 'proof', but that on that very account it was unassailable by the 'mere' reason; a faith which rested on demonstration would be either compulsory and mechanical, or would be exposed to disproof by other demonstrations. Faith, like Imagination, is alive and creative, ever *realizing* its own objects. This was Newman's position in the *University Sermons* and the *Grammar of Assent*; let us illustrate first from the *Sermons*. In No. IV, for example, on 'The Usurpations of Reason', Newman says of 'Reason' what Coleridge had said of 'Understanding': he means by it 'secular reason' or 'the wisdom of this world' (Coleridge's 'mind of the flesh'). It is not on this that faith is founded; Christ does not assume or expect intellectual ability in his hearers; the Bible makes no appeal to this faculty as a means of suasion. Faith may, indeed, encroach upon reason's legitimate sphere, as when men 'apply such Scripture communications as are intended for religious purposes to the determination of physical questions. ... This was the usurpation of the schools of theology in former ages, to issue their decrees to the subjects of the Senses and the Intellect.'[1] The reverse happens, and has disastrously happened since the Reformation, when reason presumes to deal with matters belonging to religion and morals—when it works on 'assumptions foreign and injurious' to religion. What Hume said in irony is most sober truth—'it is true as far as every important question in Revelation is concerned, and to forget this is the error which is at present under consideration'. A Worldly-Wiseman discoursing on religion, whether for or against, is like a blind man lecturing on colours; the necessary assumptions of religion are supplied, not by reason, but by the moral sense, and by 'spiritual discernment'. Reasonings on 'evidences' may be plausible, but they do not *convince*. The modern 'usurpations' of reason have typically consisted, since the Reformation, in trying to make the proof of Christianity independent of its only true foundations: the Church and the Conscience—the external and internal witnesses. Scripture was set up in place of the first—with what results we

[1] *Oxford Univ. Sermons* (3rd ed., 1872), p. 59.

know; Conscience was resolved into Utilitarian expediencies, and increasing reliance was placed on 'evidences from Nature'. On this last point Newman repeats (without mentioning him) the declaration of Pascal, who, at a time when it was becoming the vogue in philosophic circles to look to Nature as the surest evidence of Nature's God, had seen that Nature only proves God to those who already believe in Him on other grounds. Evidences from Nature? Yes, says Newman: 'beautiful and interesting to the believer in a God; but, when men have not already recognized God's voice within them, ineffective'. In Sermon X he goes even further:

> 'It is indeed a great question whether Atheism is not as philosophically consistent with the phenomena of the physical world, taken by themselves, as the doctrine of a creative and governing Power. But, however this be, the practical safeguard against Atheism in the case of scientific enquirers is the inward need and desire, the inward experience of that Power, existing in the mind before and independently of their examination of His material world.'[1]

The eighteenth century, 'a time when love was cold', was the great Age of Evidences; but the history even of that age shows that when men do embrace the Gospel it is because it meets their needs, not because it convinces their minds; while, on the irreligious, evidences are always wasted. This tenth Sermon has significantly as its text: 'Now Faith is the substance of things hoped for, the evidence of things not seen.' Faith has to make its own objects real; it must realize them and make them substantial; it is not a mere believing upon evidence, or assenting to the conclusion of a chain of arguments. 'Mere facts have no warmth', and reason, which deals with them, is cold and critical, not creative. Faith, like Coleridge's Imagination, is essentially vital, while objects and inferences, as such, are fixed and dead. It follows from this that faith, springing from the conscience, from an antecedent habit or predisposition, is content with proofs which from the point of view of reason are defective or insufficient; religious certainty cannot be had ready-made—it has to be

[1] *Ibid.*, p. 194.

hungered and thirsted after, and so *deserved*. On the level of reason, proofs *constrain* assent; on that of faith, love and purity *produce* it. Faith may be justified by reason without originating in it, just as reason may analyse motives without itself being a motive. Logical proofs are made for us by the nature of the mind; proofs of faith we must make for ourselves in the course of our struggle towards a holier life; faith arises out of the hunger and thirst after righteousness, and is part of its blessedness.

'A mutilated and defective evidence suffices for persuasion where the heart is alive; but dead evidences, however perfect, can but create a dead faith.'[1]

Newman, feeling this theme to be vital to his defence of the believing temper in an unbelieving age, devoted very great attention to the process whereby 'probabilities' are transmuted by faith into certainties. In the *University Sermons* he had already indicated his position, but the final distillation of his thought is to be found in the *Grammar of Assent* (1870). I do not propose to analyse this closely wrought book in any detail; it must suffice to indicate briefly how the earlier ideas are there developed. The main theme of the work is that religious truth is 'proved', not by scientific demonstration, but by an accumulation of probabilities 'sufficient for certitude'. Even in matters of science and of everyday life we can and must assent to certain strong probabilities on evidence short of demonstration; in religion this is not only inevitable but essential.

'As in mathematics we are justified by the dictate of nature in withholding our assent from a conclusion of which we have not yet a strict logical demonstration, so by a like dictate we are not justified, in the case of concrete reasoning and especially of religious enquiry, in waiting till such logical demonstration is ours, but on the contrary are bound in conscience to seek truth and to look for certainty by modes of proof which, when reduced to the shape of formal propositions, fail to satisfy the severe requisitions of science.'[2]

[1] *Ibid.*, p. 200.
[2] *An Essay in Aid of a Grammar of Assent* (1870), p. 407.

The distinction between 'notional' and 'real' assents, which is elaborated at the outset, corresponds to Keats's distinction between 'axioms of philosophy' before and after they have been 'proved upon the pulses', and to D. H. Lawrence's distinction between mental knowledge which is scientific—knowledge in terms of 'apartness', and religious or poetic knowledge, which is knowledge in terms of 'togetherness'. The world of notions is 'the dry and sterile little world the abstracted mind inhabits'[1]; it is the world of catchwords, clichés and unexamined assumptions—'progress', 'liberalism', 'civilization', 'justification by faith only', 'private judgment', 'the Bible and nothing but the Bible'. Most religion in England now, says Newman, is mere notional assent, and involves little beyond correct behaviour, pious sentiments and a decent reverence for 'sacred scenes'. It is one thing, then, to accept a notion, and quite another thing to realize a fact; one thing to 'acquiesce in an abstract truth', and quite another to give it 'practical expression' in action. A 'real' assent is one which is 'felt in the heart, and felt along the blood', one which affects the imagination, and impels the will towards relevant action. Notional demonstrations cannot produce these results, and real assents therefore —religious beliefs above all—cannot be their outcome. Religious assent has always been enjoined upon us by revelation or by authority: 'it never has been a deduction from what we know; it has ever been an assertion of what we are to believe'.[2] It cannot be too emphatically stated, however, that Newman builds revealed religion upon the foundation of natural religion; the primary assumptions of religion are supplied by the Conscience. In our awareness of right and wrong, of good and bad, of a higher and a lower quality of living, in our sense of sin and failure, in our sense of obligation, in our yearnings after deliverance and a holier life— here, and not in brittle reasonings, lie the materials for a *real* apprehension of a Divine Sovereign and Judge. This apprehension is independent of Revelation or dogma; it is independent of theological formulations. That is not to say that dogma and theology are superfluous; on the contrary, being

---

[1] Lawrence's phrase, cf. above, p. 28. [2] *Grammar*, p. 93.

the intellectual expressions of religious experience, they strengthen and define it: 'devotion falls back upon dogma as its intellectual stay'. Theology is the notional formulation of what the experience seems to mean; 'the firmest hold of theological truths', accordingly, 'is gained by habits of personal religion'. It is here that Newman makes the transition from natural to revealed religion, a transition rendered imperative for him by his wider vision of human nature in its fallen state, by his sombre and tragic view of our weakness and sinfulness. Conscience, the inner witness, can become feeble through neglect, and almost fade away; on the other hand, it can be strengthened and illuminated. Starting from the belief in God, we are predisposed to assent to the probability that God will have provided some extraordinary means to redeem us, and to define and clarify the dim conception of Himself which is all that Nature affords. The probability that a revelation has been vouchsafed deepens into certainty when, obedient to the heavenly intimation, we advance further and further towards sanctity.

> 'If religion is to be devotion, and not a mere matter of sentiment, if it is to be made the ruling principle of our lives, if our actions, one by one, and our daily conduct, are to be consistently directed towards an Invisible Being, we need something higher than a balance of arguments to fix and to control our minds. Sacrifice of wealth, name, or position, faith and hope, self-conquest, communion with the spiritual world, presuppose a real hold and habitual intuition of the objects of Revelation, which is certitude under another name.'[1]

A real assent to the truths of natural religion, then, will lead to a real assent to those of revealed religion, and our sense of probability, our 'illative' sense (which judges degrees of truth), will further lead us to acknowledge the Church to which, under His divine guidance, God has committed the task of preserving and interpreting the revelation. To reach this ultimate certainty, and the 'triumphant repose' which it brings, we have but to begin obeying conscience; if we persevere—one step at a time—the kindly light will lead us on.

[1] *Ibid.*, p. 230.

In this rejection, then, of the flimsy evidences which had satisfied a more superficial age, and in this disclosure of a deeper and firmer foundation for religious faith, Newman was carrying on the main, the vital task of the nineteenth century, the work which had been begun by Coleridge. Its importance can be appreciated even by those who cannot admit its necessary connexion with the Catholic system with which, for Newman, it was all of a piece. We have seen how, in Newman's thought, assent to the dictates of conscience led on towards Catholic dogma. The pattern of this development is repeated, with even greater clarity of outline, in the life of his disciple W. G. Ward, and for this reason—but also because Ward moved from Arnoldism to Newmanism, and thus links our previous chapter with this—I will conclude with a few allusions to his biography.[1]

Ward (1812-1882), though not a Rugbeian, had in early life been deeply impressed by Arnold's high ethical earnestness, by his unworldliness, and by the note of reality in all his words and works. Arnoldism, 'by its rejection or disparagement of all in religion which did not directly tend to bring the soul nearer to God and farther from sin', was to Ward a 'wholesome antidote' to two kinds of formalism: the old Protestant religion of respectability, and the new romantic 'antiquarianism'. He trusted Arnold as a man of higher moral perception than himself. But Arnold was touched by the spirit of 'free enquiry', and Ward soon began to ask himself how much doctrine would free enquiry really support? how much would it leave undamaged? He began to attend Newman's Oxford sermons, and the very first one he heard changed his life. He became convinced that the answer to his question was, *None*.

'When as time went on he came to feel that that very *minimum* of doctrine which was necessary as a support and sanction to the moral law must fade away before the consistent application of the latitudinarian intellectual principles, the question presented itself:

[1] Wilfrid Ward, *W. G. Ward and the Oxford Movement* (2nd ed., 1890).

May there not be after all some indissoluble connection between the plenitude of doctrine and the highest morality?'[1]

Might not Church authority be a necessary, and a divinely appointed, external embodiment and safeguard of conscience? The principles of free enquiry and private judgment falsely assume that belief is the outcome of a balancing of pros and cons. Moreover, the Protestants, who claim this liberty, do not consistently employ it; they leave their own positions unexamined; they shrink from German biblical criticism; they fail to see that their arguments against Rome would, if rigorously applied, undermine their own faith, and probably theism itself. The true genesis of religious belief, as Newman taught Ward to see it, was in obedience to conscience: 'Obedience comes first, knowledge afterwards. It is by being pure in heart that we see God, not by seeing God that we become pure in heart. . . . He who learns the truth from argument or mere trust in men may lose it again by argument or by trust in men; but he who learns it by obedience can lose it only by disobedience.'[2] But we need an external guide to correct our private idiosyncrasies: we need the funded wisdom of the ages to give us the true sense of Scripture, we need a visible symbol of the unseen world—the unseen world which, alas! so often and so easily fades into seeming unreality. 'An unseen Church would be a very sorry antagonist against so very visible a world.' Ward read Froude's *Remains* in 1838, and noted with approval its clarity and above all its *thoroughness*; Froude, as we have seen, was not afraid of inferences. Arnoldism, by contrast, seemed to 'stop short'; like the Protestantism of which it was a typical product, it took the first steps towards belief, but shrank from its 'plenitude'. It could accept the Incarnation, and the mystery of the Trinity, but not the developments of these doctrines—not the Eucharist, not the priesthood, not saints, not angels. Arnold substituted Porson and Hermann for the 'prophetical office of the Church', and in interpreting Scripture he relied, not on Church tradition, but on his own private intuitions. Gradually, then, and

[1] *Ibid.*, p. 74. [2] W. G. Ward, quoted *ibid.*, p. 77.

especially as the storm over Tract xc moved to its climax, Ward began to see the whole corpus of Catholic doctrine and practice, not only as an organic and legitimate development from the origins which Protestantism also acknowledged, but as a necessary *succedaneum* to the spiritual life.

'The more a person feels his deficiency in the apprehension of unseen things', he wrote to Pusey, 'the more painfully he feels the want of "so consoling and impressive" an image of a visible Church, as even Rome displays; the more difficult he finds his contest with his old nature; the more he regrets that he has not been trained from the first in regular confession; the more he misses the practical rules of conduct in which Roman books of devotion abound, drawn from the stores, which they have retained, of traditional teaching; the more he misses the guidance of a priest carefully trained with a view to the confessional.'[1]

In his book *The Ideal of a Christian Church* (1844), published the year before he entered the Roman Catholic Church (a book which has been called 'Tract xc writ large'), Ward gave systematic expression to the insights he had by then attained. The aim of the Church is the personal sanctification and salvation of each believer; now, in the Church of England the general standard of Christian attainment was lamentably low. Moreover, the spirit of questioning and the reliance on private judgment, set in motion by Protestantism, lead eventually to scepticism; contemporary unbelief was implicit in the Reformation, and for this the only antidote is in Catholic principles. Existing religions, however, must be saved, not destroyed. How? by returning to fundamentals, and building up the Catholic life thereon. The starting-point with Ward, as with Newman, is the appeal to the facts of our moral experience; religious truth may be brought to life again by realizing its indissoluble connexion with moral truth. The category 'ought'—Kant's 'Thou Shalt'—is a primary fact of our consciousness as moral beings; this sense of unconditional obligation, which is present with us all, points beyond ourselves to a region infinitely higher than

[1] *Ibid.*, p. 183.

the sensible world, and informs us of an unseen reality, the objective source of the moral imperative. An earnest man will cultivate an attitude of faith in this unseen reality; he will give 'watchful and reverent attention' to the voice of conscience. This attitude of faith is distinguished from the Evangelical 'sense of assurance': the latter is passive and subjective, while the former involves effort to do God's will. In opposition to Luther, Ward argues that moral effort *has* intrinsic worth, and that the function of revealed religion is to develop, not to abrogate or supersede, natural religion. He finds in the Catholic Church this natural fulfilment; its credentials are established, above all, by its superior standards of sanctity. These insights lead the enquirer to expect

> 'some home in which this moral reality may have a secure rest and lodgment',[1]

and he will be inclined to seek this where there are Unity, Sanctity, Catholicity, Apostolicity. 'The saints of the Church are the great witnesses to her divinity.'

Wilfrid Ward, reviewing this argument, indicates as follows what is for us its most significant note:

> 'Religious belief is nowhere allowed to be normally the result of the impartial review of certain considerations, but is uniformly maintained to depend finally upon an insight given by a special course of action.'[2]

We may round this off by a quotation from W. G. Ward himself—it is a deliverance which might well have come from Coleridge (or Kant):

> 'Knowledge of phenomena is obtained by the intellect, knowledge of realities by the conscience; knowledge of phenomena by inquiry, knowledge of reality by obedience; ... the one pursuit tends to pride, the other indispensably requires and infallibly increases humility.'[3]

Critics of the Oxford Movement, then as now, attended too exclusively to its 'objectionable' and 'Romanizing' manifestations, and failed to appreciate that the 'Catholicity'

---

[1] *Ibid.*, p. 259.   [2] *Ibid.*, p. 257.   [3] *Ibid.*, p. 258.

of men like Newman and Ward was no piece of fastidious or wanton Romanticism, but an organic outgrowth from their searching critique of religious foundations. After even so perfunctory a hearing as we have here allowed these men, how woefully superficial seem the strictures of Arnold or Stanley!

> 'A dress, a ritual, a name, a ceremony ... objects so pitiful that if gained ever so completely they would make no man the wiser or the better.' [Arnold]

> 'It is curious to look back upon the trivial elements which produced so much excitement. ... The apostolical succession, the revival of obsolete rubrics, together with one or two Patristic tendencies, such as the doctrine of reserve and of mysticism, were the staple of their teaching.' [Stanley][1]

The fact is, on the contrary, that Newman and Ward, led by a profound spiritual instinct, placed religion on a surer basis than any afforded by scriptural fundamentalism or evangelical 'assurance'. The perennial strength of Catholicism was never more strikingly displayed than when, by-passing the new scriptural criticism and forestalling scientific agnosticism, it showed itself—what popular Protestantism in general certainly was not—invulnerable to both. 'Religious belief is nowhere allowed to be normally the result of the impartial review of certain considerations'—to take up this ground was indeed to perfect strength in weakness; it was indeed to steal the enemy's thunder: for the impossibility of extracting religion out of 'candid' enquiry on the level of reason was the commonest topic of unbelievers. To the other part of their teaching, that the moral foundation must needs sustain a Catholic superstructure, that the path of consistent sanctity must inevitably lead to Rome, a non-Catholic cannot accord the same praise. The fascination, the compulsive power of Rome were and are irresistible exactly in proportion to the weakness or degeneracy of alternative disciplines. Others than Catholics could learn, and learn from Catholic-

---

[1] Quoted *ibid.*, p. 374.

ism itself, to ground their faith upon 'an insight given by a special course of action'; to deserve, by purity of heart, the vision of God. They could, and can, do this without ceasing to honour, and even to envy, those to whom the Catholic solution is *not* 'frankly impossible'.

CHAPTER IV

THOMAS CARLYLE

1. Introductory

CARLYLE was born in the same year as Keats (1795), and died only six years before the Jubilee of Queen Victoria. His life illustrates with special clearness what can happen to a Romantic when he survives into the latter-days of the nineteenth century. He had seen his visions and dreamt his dreams in the days of Goethe, Wordsworth and Coleridge; then, living on deep into an 'iron time of doubts, disputes, distractions, fears', he strove, in tones at first ringing, but later becoming shrill or strident, to prevent a faithless generation from following false lights. Carlyle was a man with a message, if ever there was one, and the message was essentially that of the great Romantic poets and thinkers, applied to the condition of England in the days of Chartism and the dismal science. He is neglected now, but his influence in his own lifetime was enormous. J. A. Froude, writing in 1849, classed him as one of the two most greatly gifted men then living in England, the other being Newman; and R. H. Hutton writes that 'for many years before his death Carlyle was to England what his great hero, Goethe, long was to Germany,—the aged seer whose personal judgments on men and things were eagerly sought after, and eagerly chronicled and retailed'.[1] To those who were young in the '30's and '40's, to those especially who were adrift in the cross-currents of Newmanism and Benthamism, and had lost their sense of direction, Carlyle's early prophesyings (notably *Sartor* and *Heroes*) came with the force of a revelation, and 'Carlyle is my religion' was heard as often as 'credo in Newmannum'. Froude, who is a representative of the honest doubters of that time, tells us that 'amidst the controversies, the arguments,

---

[1] *Modern Guides of English Thought* (1887), p. 1.

the doubts, the crowding uncertainties of forty years ago, Carlyle's voice was to the young generation of Englishmen like the sound of "ten thousand trumpets" in their ears, as the Knight of Orange said of John Knox'. 'I, for one', Froude continues, 'was saved by Carlyle's writings from Positivism, or Romanism, or Atheism, or any other of the creeds or no creeds which in those years were whirling us about in Oxford like leaves in an autumn storm.'[1] Speaking as one having authority, and setting aside all traditional doctrines or demonstrations, he taught such men as Froude to believe in a living God even though the creeds were outworn. 'To him' (if I may quote once more from Froude's biography) 'God's existence was not an arguable probability, a fact dependent for its certainty on Church authority, or on Apostolic succession, or on so-called histories which might possibly prove to be no more than legends; but an awful reality to which the fates of nations, the fate of each individual man, bore perpetual witness.'[2] It was this, too, which gave Carlyle his power over the many Puritans who were longing for emancipation but who were afraid to venture forth. Of these William White, the father of 'Mark Rutherford', may be taken as typical; 'it was the *Heroes and Hero-Worship* and the *Sartor Resartus* which drew him away from the meeting house' (writes his son). 'There is nothing in these two books directly hostile to either church or dissent, but they laid hold on him as no books had ever held, and the expansion they wrought in him could not possibly tolerate the limitations of orthodoxy.'[3] James Martineau, writing in 1856, ranked Carlyle, with Coleridge, Newman and Maurice, as one of the main influences upon the religious sentiment of the time, and said that although by then his 'pentecostal power' had abated, he had delivered 'captives out of number', giving them faith and life and aspiration in place of mean scepticisms.[4]

A full examination of Carlyle's teaching has to include an

---

[1] Froude, *Carlyle's Life in London* (1884), vol. i, pp. 292 and 295.
[2] *Ibid.*, p. 293.
[3] *Early Life of Mark Rutherford*, p. 38.
[4] *Essays, Reviews and Addresses*, vol. i, p. 266.

analysis of his style, for of him it is abundantly true that the style *is* the man. Carlylese is as distinct a dialect as Miltonics, though a style as Gothic in its chiaroscuro as Milton's is classical in its inversions and intonations. It is certainly (as Keats said of *Paradise Lost*) 'unique', a 'curiosity', and not to be taken as a model. But it has a strange vitality, and indeed it is only great energy of intellect and imagination which can thus make for itself a new language out of an old one. Like others who have forged a highly individual style, Carlyle began by writing the ordinary English of his time, and those who find his mature work unreadable may prefer his early manner. But there can be no doubt that Carlylese, with all its faults, was intensely expressive both of Carlyle's personality and of his relationship to his age: that, namely, of a prophet-sage who, in virtue of a few simple and profound intuitions, hurls lifelong defiance at all the main tendencies of the modern world. Carlyle can never write urbanely; he is always on the stretch. He will not consent to use the current verbal coin; every phrase (and many actual words) must come molten from the forge. For Carlyle writes almost exclusively from the heart or the solar-plexus, not from the head. He sees by flashes and does not think connectedly; summer-lightning, not sunshine, is the light that guides him. So anxious is he not to occupy common ground with his reader, so anxious to keep clear of accepted assumptions and catchwords, that the use of standard English, which implies a certain solidarity between writer and reader, a sharing of presuppositions as between man and man (not to say 'gentleman and gentleman'), becomes impossible for him. Everything he says must be said uniquely, as if for the first time; the constant implication being: 'when I say anything, I mean unspoken volumes, and not the cliché anyone else would mean'. All this makes him fatiguing to read, but it is also the secret of his extraordinary power of transmuting any person, scene or object, at a touch, into an emanation of the Carlylean vision. I hope to recur to this subject from time to time while illustrating various aspects of his thought.

11. Carlyle's Religion

1. 'A man's religion' (he said in *Heroes*) 'is the chief fact with regard to him'; let us follow his lead and take his own religion first. It is not easy to divide his thought into 'aspects', for to him, as to Coleridge, 'the unity of all had been revealed', and one of the main sources of his influence was his power of suggesting that all topics were aspects of one topic, and that the most important of all. God and man, supernatural and natural, spirit and matter, sacred and profane:—it was precisely by fusing and obliterating all these time-honoured distinctions in his visionary furnace that he cast a spell over his listeners, and gave them a sense of deepened insight. It is thus impossible to consider his religion without considering the whole of his thought, even if for the sake of presentation we must make some subdivisions.

Carlyle is remembered, and his influence was felt, as an upholder of the spiritual view of the world in an age of increasing materialism and unbelief. Yet he is the most remarkable example of a phenomenon which I take to be typical of the nineteenth century, that of the religious temperament severed from 'religion'. Few 'secular' writers of his time can have used the name of God more constantly, yet he meant by this word, as Sterling pointed out, something other than the God of Christianity. Sterling, criticizing the trend of Teufelsdröckh's philosophy from the standpoint of a Christian minister, wrote as follows:

> 'What we find everywhere, with an abundant use of the name of God, is the conception of a formless Infinite, whether in time or space; of a high inscrutable Necessity, which it is the chief wisdom and virtue to submit to, which is the mysterious impersonal base of all Existence,—shows itself in the laws of every separate being's nature; and for man in the shape of duty.'[1]

A far more eminent Christian contemporary, F. D. Maurice, said of Carlyle that 'a profound theocratic belief was really

[1] Carlyle's *Life of Sterling* (Chapman & Hall, 1907), p. 102.

at the basis of his mind'[1], and to Maurice it was a matter of regret and concern that so powerful a spiritual influence as Carlyle's should not be working on the side of the Church. After reading *The French Revolution*, Maurice described Carlyle as a man who, although opposed to the Church, was teaching the reality of a divine order in history; elsewhere, however, he accuses him of treating Christian doctrine as a mere mythical vesture, and of indulging in 'wild pantheistic rant'.

Carlyle belonged to the company of the escaped Puritans. Rejecting Church, creed and sacrament—all that he described as 'Hebrew Old-Clothes'—he yet retained the deep intuitions of his Calvinistic peasant-childhood, and it was from the unquestioned moral certainties of Puritanism that he derived both his satiric animus and his prophetic energy. It would be simpler and truer to say that he derived them from his mother, to whom he was bound by the strongest affection of his life, and whose love and anxious care for him continued unbroken until her death, when he himself was nearly sixty. It is touching as well as illuminating to read the extracts from their correspondence given by Froude. Margaret Carlyle, ever afraid that Tom's strange new books —his *Wilhelm Meister*, his Voltaire and his D'Alembert— will lead him astray and shake his faith, implores him to read his Bible and make religion his main concern; Carlyle, sure of his own fundamental faith, yet estranged from the old forms, tries to reassure her in words which will neither compromise him nor distress her, but be true for them both.

> 'I am rather afraid', he writes (March 29, 1819), 'that I have not been quite regular in reading that best of books which you recommended to me. However, last night I was reading upon my favourite Job, and I hope to do better in time to come. I entreat you to believe that I am sincerely desirous of being a good man; and though we may differ in some few unimportant particulars, yet I firmly trust that the same power which created us with imperfect faculties will pardon the errors of every one (and none are without them) who seeks truth and righteousness with a simple heart.'

[1] *Life of F. D. M.* by his son, vol. ii, p. 404.

'Oh, my dear, dear son,' she answers, 'I would pray for a blessing on your learning. I beg you with all the feeling of an affectionate mother that you would study the Word of God. . . . Do make religion your great study, Tom; if you repent it, I will bear the blame for ever.'

And so it continues, right on into Carlyle's late middle-age; their hearts are in the same place, though their intellects are wide asunder. When his mother died (in 1854) his grief expressed itself in a prayer that God would make him thankful for such a mother and more worthy of her in the years that might remain to him. In his Journal he wrote:

'Oh pious mother! Kind, good, brave, and truthful soul as I have ever found, and more than I have ever elsewhere found in this world, your poor Tom, long out of his schooldays now, has fallen very lonely, very lame and broken in this pilgrimage of his, and you cannot help him or cheer him by a kind word any more. From your grave in Ecclefechan Kirkyard yonder you bid him trust in God, and that also he will try if he can understand, and *do*. The conquest of the world and of death and hell does verily yet lie in that, if one can understand and do it.' [1]

In a real sense Carlyle *did* make religion his great lifelong study; all the positives in his teaching are on the side of faith and against unbelief. The evils which he denounced were all due, he taught, to spiritual paralysis, lack of reverence, lack of wonder—in a word, to lack of religious belief. Like a Hebrew prophet, he recalls his age from following the idols of materialism, utilitarianism, democracy and the like, to the worship of the true God. Men's hearts and minds were stricken with the blight of eighteenth century rationalism; the universe had gone dead and mechanical; the nations would perish unless they could recapture the vision of God working in Nature and history, and learn that the meaning of life lay in dutiful service, and not in motive-grinding or the felicific calculus. In all this Carlyle's affinity with the religious side of Romanticism is manifest enough. In so far as the Romantic Movement meant a rejection of

[1] *Life in London*, vol. ii, p. 149.

the flimsy superficialities of the age of reason, an awakening to fuller and richer insights into reality and into the relation of past and present, and an acknowledgment of the authenticity of Imagination and of Faith—then Carlyle's work can be seen as a vigorous continuation of that movement. The same forces led Coleridge from Unitarianism to Anglicanism, and Newman from the Church of England to Rome. The path of Carlyle's pilgrimage diverged widely from theirs, but his starting-point was the same: the demand for a deeper and more spiritual interpretation of experience than had been available in the previous century.

2. The affinities between Carlyle and Coleridge, in particular, are striking enough to deserve consideration. Both denounced the poisonous legacy of the century of unbelief: atheism, materialism, mechanical philosophy, utilitarian ethics, false optimism, progress-worship, and a shallow interpretation of history (especially of the Middle Ages); both pleaded for life against mechanism, for Reason against Understanding, for the eye of the soul against the eye of the flesh; both proclaimed the reality of the invisible; both summoned their age to leave Mammon-worship and return to God; both derived their inspiration jointly from Christianity and German idealism. Why then do we not get from Carlyle, as we do from many others (Sterling, Hare, Thomas Arnold, Newman, Maurice and even J. S. Mill), a clear acknowledgment of reverence or respect for Coleridge? The answer is to be sought in his recorded impressions of Coleridge, which reveal his inmost mind as clearly as anything in his writings. We encounter here a blend of admiration for the seer, with pitying contempt for the man, and deep distrust for his attempt to rehabilitate the Church and its theology. In 1824, having finished *Wilhelm Meister*, Carlyle descended upon London. He viewed and measured up its literary society like some clear-eyed Brobdingnagian dropped by accident into Lilliput. Here are some of his satiric sketches of notabilities, Coleridge amongst them:

'Thomas Campbell has . . . no living well of thought or feeling in him. His head is a shop, not a manufactory; and for his heart, it is as dry as a Greenock kipper. . . . He is not so much a man as the editor of a magazine. His life is that of an exotic. He exists in London, as most Scotsmen do, like a shrub disrooted and stuck into a bottle of water. . . . Coleridge is sunk inextricably in the depths of putrescent indolence. Southey and Wordsworth have retired far from the din of this monstrous city; so has Thomas Moore. Whom have we left? The dwarf Opium-eater. . . . He carries a laudanum bottle in his pocket, and the venom of a wasp in his heart. . . . Hazlitt is writing his way through France and Italy. The ginshops and pawnbrokers bewail his absence. . . . "Good heavens!" I often inwardly exclaim, "and is this the literary world?"' [1]

In all this we hear the voice of the Scottish peasant and Puritan accustomed to plain living and high thinking, honest toil up the Hill Difficulty, and deadly struggles with Apollyon: the voice, too, we may add, of the as yet unrecognized literary aspirant. This is how he describes a visit to Coleridge:

'I have seen many curiosities; not the least of them I reckon Coleridge, the Kantian metaphysician and quondam Lake poet. . . . Figure a fat, flabby, incurvated personage, at once short, rotund, and relaxed, with a watery mouth, a snuffy nose, a pair of strange brown, timid, yet earnest-looking eyes, a high tapering brow, and a great bush of grey hair; and you have some faint idea of Coleridge. He is a kind good soul, full of religion and affection and poetry and animal magnetism. His cardinal sin is that he wants *will*. He has no resolution. He shrinks from pain or labour in any of its shapes. His very attitude bespeaks this. He never straightens his knee-joints. He stoops with his fat, ill-shapen shoulders, and in walking he does not tread, but shovel and slide. . . . The conversation of the man is much as I anticipated—a forest of thoughts, some true, many false, more *part* dubious, all of them ingenious in some degree, often in a high degree. But there is no method in his talk: he wanders like a man sailing among many currents, whithersoever his lazy mind directs him; and what is more unpleasant, he preaches, or rather soliloquises. Hence I found him unprofitable, even tedious;

---

[1] Letter to Jane Welsh, in Froude's *T. C., A History of the First Forty Years of his Life* (1882) (referred to henceforth as *Early Life*), vol. i, pp. 263-4.

but we parted very good friends. . . . I reckon him a man of great and useless genius: a strange, not at all a great man.'[1]

Next year, on his second visit to London (1825), he calls Coleridge 'a mass of richest spices putrefied into a dunghill', and after another caustic commentary on the literary world he breaks out:

'The Devil in his own good time take all such literary men. One sterling fellow like Schiller, or even old Johnson, would take half a dozen such creatures by the nape of the neck, between his finger and thumb, and carry them forth to the nearest common sink. Save Allan Cunningham, our honest Nithsdale peasant, there is not one *man* among them.'[2]

So much for the personal estimate. Carlyle's opinion of Coleridge's thought and influence is expressed in the *Life of Sterling*, where Coleridge becomes a symbol of the mediaeval enchantments which have allured young Sterling into the clerical dream-world. Some quotations from the celebrated eighth chapter of *Sterling* (part I) will show why Carlyle could not be Coleridge's disciple:

'Coleridge sat on the brow of Highgate Hill, in those years, looking down on London and its smoke-tumult, like a sage escaped from the inanity of life's battle . . . he had, especially among young inquiring men, a higher than literary, a kind of prophetic or magician character. He was thought to hold, he alone in England, the key of German and other Transcendentalisms; knew the sublime secret of believing by "the reason" what "the understanding" had been obliged to fling out as incredible; and could still, after Hume and Voltaire had done their best and worst with him, profess himself an orthodox Christian, and say and point to the Church of England, with its singular old rubrics and surplices at Allhallowtide, *Esto perpetua*. A sublime man; who, alone in these dark days, had saved his crown of spiritual manhood; escaping from the black materialisms, and revolutionary deluges, with "God, Freedom, Immortality" still his; a king of men.'

With Coleridge's diagnosis of the world's sickness Carlyle had no quarrel; after all, it was his own:

[1] Ibid., p. 222. [2] Ibid., pp. 292-3.

'All Science had become mechanical; the science not of men, but of a kind of human beavers. Churches themselves had died away into a godless mechanical condition. Men's souls were blinded, hebetated; and sunk under the influence of Atheism and Materialism, and Hume and Voltaire: the world for the present was as an extinct world, deserted of God, and incapable of well-doing till it changed its heart and spirit.'

All this Carlyle, like any Coleridgean, recognizes as a 'too sorrowful truth'. To him it seemed manifest, however, that Coleridge's subtle mind harboured, along with this insight, a 'fatal delusion'. The insight discerned that

'in spite of beaver sciences and temporary spiritual hebetude and cecity, man and his Universe were eternally divine; and that no past nobleness, or revelation of the divine, could or would ever be lost to him.'

It also rightly insisted that it is good 'to do what you can with old Churches and practical Symbols of the Noble'. The 'fatal delusion' came in with Coleridge's proposed remedy, namely to bring the 'dead Churches, this dead English Church especially', to life again. Gold lies amongst their ruins, but

'on the whole, do not think that you can, by logical alchymy, distil astral spirits from them. ... What the light of your mind, which is the direct inspiration of the Almighty, pronounces incredible,— that, in God's name, leave uncredited; at your peril do not try believing that. No subtlest hocus-pocus of "reason" *versus* "understanding" will avail for that feat ...!'

The Past is the past; the Present is something different, if worse; the Church must be consigned, though with melancholy reverence and respect, to the Past. One is reminded of his journal-comment on the Church, the Mass and the priests at Bruges (1842); his feelings, as usual, were mixed. The sight of the worshippers and their devotion touched him deeply; the fat priests revolted him: he wanted to kick them into the canal.

'Things are long-lived, and God above appoints their term. Yet when the brains of a thing have been out for three centuries and odd, one does wish that it would be kind enough to die.'

Even so he returns upon himself, writhing as ever in his life-long dilemma:

'At bottom one cannot wish these men kicked into the canals, for what would follow were they gone? Atheistic Benthamism, French Editorial "rights of man", and "Grande Nation". That is a far worse thing, a far untruer thing. God pity the generation in which you have to see deluded and deluding *simulacra*, Tartuffes and semi-Tartuffes, and to *stay* the uplifted foot, and not kick them into the canal.'[1]

Carlyle, then, rejects Coleridge's remedy as moonshine, but what was his own? Faith, Belief, Wonder, Reverence—yes, but faith in what? Nearly all his work implies or states his answer, but it is partly set forth in the same chapter on Coleridge:

'For the old Eternal Powers do live forever; nor do their laws know any change, however we in our poor wigs and church-tippets may attempt to read their laws. To *steal* into Heaven,—by the modern method, of sticking ostrich-like your head into fallacies on Earth, . . . is forever forbidden. High-treason is the name of that attempt; and it continues to be punished as such. Strange enough: here once more was a kind of Heaven-scaling Ixion; and to him, as to the old one, the just Gods were very stern! The ever-revolving, never-advancing Wheel (of a kind) was his, through life; and from his Cloud-Juno did not he too procreate strange Centaurs, spectral Puseyisms, monstrous illusory Hybrids, and ecclesiastical Chimaeras,—which now roam the earth in a very lamentable manner!'

The 'old Eternal Powers', 'the just gods', in these, then, we may and must trust, but

'Speedy end to Superstition,—a gentle one if you can contrive it, but an end. What can it profit any mortal to adopt locutions and imaginations which do *not* correspond to fact; which no sane mortal can deliberately adopt in his soul as true; which the most orthodox of mortals can only, and this after infinite essentially *impious* effort

[1] *Life in London*, vol. i, pp. 264-5.

to put-out the eyes of his mind, persuade himself to "believe that he believes"? Away with it; in the name of God, come out of it, all true men!'[1]

These are brave Protestant words, and we can still respond approvingly to Carlyle's appeal for honesty, especially if we are sure what such terms as 'superstition', 'imagination' and 'fact' precisely mean. But I doubt whether Carlyle's own faith was really more intelligible or demonstrable than Coleridge's; it was certainly less definite. It was perhaps fortunate for his polemical purpose that he could represent orthodoxy as the view of a man who lacked will-power, whose conversation was bewildering, and whose knee-joints were never straightened.

Carlyle's position resembles that of Arnold in *Literature and Dogma*; it is so differently stated as to be hardly recognizable as similar, yet essentially it is so. It is a position common to liberal Victorians w,th a religious temper; the old certainties stand firm even when the dogmatic supports are removed, and all clear-sighted, honest men must see, or soon will see, that they *have* been removed. Carlyle does not talk of 'the eternal not ourselves that makes for righteousness', nor of the 'stream of tendency', he uses language compounded out of Hebrew prophecy and German transcendentalism. Indeed, his divinity is a sort of amalgam of Jehovah, Odin, Calvin's predestinating God and the Soul of the World; his faith, a blend of Old Testament monotheism, pantheism and philosophic necessitarianism. Yet we shall misunderstand Carlyle unless we realize that this faith, describe it as we will, was the invisible sun by which he lived, and that from the time when he conquered his youthful spirit of negation its pure flame burnt inextinguishably within him.

3. Carlyle's 'conversion' or spiritual rebirth has become familiar from the account given in *Sartor Resartus* of Teufelsdröckh's victory over the 'Everlasting No'—an account which, he has told us, is true to his own experience. As in the story of many mystics, his illumination was preceded by

[1] *Sterling*, i, ch. 7.

a dark night of the soul—the 'fixed starless Tartarean black', in which doubt has darkened into unbelief. This phase followed the discovery, through wide reading in European literature, that the religion of Annandale, though it had formed in him a pure, moral nature, and given him an unshakable, instinctive piety, was based in part upon assumptions no longer acceptable to the modern mind. His description of this ordeal reminds one of Bunyan's in *Grace Abounding*, but the *Zeitgeist* has deprived Carlyle even of the Devil:

'In the midst of their crowded streets and assemblages, I walked solitary.... Some comfort it would have been, could I, like Faust, have fancied myself tempted and tormented of the Devil ... but in our age of Down-pulling and Disbelief, the very Devil has been pulled down.... To me the Universe was all void of Life, of Purpose, of Volition; even of Hostility: it was one huge, dead, immeasurable Steam-engine, rolling on, in its dead indifference, to grind me limb from limb. O, the vast, gloomy, solitary Golgotha, and Mill of Death!...

'So had it lasted, as in bitter protracted Death-agony, through long years. The heart within me, unvisited by any heavenly dewdrop, was smouldering in sulphurous slow-consuming fire....

'Full of such humour,... was I, one sultry Dog-day, after much perambulation, toiling along the dirty little *Rue Saint-Thomas de L'Enfer*, among civic rubbish enough, in a close atmosphere, and over pavements hot as Nebuchadnezzar's Furnace; whereby doubtless my spirits were little cheered; when, all at once, there rose a Thought in me, and I asked myself: "What *art* thou afraid of?... Despicable biped! what is the sum-total of the worst that lies before thee? Death? Well, Death; and say the pangs of Tophet too, and all that the Devil and Man may, will or can do against thee! Hast thou not a heart; canst thou not suffer whatsoever it be; and, as a Child of Freedom, though outcast, trample Tophet itself under thy feet, while it consumes thee? Let it come, then; I will meet it and defy it!" And as I so thought, there rushed like a stream of fire over my whole soul; and I shook base Fear away from me forever. I was strong, of unknown strength; a spirit, almost a god. Ever from that time the temper of my misery was changed: not Fear or whining Sorrow was it, but Indignation and grim fire-eyed Defiance.

'Thus had the EVERLASTING NO (*das Ewige Nein*) pealed authoritatively through all the recesses of my Being, of my ME; and then it was that my whole ME stood up, in native God-created majesty, and with emphasis recorded its Protest. . . . The Everlasting No had said: "Behold, thou art faithless, outcast, and the Universe is mine (the Devil's)"; to which my whole Me now made answer: "*I* am not thine, but Free, and forever hate thee!"

'It is from this hour that I incline to date my Spiritual New-birth, or Baphometic Fire-baptism; perhaps I directly thereupon began to be a Man.'[1]

The Christian reader will notice, in all this, a lack of conformity with the established pattern of conversion: there is no contrition, no reliance upon grace or redeeming love, but on the contrary, much proud and passionate self-assertion. The emotion that follows release is hatred and defiance of the Devil, rather than love and gratitude towards God. Nevertheless, he had found a faith, and never afterwards lost it. Writing, in his *Reminiscences*, of his sojourn some years after this (in 1825) at Hoddam Hill ('a not ignoble russet-coated Idyll in my memory'), he expressly associates the experiences of that period with Christian conversion:

'This year I found that I had conquered all my scepticisms, agonizing doubtings, fearful wrestlings with the foul and vile and soul-murdering Mud-Gods of my Epoch . . . and was emerging, free in spirit, into the eternal blue of ether,—where, blessed be Heaven, I have, for the spiritual part, ever since lived. . . . What my pious joy and gratitude then was, let the pious soul figure. . . . I understood well what the old Christian people meant by their "Conversion", by God's Infinite Mercy to them:—I had, in effect, gained an immense victory; and, for a number of years, had, in spite of nerves and chagrins, a constant inward happiness that was quite royal and supreme; in which all temporal evil was transient and insignificant; and which essentially remains with me still, though far oftener *eclipsed*, and lying deeper *down*, than then. Once more, thank Heaven for its highest gift. I then felt, and still feel,

[1] *Sartor*, bk. ii, ch. 7.

endlessly indebted to *Goethe* in this business; he, in his fashion, I perceived, had travelled the steep rocky road before me,—the first of the moderns. . . . Meanwhile, my thoughts were very peaceable, full of pity and humanity as they had never been before. Nowhere can I recollect of myself such pious musings; communings, silent and spontaneous, with Fact and Nature, as in these poor Annandale localities.'[1]

In this later account there is more serenity and thankfulness than before, but not more Christianity; the mood is mainly Wordsworthian (suggestive of much in *Tintern Abbey* and *The Prelude*), and the 'redeemer' is Goethe. What he has attained is not humility and love, but a spiritual elevation from whence he can look down, with mingled compassion and scorn, on 'the welterings of my poor fellow-creatures, still stuck in that fatal element'—a point of vantage which removes him far above 'Puseyisms, Ritualisms, Metaphysical controversies and cobwebberies' and leaves him with no feeling 'except honest silent pity for the serious or religious part of them, and occasional indignation . . . at the frivolous, *secular* and impious part, with their Universal Suffrages, their Nigger Emancipations, Sluggard-and-Scoundrel Protection Societies, and "Unexampled Prosperities", for the time being!'

From this time onwards Carlyle increasingly assumes the tone of a religious seer, proclaiming that God lives and reigns, and executes judgment amongst the nations. His *French Revolution*, which more than any other single work won him fame, is unlike any book of history since the Pentateuch; it is a Vision of Judgment, in which the wrath of God is seen, as of old, descending upon a sinful and corrupt generation. Indeed the Revolution, the palmary modern instance of the workings of eternal divine justice, was ever in Carlyle's mind the main evidence for the reality of a moral order in the world. Believe in God, seek the Truth, and do the Duty nearest to hand! is the burden of his message. Belief is the condition of all genuine life and work:

'*Belief*, said one the other night, has done immense evil: witness

[1] *Reminiscences* (Everyman ed.), pp. 281-2.

Kipperdolling and the Anabaptists, etc. "True", rejoined I, with vehemence, almost with fury . . . "true belief has done some evil in the world; but it has done all the good that was ever done in it; from the time when Moses saw the Burning Bush and *believed* it to be God appointing him deliverer of His people, down to the last act of belief that you and I executed. Good never came from aught else."' [1]

To his younger brother Alexander he writes—almost repeating his mother's words to himself:

'I was very glad to learn that you had promised to my mother to keep religion in your house: without religion constantly present in the heart, I see not how a man can live otherwise than unreasonably, than desperately.' [2]

Belief is the condition of Life and Work, but the converse is also true; if you lack belief, 'do the duty which lies nearest'; 'he who has ever seen into the *infinite* nature of duty has seen all that costs difficulty. The universe has then become a temple for him, and the divinity and all divine things thereof will infallibly become revealed.' [3] Doubt can only be removed by action *and* by the reading of Goethe, whose works 'are as the day-spring visiting us in the dark night'.

4. The strength of Carlyle lay in the passionate sincerity with which he believed in his own 'God'. This 'God' may have been, as Sterling and others complained, a mere 'formless Infinite' or an 'inscrutable Necessity', but it was real to him, it may be conjectured, as the God of Christianity was to few 'Christians' of that age. But Carlyle's appeal to the many who were religiously inclined yet dissatisfied with orthodoxy, the exhilarating sense of release and renewal he brought them, were due not merely to the fiery energy of his own conviction. They were due also to this; that Carlyle's teaching powerfully reinforced two tendencies which had for long been gathering momentum in the mind of Europe

---

[1] *Early Life*, vol. ii, p. 331 (Journal, Feb. 1833).
[2] *Ibid.*, p. 264. [3] *Ibid.*, p. 259.

—the tendency to find God in Nature, and the tendency (produced, like the former, by the scientific movement) to regard all translations of picture-thinking into concept and law as closer approximations to Truth. Substitute 'the Immensities and Eternities' for God, substitute 'the Temple of the Universe' for the Church, 'Literature' for the Bible, 'Heroes' for saints, 'Work' for prayer, and the like: do all this, and you have at one stroke destroyed 'superstition' and provided a true religion for honest men in these latter days. Here at last was a creed which *did* 'correspond to fact'; which could be believed without putting out the eyes of the mind. What Mark Rutherford has said of Wordsworth may here be applied to Carlyle; speaking of his first reading of *Lyrical Ballads*, he says:

> 'it excited a movement and a growth which went on till, by degrees, all the systems which enveloped me like a body gradually decayed from me and fell away into nothing. . . . God is nowhere formally deposed, and Wordsworth would have been the last man to say that he had lost his faith in the God of his fathers. But his real God is not the God of the Church, but the God of the hills, the abstraction Nature, and to this my reverence was transferred. Instead of an object of worship which was altogether artificial, remote, never coming into genuine contact with me, I now had one which I thought to be real, one in which literally I could live and move and have my being, an actual fact present before my eyes. God was brought from that heaven of the books, and dwelt on the downs in the far-away distances, and in every cloud-shadow which wandered across the valley. Wordsworth unconsciously did for me what every spiritual reformer has done—he recreated my Supreme Divinity; substituting a new and living spirit for the old deity, once alive, but gradually hardened into an idol.'[1]

We can watch this process going on in a passage like the following (from *Sartor*, bk. ii, ch. 9—'The Everlasting Yea'):

> 'Often also could I see the black Tempest marching in anger through the distance: round some Schreckhorn, as yet grim-blue,

---

[1] *Autobiography of Mark Rutherford*, pp. 18-19.

would the eddying vapour gather, and there tumultuously eddy, and flow down like a mad witch's hair; till, after a space, it vanished, and, in the clear sunbeam, your Schreckhorn stood smiling grim-white, for the vapour had held snow. How thou fermentest and elaboratest in thy great fermenting vat and laboratory of an Atmosphere, of a World, O Nature!—Or what is Nature? Ha! why do I not name thee GOD? Art not thou the "Living Garment of God"? O Heavens, is it, in very deed, HE, then, that ever speaks through thee; that lives and loves in thee, that lives and loves in me?'

Thus does Carlyle translate the old conversion-story into the language of Nature-worship. Many of the characteristics of his style, too, are here illustrated: the tone of rapt soliloquy; the touch of Gothic terror; the poetic fury, checked however by the abrupt changes of rhythm and by such a phrase as 'your Schreckhorn'; the volte-face at 'Ha!'; the catch in the throat, and the freely flowing unction of the final rhetorical question. Having thus woven his spell, and won your emotional assent, he can then complete the incantation in a strain of exalted tenderness, leading up to a clinching affirmative:

'Fore-shadows, call them rather fore-splendours, of that Truth, and Beginning of Truths, fell mysteriously over my soul. Sweeter than Dayspring to the Shipwrecked in Nova Zembla; ah, like the mother's voice to her little child that strays bewildered, weeping, in unknown tumults; like soft streamings of celestial music to my too-exasperated heart, came that Evangel. The Universe is not dead and demoniacal, a charnel house with spectres; but godlike, and my Father's!'

It was in this way that Carlyle offered to his readers 'God's Universe' as a 'Symbol of the Godlike', and 'Immensity' for a Temple; it was an appeal which (as Pascal had long ago declared) could influence only those who already believed in God on other grounds. But there were plenty of these, and the appeal met with eager response.

'Listen, and for organ-music thou wilt ever, as of old, hear the Morning Stars sing together.'

Another characteristic passage (from *Past and Present*, part ii, ch. 2) will illustrate Carlyle's effort to present the 'Truth' that underlies a traditional 'picture': his way of prophesying in the name of a belief from which he at the same time strips off the 'Hebrew old-clothes'. This time it is 'Heaven' and 'Hell':

> 'Reader, even Christian Reader as thy title goes, hast thou any notion of Heaven and Hell? I rather apprehend, not. Often as the words are on our tongue, they have got a fabulous or semi-fabulous character for most of us, and pass on like a kind of transient similitude, like a sound signifying little.
>
> 'Yet it is well worth while for us to know, once and always, that they are not a similitude, nor a fable nor semi-fable; that they are an everlasting highest fact! "No Lake of Sicilian or other sulphur burns now anywhere in these ages", sayest thou? Well, and if there did not! Believe that there does not; believe it if thou wilt, nay hold by it as a real increase, a rise to higher stages, to wider horizons and empires. All this has vanished, or has not vanished; believe as thou wilt as to all this. But that an Infinite of Practical Importance, speaking with strict arithmetical exactness, an *Infinite*, has vanished or can vanish from the Life of any Man: this thou shalt not believe! O brother, the Infinite of Terror, of Hope, of Pity, did it not at any moment disclose itself to thee, indubitable, unnameable? Came it never, like the gleam of *preter*natural eternal Oceans, like the voice of old Eternities, far-sounding through thy heart of hearts? Never? Alas, it was not thy Liberalism, then; it was thy Animalism! The Infinite is more sure than any other fact. But only men can discern it; mere building beavers, spinning arachnes, much more the predatory vulturous and vulpine species, do not discern it well!—'

We have here the suasive rhetoric of an evangelistic preacher, who is offering (however) not free grace to repentant sinners, but a vision of the Infinite to a generation of purblind mechanics and exploiters. Once again the technique is to win assent, not by argument, but by a subtly shifting attack on the heart. First, there is the confidence-winning irony of the exordium to the reader—'I rather apprehend, not', and 'it is well worth while for us to know'. Then, the concession to the time-spirit: it is a *real* advance to discard the picture of a sulphuric lake. Then, with the transition to *but Hell is real all the same*, comes the abrupt apostrophe, uttered with tears in the voice—'O brother!' The afflatus thereupon descends with power, and swells to a pathetic climax in the question 'Never?' Finally, in the hush that ensues, he swallows a sob, and returns to satire, ending with the grave headshake, the ejaculated understatement (conveying pent-up significance): 'do not discern it well!' And where, after all this, do we stand? We have been shaken, perhaps even moved to tears; we have been shamed out of our preoccupation with winning, spinning and building, and reminded that there is an unseen reality beneath and above our transitory world. But we are left, in effect, only with a wistful echo from the 'old Eternities'; a melancholy gleam from 'preternatural Oceans'.

The man to whom the Universe has become a Temple will pass through life in a marvelling temper; he will know that 'in every object there is inexhaustible meaning', and that 'the eye sees in it what the eye brings means of seeing'. Wonder is the basis of all true worship, and Carlyle, anticipating D. H. Lawrence here (as often), attacks Science for having killed the emotion of wonder:

> 'The man who cannot wonder... were he President of innumerable Royal Societies ... is but a Pair of Spectacles behind which is no Eye.... Doth not thy cow calve, doth not thy bull gender? Thou thyself, wert thou not born, wilt thou not die? "Explain" me all this ... or, what were better, give it up, and weep not that the reign of wonder is done, and God's world all disembellished and prosaic, but that thou hitherto art a Dilettante and sandblind Pedant!'[1]

If Carlyle here looks forward to Lawrence, he looks back also to Wordsworth and Coleridge: 'to excite a feeling analogous to the supernatural by awakening the mind's attention from the lethargy of custom'[2]—this was continually his aim. He developed, indeed, an explicit doctrine of the identity of natural and supernatural, not by denying

[1] *Sartor*, bk. i, ch. 10. [2] *Biog. Lit.*, ed. Shawcross, ii, p. 6.

the supernatural, but by raising the natural to the higher level. In his Journal for February 1, 1833, he writes:

'That the Supernatural differs not from the Natural is a great Truth, which the last century (especially in France) has been engaged in demonstrating. The Philosophers went far wrong, however, in this, that instead of raising the natural to the supernatural, they strove to sink the supernatural to the natural. The gist of my whole way of thought is to do not the latter but the *former*.'[1]

It was indeed the 'gist' of his whole message, for by means of it he was able to reconcile the contraries that met in him: the impulse to deny, and the impulse to affirm. The Church is dead?—then worship in the temple of the universe; Heaven is a fable? but Infinitude remains; miracles are discredited? but Nature is a miracle; the Bible is incredible? but History is a Bible; Revelation is a fairy-tale? but the true Shekinah is Man, and in worshipping Heroes we are acknowledging the godlike in human form.

5. Carlyle possessed a power of double-vision or second-sight which, in another age, might have made him a great satirist. He had the satirist's awareness of the disparities between the ideal and the actual, the real and the illusory, the genuine and the spurious; but, though satire abounds in his work, he was too much a Romantic to maintain the satiric poise. Tenderness and *Schwärmerei* were continually breaking in, so that he remains on the whole a humorist. But this second-sight gave him the power to see persons, things and events in a spectral and visionary light; when this clairvoyance was upon him he beheld objects not as objects, but as symbols of invisible forces, or as patterns in a divine drama. From this kind of insight springs much of the power and pathos of his historical work, and his portraits of men and women; people in action, while remaining human, are simultaneously seen as impelled to glory or disaster by unalterable invisible law, as the human units in Hardy's *Dynasts* are unwitting agents of the Immanent Will. To Carlyle this visionary power often brought great suffering:

[1] *Early Life*, vol. ii, p. 330.

he speaks of it as a 'detestable state of enchantment'. Yet, now that the force of his 'message' is spent, this power may well seem to be the most unequivocal sign of his greatness. I mention it while speaking of his 'religion', because it was closely connected with his grasp of unseen realities. A few examples will be of service here: London in 1835, like the Paris of the Revolution, is pictured as a Dance of Death—

> 'The world looks often quite spectral to me; sometimes, as in Regent Street the other night (my nerves being all shattered), quite hideous, discordant, almost infernal. I had been at Mrs Austin's, heard Sidney Smith for the first time guffawing, other persons prating, jargoning. To me through these thin cobwebs Death and Eternity sate glaring.' [1]

'I feel', he says again, 'a fierce glare of insight in me into many things'; and later: 'As I live, and have long lived, death and Hades differ little to me from the earth and life. The human figure I meet is wild, wondrous, ghastly to me, almost as if it were a spectre and I a spectre—*Taisons*.' [2] When he is in a more tranquil mood, the same gift will sometimes sharpen his perception, and we get descriptive passages alive with realized detail, yet subdued to unity by a predominant vision:

> 'It was a day of tempestuous wind; but the sun occasionally shone; the country was green, bright; the hills of an almost spiritual clearness, and broad swift storms of hail came dashing down from them on this hand and that. It was a kind of *preternatural* walk, full of sadness, full of purity.
>
> 'The Scaur Water ... came brawling down, the voice of it like a lamentation among the winds, answering me as the voice of a brother wanderer and lamenter, wanderers like me through a certain portion of eternity and infinite space. Poor brook! yet it was nothing but drops of water.' [3]

Or this, written to Sterling from the shore of the Solway Firth:

> 'There is no idler, sadder, quieter, more *ghostlike* man in the

[1] *Life in London*, vol. i, p. 54.   [2] *Ibid.*, p. 201.   [3] *Ibid.*, p. 244.

world even now than I. Most weary, flat, stale, seem to me all the electioneerings, and screechings, and jibberings, that the earth is filled with, in these, or indeed in any days. Men's very sorrows, and the tears one's heart weeps when the eye is dry, what is in that either? In an hour, will not death make it all still again? ... I look on the sapphire of St. Bees head and the Solway mirror from the gable window. I ride to the top of Blaweery, and see all round from Ettrick Pen to Helvellyn, from Tyndale and Northumberland to Cairnsmuir and Ayrshire. *Voir c'est avoir*. A brave old earth, in which, as above said, I am content to acquiesce without quarrel, and, at lowest, hold my peace. One night, late, I rode through the village where I was born. The old Kirkyard tree, a huge old gnarled ash, was nestling itself softly against the great twilight in the north. A star or two looked out, and the old graves were all there, and my father and my sister; and God was above us all.'[1]

6 The reaction of the conventionally religious mind of the time to Carlyle's teaching is well seen in R. H. Hutton's *Spectator* articles. Hutton objects to the 'Abysses' and 'Eternities'; such periphrases are a cloak for Carlyle's ambiguous position. They are terms of vague, mystic potency, really referring to some impersonal law or world-process, yet at the same time implying a spiritual power which Carlyle will not explicitly avow. Hutton means, I think, that Carlyle has no right to use darkly religiose language while rejecting 'religion'.[2] This would be a valid criticism if what Carlyle rejected had been the *whole* of 'religion', and if that 'whole' had been fully alive and active in the established forms of the time. But the same criticism could be used to depreciate all spiritual insight not expressed through official channels. It seems to me that Sterling [3] came nearer to the truth when he compared Carlyle with Luther, adding that Carlyle had the much more difficult task of asserting Divine reality in an age of clear but shallow thinking, when men

---

[1] *Ibid.*, p. 110.
[2] R. H. Hutton, *Criticisms on Contemporary Thought and Thinkers, selected from the Spectator*, 1894.
[3] See *On the Writings of T. C.* (*London and Westminster Review*, 1839), in *Essays and Tales*, vol. i, 1848.

commonly had knowledge without belief, and belief without knowledge, and when, though understandings were quick, hearts were often empty of love, hope and awe. As he truly says, Carlyle had, above most men, that sense of a 'higher unseen Subsistence', of a 'supersensual, infinite Reality', of 'Being itself', which is at the heart of all religious experience. Carlyle was not writing for those who had faith, but for those who had lost it, and who considered such loss to be 'progress'. In his old age he showed himself fully alive to the issues raised by men like Hutton:

> 'The name [of God] has become as if obsolete to the most devout of us; and it is, to the huge idly impious million of writing, preaching, and talking people as if the *fact* too had quite ceased to be certain. "The Eternities", "the Silences", etc. I myself have tried various shifts to avoid mentioning the "Name" to such an audience —audience which merely sneers in return—and is more convinced of its delusion than ever. "No more humbug!" "Let us go ahead!" "All descended from gorillas seemingly." "Sun made by collision of huge masses of planets, asteroids, etc., in the infinite of space." Very possibly say I! "Then where is the place for a Creator?" The *fool* hath said in his heart there is no God. . . . The *fool* hath said it—he and nobody else; and with dismal results in our days— as in all days; which often makes me sad to think of, coming nearer myself and the end of my own life than I ever expected they would do. [Froude here adds a footnote: 'Carlyle did not deny his own responsibilities in the matter. In his desire to extricate the kernel from the shell in which it was rotting, he had shaken existing beliefs as much as any man, and, he admitted to me, "had given a considerable shove to all that".'] That of the sun, and his possibly being made in that manner, seemed to me a real triumph of science, indefinitely widening the horizon of our *theological* ideas withal . . . I suppose the finest stroke that "Science", poor creature, has or may have succeeded in making during my time—welcome to me if it be a truth—honourably welcome! But what has it to do with the existence of the Eternal Unnameable? Fools! Fools! It widens the horizon of my imagination, fills me with deeper and deeper wonder and devout awe.'[1]

[1] *Life in London*, vol. ii, pp. 370-1.

III. Carlyle's Moral and Political Ideas

In the light of the foregoing we may now briefly consider some of Carlyle's moral and political ideas. His idealism was a part of his religiosity: The World is the vesture of God, matter of thought, the transient of the eternal; every object is 'a window through which we may look into Infinitude itself'. The clue to History is the account of men's inmost thoughts—hence, of their religion: 'the thoughts they had were the parents of the actions they did . . . it was the unseen and spiritual in them that determined the outward and actual'.[1] Indeed, History is essentially Biography, and above all the Biography of Great Men. Thus unequivocally does Carlyle deny the doctrine of 'historical materialism', which asserts that thoughts, ideals, religions, arts and the like are epiphenomena: mirages floating upon the economic sands. But I have found no hint that Carlyle knew the writings of Marx; the enemy, for him as for Coleridge, was 'The Unbelieving Century' (the eighteenth), and its legacy in his own time. The eighteenth century suffered from 'spiritual paralysis'; it was sceptical, utilitarian, mechanical:

> 'How mean, dwarfish are their ways of thinking, in this time,—compared not with the Christian Shakespeares and Miltons, but with the old Pagan Skalds, with any species of believing men! The living TREE Igdrasil, with the melodious prophetic waving of its world-wide boughs, deep-rooted as Hela, has died-out into the clanking of a World-MACHINE. "Tree" and "Machine": contrast these two things. I, for my share, declare the world to be no machine! I say that it does *not* go by the wheel-and-pinion "motives", self-interests, checks, balances; that there is something far other in it than the clank of spinning-jennies and parliamentary majorities; and, on the whole, that it is not a machine at all!'[2]

The battle of Belief against Unbelief is never-ending; in the eighteenth century Unbelief was in the ascendant, for the old ways of believing were in decay. Carlyle can find a word of negative praise for Benthamism, as an honest attempt to make whatever could be made of a 'dead iron machine'

---

[1] *Heroes*, Lecture I.   [2] *Heroes*, Lecture V.

worked by 'Gravitation and selfish Hunger'. But the 'doctrine of motives', the view that the ultimate springs of action are love of pleasure and fear of pain, was the object of his special abhorrence. 'Foolish Wordmonger and Motive-grinder, who in thy Logic-mill hast an earthly mechanism for the Godlike itself, and wouldst fain grind me out Virtue from the husks of Pleasure,—I tell thee, Nay!' [1]

> 'God's absolute Laws, sanctioned by an eternal Heaven and an eternal Hell, have become Moral Philosophies, sanctioned by able computations of Profit and Loss, by weak considerations of Pleasures of Virtue and the Moral Sublime.' . . . 'God's Laws are become a Greatest-Happiness Principle, a Parliamentary Expediency: the Heavens over-arch us only as an Astronomical Time-keeper.' [2]

Enlightened egoism 'is not the rule by which man's life can be led'; *Laissez-faire*', 'Supply-and-demand', and 'Cash-payment for the sole nexus' are not valid laws of union for a society of human beings. The true laws were understood in the age of Abbot Samson, when wild-fowl screamed over Lancashire, the coal and iron seams slept undisturbed side by side, and the Ribble and the Aire were 'as yet unpolluted by dyer's chemistry'; when Religion was 'not yet a horrible restless Doubt, still less a far horribler composed Cant; but a great heaven-high Unquestionability, encompassing, interpenetrating the whole of Life'.[3]

Carlyle's analysis of modern society resembles Arnold's, but with a change of nomenclature; the 'Barbarians' become the exponents of Dilettantism or Donothingism, and the 'Philistines' of Mammonism. The latter have this superiority over an idle, game-preserving aristocracy, that their Mammonism at least makes them *work*; for Plugson of Undershot, therefore, Carlyle has a measure of respect—he, at any rate, is 'real'. 'Not that we want *no* aristocracy', he wrote in his Journal, Oct. 1830, 'but that we want a *true* one.' [4] Carlyle's view of our present aristocracy varied considerably from the days of his tutorship in the Buller family to the later frequentings of Bath House or Alverstoke. His

---
[1] *Sartor*, bk. ii, ch. 7. [2] *Past and Present*, bk. iii, ch. 1.
[3] *Ibid.*, bk. ii, ch. 5 and 6. [4] *Early Life*, vol. ii, p. 92.

first impressions of fashionable life and people may be seen in this passage of a letter to Jane Welsh (from Kinnaird, June 1823):

> 'I see something of fashionable people here, and truly to my plebeian conception there is not a more futile class of persons on the face of the earth. If I were doomed to exist as a man of fashion, I do honestly believe I should swallow ratsbane, or apply to hemp or steel before three months were over. From day to day and year to year the problem is, not how to use time, but how to waste it least painfully.... They move heaven and earth to get everything arranged and enacted properly; and when the whole is done what is it? Had the parties all wrapped themselves in warm blankets and kept their beds, much peace had been among several hundreds of his Majesty's subjects, and the same result, the uneasy destruction of half a dozen hours, had been quite as well attained.... There is something in the life of a sturdy peasant toiling from sun to sun for a plump wife and six eating children; but as for the Lady Jerseys and the Lord Petershams, peace be with them.'[1]

In later days, when he had long enjoyed the freedom of great houses and drawing-rooms, he came to feel differently. Not that he succumbed to flattery and blandishments; he learned to respect what was distinguished in the tone and morale of high society. In the Journal for February 8, 1848,[2] we find:

> 'Our Aristocracy, I rather take it, are the *best*, or as good as any class we have; but their position is fatally awry,—their whole breeding and way of life, "To go gracefully idle" (most tragically *so*), and which of them can mend it?'

His final judgment is given in the *Reminiscences*:

> 'Certain of the Aristocracy, however, did seem to me still very *noble*; and, with due elimination of the grossly worthless (none of whom had we to do with), I should vote at present that, of *classes* known to me in England, the Aristocracy (with its perfection of human politeness, its continual grace of bearing and of acting,

---

[1] *Ibid.*, vol. i, pp. 186-7.
[2] Froude quotes this under Feb. 9 (*Life in London*, vol. i, p. 422).

steadfast "honour", light address and cheery *stoicism*, if you see *well* into it), is actually yet the best of English Classes.' [1]

Carlyle's attitude towards the Masses is like that of Langland: a blend of compassion for human misery with scorn for the nostrums of 'democracy'. It is in the name of the toiling millions that he denounces *laissez-faire* and the cash nexus, but the remedy is not to be found in mere political enfranchisement. The Reform Bill has proved a Barmecide Feast; the franchise has been extended, but there remain as before hunger, unemployment, lack of security, lack of hope, sense of injustice.

> 'The notion that a man's liberty consists in giving his vote at election-hustings, and saying, "Behold, now I too have my twenty-thousandth part of a Talker in our National Palaver; will not all the Gods be good to me?"—is one of the pleasantest!'
>
> 'This liberty turns out, before it have long continued in action, with all men flinging up their caps round it, to be, for the Working Millions a liberty to die by want of food; for the Idle Thousands and Units, alas, a still more fatal liberty to live in want of work.' [2]

What is needed is a true Aristocracy, an Aristocracy of the Wise, and a true Priesthood; the only 'right' of man is the right to be wisely governed. God made the world for 'degree' (hierarchy), and in feudal times, before cash became the sole nexus, an Idea was really at work in the actual, that, namely, of the organic Christian society. Rebellion is an ugly thing, but if our present nobility and clergy can do nothing, others will. The 'Toiling Millions' are in 'most vital need and passionate instinctive desire'—not of Votes, but of 'Guidance'; guidance by 'Real Superiors'. England will either learn how to find its Heroes, or it will cease to exist among Nations. Hero-worship is the essence and practical perfection of all manner of worship; it has a mystical foundation, for in the Great Man Heaven reveals itself.

This of course is the part of Carlyle's teaching which is least endurable to us today. He correctly diagnosed the

---

[1] *Op. cit.*, p. 80 (Everyman ed.).
[2] *Past and Present*, bk. iii, ch. 13.

weaknesses and exposed the cant of Victorian 'democracy': its reliance upon *laissez-faire* economics, its superficial conception of freedom, its belief in the virtues of political enfranchisement, its deficiency in purpose, idea or soul. Given such defects (and most agree that it had these defects), 'democracy' was likely enough to relapse into dictatorship. But Carlyle's heroes, it must be remembered, are not all Führers: they are also the Prophets—Buddha, Mahomet, Christ; the poets—Dante, Shakespeare, Goethe, Burns; the men of letters—Johnson or Rousseau. True, they are above all the kings, soldiers and governors: Caesar, Cromwell, Frederick, Napoleon; but Cromwell was the chief of Heroes, because he was the soldier of God. I do not think that Carlyle would have mistaken Hitler for a Cromwell, any more than Plato would have mistaken him for a Philosopher-king. He is commonly supposed, indeed, to have believed and taught that 'Might is Right', and even some of his devoted admirers were shocked at his apparent 'abdication of all moral judgment on atrocious actions and abandoned men, —a Mirabeau and a September massacre'.[1] Carlyle had an imagination too dramatic and superheated ('my work', he said, 'needs all to be done with my nerves in a kind of blaze'); he often delights in exhibitions of mere energy, or in historical convulsions wherein judgment is executed by fire and whirlwind. But, as he was careful to explain, what he really meant was that in a world governed by a righteous Providence, might is right *in the long run*; Injustice and Untruth cannot long flourish in such a world (witness the French Revolution, the supreme object-lesson). The strong class, nation or man, will in the long view be the just and the righteous, because to be strong *means* to be righteous. He admits that 'Might and Right do differ frightfully from hour to hour; but give them centuries to try it in, they are found to be identical'[2]—which is small comfort, perhaps, to dwellers in one of the intermediate centuries. To Lecky, who had accused him of supposing all might as such to be right, he replied: 'I shall have to tell Lecky one day that quite the

---

[1] J. Martineau, *op. cit.*, p. 274 (cf. also Sterling, *loc. cit.*).
[2] *Chartism* (1839), ch. 8 (cf. *Past and Present*, bk. iii, ch. 10).

converse or *re*verse is the great and venerable author's real opinion—namely, that right is the eternal symbol of might ... and that, in fact, he probably never met with a son of Adam more contemptuous of might except where it rests on the above origin.'

Carlyle could not be expected to see (what we see so clearly as to make discussion tiresome) that hero-worship, as a cure for democracy, might be far worse than the disease, or that the 'passionate instinctive desire' for a Leader might be satisfied quite as easily by a Hitler as by a Cromwell. What we can learn from Carlyle is that 'democracy', in order to survive, must be born again; it must unlearn its economic idolatries, cease to be self-seeking and mechanical, and recapture its soul by returning to its own inmost ideas, which will turn out, on reflexion, to be those of Christianity. We seem to discern now that the old 'liberal' values—Liberty, Equality, Fraternity, the Rights of Man, tolerance, reverence for each individual as an end and not a means—can only flourish if they are rooted in the religion from which they originally sprang, and that the instinctive need for an object of worship, if not properly satisfied, will send us seeking after strange gods.

CHAPTER V

A NOTE ON BENTHAM'S DEONTOLOGY

IT is not my present intention to devote any lengthy discussion to Bentham, who belongs essentially to the eighteenth century. Greater attention will be given to J. S. Mill (Chapter VI) in whom the Benthamite tradition is modified by the nineteenth century climate, and through whom it exerted its most powerful influence on the age. But I propose, by way of introduction, to glance at the *Deontology*, that popular exposition of Benthamism, 'arranged and edited' by his disciple John Bowring (1834), which appears to have been generally regarded as sufficiently representative of the master's moral outlook.

Benthamism, according to Henry Sidgwick, 'is the one outcome of the Seculum Rationalisticum against which the philosophy of Restoration and Reaction has had to struggle continually with varying degrees of success'.[1] The vitality of any teaching, or historical movement, depends upon what it affirms rather than upon what it denies, and its survival and continued power will often mean that its positives are insufficiently regarded by opposing schools. The grand positives of Bentham were benevolence and veracity: the passion for the relief of man's estate, and the passion for truth. Bentham's multifarious activities, pursued without abatement to the end of a long life, were inspired by a 'dominant and all-comprehensive desire for the amelioration of human life'; they were inspired, too, by the belief that he had found the key to all moral truth. This institution, this custom, this code, this system of legislation—does it promote human happiness? then it is sound. This theory, this creed, this moral teaching—does it rightly explain why virtue is admirable, or why duty is obligatory? then it is true: all else is misrepresentation. The limitations of Bentham can be gauged by his dismissal of all poetry (and most religion) as 'misrepresentation'; this is his negative side. But benevolence and

[1] *Miscellaneous Essays and Addresses* (1904), p. 137.

veracity are supreme values, and if it falls to one of the deniers to be their special advocate, the believers must have long been drowsed. When Evangelical religion has become so 'other-worldly' that a Hannah More can regard poverty as being (like niggerhood) 'ordained', or a Wilberforce can oppose reform on the ground that the existing order 'combines the greatest measure of temporal comforts and spiritual privileges', and can encourage the poor to submission because 'their situation, with all its evils, is better than they have deserved at the hands of God',—when things are thus, the neglected work will generally be undertaken by secularists and infidels. They will carry it on, pardonably unaware that their own passion for humanity is derived from the very tradition they despise—that it is, in fact, the living spirit of a religion which has deserted its official mansion to dwell for a time in them. Most of the revolutionary movements of the last two hundred years—Encyclopaedism, Chartism, Marxism—in so far as they were anti-Christian in doctrine, can be regarded in this way; their strength is the measure of the failure of 'Christianity' to mediate its own impulse. Bentham was of course no revolutionary; he was, to adapt a phrase of Sidgwick, at once one of the most and one of the least idealistic of 'practical philosophers'. He was, however, anti-Christian, in the sense that he rejected what was then supposed to be Christianity, namely a number of insufficient 'evidences' and untenable dogmas, and an obsolete political and social structure. A mere glance at his *Church of England Catechism Explained*[1] reveals the quality of his animus against the pseudo-Christianity of the day. The Church teaches children 'insincerity', he says, by making them affirm what they cannot possibly understand or mean. They promise, for example, to fulfil the undertaking of their god-parents, that they will 'renounce the devil and all his works, the pomps and vanity of this wicked world', etc. 'The Devil', Bentham comments: 'who or what is he, and how is it that he is renounced?' Has the child happened to have any dealings with him? Let the Archbishop of Canterbury tell us, and let him further explain how his own 'works' are distinguished

[1] 1824 ed., pp. 1-25.

from the aforesaid 'pomps and vanity'. What King, what Lords Temporal or Spiritual, have ever renounced them? The child also rehearses the Apostles' Creed: but who believes it to have been formed by the Apostles? who can afford to buy *Pearson on the Creed*, or understands it if he can? Bentham waives the question of the truth of the assertions about Christ's birth and death, and insists that the mischief lies in making a child *say* that he believes such mysteries.

In Bentham's time it was not prudent—it was even illegal —to publish attacks on the established religion. The booklet on the Catechism appeared anonymously, and the main manifesto of the Utilitarian party came out under the pseudonym of 'Philip Beauchamp'. This was *The Analysis of the Influence of Natural Religion on the Temporal Happiness of Mankind* (1822)[1], published by Richard Carlile (then 'safe in Dorchester gaol'—for other like indiscretions), and composed by Bentham and George Grote. Its purpose was to apply the test of utility to religious belief: what results does it produce, in terms of human happiness? The definition of religion offered by these authors may well make a modern reader gasp, or at least raise his eyebrows: belief in the existence of 'an Almighty Being, by whom pains and pleasures will be dispensed to mankind during an infinite and future state of existence'. True, it is 'natural' religion which they so define, but then 'revelation' to them was fiction, and this too is significant. This doctrine of a future state, to begin with, so far from bringing comfort, produces an overplus of fear. How are we to know the character of the divine despot? Though He is said to be benevolent, His conduct as expressed in orthodox formulae is that of a capricious autocrat. How can belief in such a Being supply a motive—'and the only adequate motive', as is commonly asserted—for moral conduct? It is claimed that we should cease to be virtuous if we ceased to believe: then we evidently derive no temporal happiness from our belief? and as to a future state, we are completely in the dark. Supernatural hopes and fears have really no effect upon our behaviour, however; what really influences us is public opinion, and our desire to be well-

[1] See the summary in Leslie Stephen, *The English Utilitarians*, vol. ii, pp. 338 ff.

thought-of by our fellows. Meanwhile, religion reduces happiness by forbidding many harmless pleasures, and by subtracting 'duty to God' from duty to man. It impedes intellectual progress by separating belief from 'its only safe ground, experience', and by rejecting the test of utility it overclouds moral science with fictitious 'intuitions'. Finally, religion 'subsidizes a standing-army' of wonder-working priests, who deprave the intellect and cherish superstition, and who (to crown their infamy) form an 'unholy alliance' with the 'sinister interests of the earth'. Here, then, we have the infidel version of 'Church and State'. To compare it with Coleridge's is to realize the full significance of Mill's famous contrast between him and Bentham; it also helps the imagination to grasp the magnitude of the task confronting any genuine defence of the faith at a time when its alleged defences were so utterly frail. A religion which was supposed to be 'proved' by Paley's evidences and by several miracles wrought two thousand years ago, and whose main present function was to consecrate the existing social order, was manifestly exposed to all the infidel artillery; and one wonders now whether the enemy, by smashing its useless and ruinous outworks, were not rendering it the most important and lasting of services. The new fortress which Coleridge began to build was made of other materials, and founded upon a deeper rock-stratum. But without the preliminary attack it might not have been built at all.

'Deontology' ($\tau\grave{o}$ $\delta\acute{e}o\nu$, that which is proper) means the science of private Ethics, by which 'happiness is created out of motives extra-legislatorial', while Jurisprudence is 'the science by which law is applied to the production of felicity'. Bowring explains that his aim is 'to place prominently forward the connexion between interest and duty in all the concerns of private life'. 'The first law of nature is to wish our own happiness; and the united voices of prudence and efficient benevolence add—Seek the happiness of others,—seek your own happiness in the happiness of others.' What is happiness? it is 'the possession of pleasure with the exemption from pain'. And what is virtue? 'that which maximizes pleasures and minimizes pains'. The moralist must therefore be 'a man hunting for consequences'; there is no 'duty' except to produce happiness, and except in this sense the word *ought* 'ought' to be abolished. Pleasure and Pain being identified respectively with good and evil, it becomes the province of Deontology to 'weigh' pleasures and pains, and to estimate their quantitative value. 'Lots' of pleasure (or pain) are measured by their intensity, duration, certainty, proximity, fruitfulness (i.e. chance of being followed by sensations of a like kind) and extent (i.e. the number of persons to whom they extend). Having weighed these, Deontology draws the rule of conduct from the result. Bentham himself expresses it thus:

> 'Sum up all the values of all the *pleasures* on the one side, and those of all the pains on the other. The balance, if it be on the side of pleasure, will give the *good* tendency of the act upon the whole . . .; if on the side of pain, the *bad* tendency of it upon the whole.'[1]

The 'pleasures' (and corresponding 'pains') are catalogued as those of Sense, Wealth, Skill, Amity, Good Reputation, Power, Piety, Sympathy, Malevolence [*sic*], Memory, Imagination, Expectation, Association. As Mill later pointed out, 'Conscience', 'Sense of Duty', 'Pleasure in Doing Right', etc., are not amongst Bentham's springs of action; they were, to him, Fictitious Entities, and it was precisely his aim to analyse every moral judgment into 'this will increase or diminish the sum of human happiness' (the 'felicific calculus'). 'Conscience' is not an ultimate; it is derivative from this calculus. 'Nature', says Bentham, 'has placed mankind under the governance of two sovereign masters, pain and pleasure. It is for them alone to point out what we ought to do, as well as to determine what we shall do.'[2] Bowring urges that men have always really known this, and have always applied the utilitarian test even while decrying it. Why then bother about what everybody knows? Because the world is still infested with spectral entities, and Deontology alone can exorcize them, and enable us 'more correctly to estimate what con-

[1] *Introduction to the Principles of Morals and Legislation* (1907 reprint), p. 31.
[2] *Ibid.*, p. 1.

duct will leave the greatest results of good'. 'Illuminated by the Deontological principle, the field of action will assume a new appearance'; 'scornful dogmas' and 'solemn mootings' will vanish into thin air. The whole book is irradiated by a sort of gospel-brightness, a sense of truth at last discovered, and good tidings to be proclaimed. This optimism appears very clearly in the section on Moral Sanctions. Bowring is discussing Bentham's 'inducements' to morality: the Physical, the Social and Moral (domestic and public opinion), the Political or Legal, and the Religious, and (under the second of these headings) he has expressed the wish that every man's house were a Panopticon—'made of glass'. But he consoles himself by reflecting that 'the liberty of the press throws all men into the public presence'. Under such influence,

> 'it were strange if men grew not every day more virtuous than on the former day. I am satisfied they do. I am satisfied they will continue so to do, till, if ever, their nature shall have arrived at its perfection. Shall they stop? Shall they turn back? The rivers shall as soon make a wall, or roll up the mountains to their source. . . .
>
> 'The constitution of the human mind being opened by degrees, the labyrinth is explored, a clue is found out for it. That clue is the influence of interest; of interest, not in that partial and sordid sense in which it is the tyrant of sordid souls, but in the enlarged and beneficent sense in which it is the common master of all spirits, and especially of the enlightened. It is put into the hands of every man. The designs by which short-sighted iniquity would mask its projects, are every day laid open. *There will be no moral enigmas by and by.*'[1]

Thus, in rhetoric worthy of Peacock's Mr Foster, Bowring virtually proclaims that the Press will finish what the Church —perhaps *began*, but has for a very long time done its best to retard.

On the question of 'religious sanctions' Bowring follows 'Philip Beauchamp'. Like any eighteenth century freethinker, he pleads to be regarded as the friend, and not the foe, of religion. 'True religion' (that recurrent label for 'my

[1] *Deontology* (1834), pp. 100-101 (my italics).

religion', or for 'no religion') can never be hostile to happiness; if any belief is so, it is thereby shown to be false. He then blandly proceeds to show the ineffectiveness of the religious sanction; it works by delayed action, and in any case the 'future state' is remote and uncertain. Religious sanctions are also often attached to 'useless' duties (ceremonial or credal). False notions are entertained of a vindictive Deity, whereas if the divine Being did not desire the happiness of all, He would be neither just nor benevolent, and so not divine. Bowring has discovered the true motive of 'classical' education: the theologians are afraid of scientific enlightenment, and so encourage the young to linger 'where the lotus grows'—in the academic groves and avenues. He gracefully explains that nothing is further from his intention and conviction than to deny a future state 'whose object shall be to maximize happiness and to develop the benevolent attributes of the Deity': he only wants to show that orthodoxy does not always agree with 'the true principles of morality', and 'the production and progress of that felicity which it is the object of morality to accomplish'. At the conclusion of the pretty parable of Timothy Thoughtless and Walter Wise (the foolish and virtuous apprentices) with which the argument is here embellished, Bowring relates that Timothy, at the end of a career which the religious sanction has been powerless to redeem, was obsessed (on his voyage to Botany Bay) with thoughts of 'an angry and avenging Deity'; while Walter, as his bank-balance mounted ever higher, 'dwelt with constant delight' on His benign attributes.

What, next, of 'motive', which has traditionally been held to give the moral index to actions, irrespective of consequences? Motive is a 'will-o'-the-wisp':

> 'Those who dread the light which its [i.e. utility's] radiance throws upon human *actions*, are fond of engaging their votaries in the chace of an inaccessible wandering will-o'-the-wisp, which they call "motive"—an entity buried in inapproachable darkness....'[1]

But nobody ever can or did have any other *motive* than 'the

[1] *Ibid.*, p. 125.

A NOTE ON BENTHAM'S *DEONTOLOGY*

pursuit of pleasure or the shunning of pain', thus the moralist has only to do with conduct 'when its consequences invade the regions of suffering and enjoyment'. How comes it, then, that men ever act wrongly, so that 'sanctions' are necessary to guide and constrain them? It is here that the sunny sky becomes a trifle overcast, though it is with clouds so deontological that we hardly perceive the change. Human nature is—not of course 'sinful', but prone to error: prone, for example, to be misled by religion (as intimated above). It is prone to Asceticism and Sympathy; from Asceticism (the principle of antipathy) comes the desire to punish vindictively, while undue Sympathy (the sentimental principle) shields misconduct from deserved blame. It is led into non-felicific side-tracks by the bogus entities—Principle, Right, Duty, Virtue, etc. But sooner or later the Deontologist must face his Apollyon, and the moment for the struggle has now come: Self-interest, we now learn, may conflict with the benevolent sympathies! And if so, what will happen? The benevolent sympathies succumb: *'there is no help for it, they are the weaker'*.[1] Men do, in their public relationships, give preference to selfish over social interests, and in their private morality they frequently prefer a lesser good which is present, to a greater which is distant. This original sinfulness is of course transposed by the Deontologist, as it had been by the early Plato, into sheer (but far from invincible) ignorance. Vice is a 'miscalculation of chances'; it is 'false moral arithmetic'. A man, for example, may be 'wedded to intoxication'; very well—Deontology not only 'entreats him not to err by an erroneous arithmetic' but demonstrates to him by reasoned proof how dearly he is purchasing his immediate pleasure. The cause of all the trouble is merely erroneous education, intellectual and moral. As for egoism in the wider field of social relationships, this is the special province of legislation. Each man seeks his own interest at the expense of others, and governors will seek to exploit their subjects and defend their own 'sinister' monopolies and privileges. Legislation must therefore be devised which shall direct each man's egoism into social channels,

[1] *Ibid.*, p. 181 (my italics).

and make it contrary to his *self*-interest to injure his fellows. Precisely because the benevolent sympathies are weaker than self-interest, the appeal of every moral injunction and every law must be an appeal to self-interest. In other words, self-love and social, though potentially and essentially the same, are not yet felt as such by our imperfectly educated fellow-creatures; we must therefore legislate in the interim, pending their final enlightenment by industrious Deontologists.

The paradox of Benthamism was well described by Sidgwick when he said that 'it is as if Hobbes or Mandeville were suddenly inspired with the social enthusiasm of Godwin'.[1] Bentham himself was nothing if not benevolent; he said of himself that he was 'as selfish as a man could be, but somehow or other selfishness had in him taken the form of benevolence'. But he did not for a moment suppose that *other* men's selfishness would often take this form; on the contrary, he believed they would always sacrifice public to private interest. It will be observed, in all this teaching, that (as Sidgwick further points out) 'there is no rational transition from the psychological part of the theory to the ethical part: from "all men seek their own happiness" to "all men *should* promote the general happiness"'—in a word, from 'is' to 'ought'. To make the theory coherent, 'all men should'—have Bentham's universal benevolence of heart, but they conspicuously lack it on his own showing. We must therefore fall back upon artificial checks and contrivances; rulers must be checked by responsibility to the people, and the people by legislation and by education. But in the absence of altruism or ethical imperatives it is hard to see how the machine could be made to grind out the general happiness; there seems to be nothing, for example, to prevent the rulers, once in power, from legislating in their own interests, or in such a way as to reduce 'responsibility' to a mere shadow.

[1] *Op. cit.*, p. 151.

CHAPTER VI

JOHN STUART MILL

1. The *Autobiography*

IN a passage already quoted (p. 1) John Stuart Mill ventured the generalization that almost every important nineteenth century mind had first learnt to think from either Coleridge or Bentham. The distinction of Mill himself was that he learned from both: from Bentham first and foremost indeed, but later from Coleridge, and from Carlyle, Comte and the contemporary *Zeitgeist* in general. His development shows how far an eighteenth century mind could suffer a nineteenth century sea-change without ever ceasing to be essentially itself—without, let us say, becoming noticeably rich or strange. In passing from Bentham to Mill we are conscious of a decline in buoyancy and an increase in subtlety; the bluff self-confidence and masculinity of the master have yielded to qualities which have been called 'feminine'—receptiveness, diffidence, self-criticism and a certain spinsterish dryness of thought and style. In Mill the old philanthropic impulse still runs strongly, but it is flowing through strange country and beginning to lose itself amongst new shallows and new deeps. Carlyle, whose early friendship with Mill illustrates and symbolizes Mill's susceptibility to new influences, wrote of him in 1833: 'he is growing quite a believer . . . yet with all his old utilitarian logic quite alive in him'.[1] How much of a 'believer' Mill became we shall enquire later, but Carlyle's remark is sufficiently apt and illuminating. Mill, the 'saint of rationalism', did try to believe much that Bentham would have dismissed as 'pushpin'; much that he himself, perhaps, had on his own principles no right to believe, but he strained in that direction without ever severing the cord that bound him to the past, and is found to the last in the company of those who are *tendentes manus ripae ulterioris amore*. Carlyle regarded him

[1] Froude, *Early Life*, vol. ii, p. 334.

at first as a disciple; when he read Mill's *The Spirit of the Age* (1831) he exclaimed (rather oddly), 'Here is a new Mystic'. But their minds were too divergent for lasting friendship. From the very first Carlyle noted Mill's essentially prosaic quality; 'furthermore, he cannot *laugh* with any compass'.[1] The two men originally found common ground in their sheer love of truth, and Charles Buller could write thus to Carlyle in 1831:

> 'To you without any fear I point out John Mill as a true Utilitarian, and as one who does honour to his creed and to his fellow-believers; because it is a creed that in him is without sectarian narrowness or unkindness, because it has not impaired his philosophy or his relish for the beautiful, or repressed any one of those good honest feelings which God gave all men before Bentham made them Utilitarians.'[2]

A few years later, however (1836), Carlyle is complaining that in Mill's home there seems to be no human spontaneity or feeling whatever: 'he seemed to me to be withering or withered into the miserablest metaphysical *scrae* [Dumfriesshire: 'old shoe'], body and mind, that I had almost ever met with in the world. His eyes go twinkling and jerking with wild lights and twitches; his head is bald, his face brown and dry—poor fellow after all.'[3] Many years afterwards (1873) Carlyle wrote thus of Mill's *Autobiography*: 'I have never read a more uninteresting book. . . . It is wholly the life of a logic-chopping engine, little more of human in it than if it had been done by a thing of mechanized iron. Autobiography of a steam-engine, perhaps, you may sometimes read it.'[4] A critic of a very different stamp —R. H. Hutton—noted, the same year, the tone of pallor and melancholy which overspreads this *Autobiography*, and attributes it to 'a certain poverty of nature' in Mill, 'in spite of the nobleness in him,—a monotonous joylessness, in spite of the hectic sanguineness of his theoretic creed'.[5] The

---

[1] *Ibid.*, p. 200.   [2] *Ibid.*, pp. 235-6.
[3] Froude, *Life in London*, vol. i, p. 74.
[4] *Ibid.*, vol. ii, p. 420.
[5] *Contemporary Thought and Thinkers* (1894), vol. i, p. 182.

JOHN STUART MILL

Autobiography remains for us one of the vital documents for the study of the nineteenth century, yet we may freely admit that its early chapters (in particular) amply confirm Carlyle's description.

Mill's recollections of early life (we cannot call it 'childhood') convey no intimations of immortality; for him, it seems, there were no 'spots of time', no 'gentle shocks of mild surprise'—nothing, in fact, but unremitting study. His father, who personally educated him, regarded his son somewhat as Lord Chesterfield regarded his own, that is, as a little blank volume in which the desired imprint could be stamped: only, instead of trying to form a man of parts and fashion, James Mill determined to produce a worthy successor in the dynasty of philosophical radicalism. When the father was threatened with early death, his most poignant thought was that he would leave the lad with his mind as yet unformed. John Stuart Mill began Greek at the age of three, and by eight he had read Herodotus, Xenophon, 'some of' Diogenes Laertius, Lucian and Isocrates, and the first six dialogues of Plato. In his twelfth year he was tackling Aristotle's Logic, and at thirteen he underwent a complete course of political economy (universal history and mathematics all the while proceeding concurrently with the rest). Before breakfast, each morning, there were those walks with his father in the Hornsey lanes, when he would repeat, from notes made on slips of paper, what he had learnt the previous day in Robertson, Hume, Gibbon or Watson. I need not further enumerate the gruesome details; Mill's education is probably the best-known thing about him. His own comment upon it is interestingly different from what we should now expect: the result of his father's experiment, he says, proves how easily a child may acquire an amount of advanced knowledge which is seldom attained, if at all, until manhood. He was not, he thinks, particularly gifted:

> 'what I could do, could assuredly be done by any boy or girl of average capacity and healthy physical constitution: and if I have accomplished anything, I owe it, among other fortunate circumstances, to the fact that through the early training bestowed upon

me by my father, I started, I may fairly say, with an advantage of a quarter of a century over my contemporaries.'[1]

What concerns us most, however, is the moral atmosphere in which Mill grew to manhood, and this can be felt in his own account of his father's principles and beliefs. His education was, he says, virtually a 'course of Benthamism' or, more exactly, a blend of Benthamism with Hartley's metaphysics and psychology, and Ricardo's political economy. The leading tenets of this body of doctrine—roughly the creed of 'philosophical radicalism'—are thus summarized by him:

(i) In *Politics*: 'an almost unbounded confidence' in the efficacy of representative government and complete freedom of discussion. The persuasiveness of reason was so irresistible, that all would be achieved if the people could meet with it in education, if they could attend discussions of every sort of opinion, and if by universal suffrage they could choose representatives to express and enforce the opinions thus formed. The legislature, as soon as it ceased to represent a mere *class* interest, would necessarily aim at the *general* interest. Aristocratic rule was the greatest obstacle to progress, and must be abolished.

(ii) *Religion:* Next after aristocracy, any established Church was regarded with the greatest abhorrence. A corporation of priests was by its nature a 'depraver of religion', and 'interested in opposing the progress of the human mind'. As a result of his exposure to this influence, Mill could say of himself:

> 'I am thus one of the very few examples, in this country, of one who has not thrown off religious belief, but never had it: I grew up in a negative state with regard to it. I looked upon the modern exactly as I did upon the ancient religion, as something which in no way concerned me.'[2]

He notes, however, that his father cautioned him against imprudent avowals of infidelity in public (a point to be

---
[1] *Autobiography* (World's Classics ed.), pp. 25-6.
[2] *Ibid.*, p. 36.

remembered in reading his Essay *On Liberty*). Mill, in this respect as in others, was (in the fashion of the old separatists, though for other reasons than theirs) always an alien in the midst of English society, and estranged from its unspoken presuppositions. He was never sent to a University, because the Mill view was that Oxford and Cambridge (like Eton and Westminster) were strongholds of bigotry and reaction. 'We regard the system of these institutions, as administered for two centuries past, with sentiments little short of utter abhorrence.'[1] His early notion of the Church of England, again, is that of the critical outsider; it may be illustrated by this passage from *The Spirit of the Age*—a passage which, by the way, might have served as text for a very different discourse by a Tractarian:

> 'From the time when the Church of England became firmly seated in its temporalities, from the period when its title to the fee-simple of our conscience acquired the sanctity of prescription, and when it was enabled to dispense with any support but what it derived from the stable foundations of the social fabric of which it formed a part; it sunk from its independent rank, into an integral part, or a kind of appendage, to the aristocracy. It merged into the higher classes: and what moral influence it possessed, was merely a portion of the general moral influence of temporal superiors.'[2]

(iii) *Psychology:* Here the fundamental doctrine was Hartley's Associationism: the belief in 'the formation of all human character by circumstances, through the universal Principle of Association, and the consequent unlimited possibility of improving the moral and intellectual condition of mankind by education'.[3]

(iv) *Ethics:* The Utilitarianism of Bentham. I will not repeat what has already been sketched under this heading; the subject will be revived when we come to examine Mill's own essay, *Utilitarianism*. How deeply Mill was influenced by Bentham can be guessed from his account of the impression made upon him when—at the age of about fifteen—

---

[1] *Dissertations and Discussions*, vol. i, p. 193 (2nd ed., 1867).
[2] See edition with Introduction by F. A. von Hayek, Univ. of Chicago, 1942.
[3] *Autobiography*, p. 91.

he first read him in Dumont's French version, the *Traité de Législation*. Although he had always been taught to apply the 'greatest happiness' formula, it then 'burst upon me with all the force of novelty'. 'The feeling rushed upon me, that all previous moralists were superseded, and that here indeed was the commencement of a new era of thought.'[1]

'The Germano-Coleridgean doctrine' (if I may recall in this context the weighty words quoted on the first page of this book) 'expresses the revolt of the human mind against the philosophy of the eighteenth century.'[2] Mill himself never revolted openly against 'that great century', but he became aware of its one-sidedness, and some of his work has consequently the hybrid quality that results from crossing Benthamism with Coleridge, Carlyle, Maurice and Comte. His awakening to the inadequacies of the eighteenth century took the form, virtually, of an awakening to the deficiencies of his own childhood and education. This 'conversion' is described by him in what is, for most readers, the most interesting—because the most 'human'—part of his *Autobiography*. Looking back upon his own early manhood, he sees that he must then have corresponded fairly closely with the popular notion of a Benthamite as a 'reasoning machine'. His zeal for the good of mankind, which he took to be his dominant passion, was really only 'zeal for speculative opinions': it had no roots in the affections. He was mentally aware of lofty ethical standards, but his head and his heart had been dissociated by his training, and especially by his father's 'undervaluing of feeling'. He could experience the emotions and enthusiasms of benevolence 'imaginatively', 'but there was at this time an intermission of its natural aliment, *poetical culture*, while there was a superabundance of the discipline antagonistic to it, that of mere logic and analysis'.[3] Shelley, it will be remembered, said that ethical science arranges the materials which poetry creates: Mill had the arranged materials without the poetry. We now

---

[1] *Ibid.*, p. 54.
[2] *Dissertations*, vol. i, p. 403.
[3] *Autobiography*, pp. 92 ff. (my italics).

regard the overforcing of the intellect in childhood as so crude an educational blunder that Mill's quiet analysis of his own case seems naïve and superficial. He proceeds to give an account of the nervous crisis which, as might have been predicted, came upon him in adolescence, and nearly destroyed him: an account which gains rather than loses in human, as in 'period' interest, through its innocence of psycho-therapy.

In the autumn of 1826 the inner tension which had doubtless long existed within him gave way, and like Bunyan—though in terms how different!—he allowed himself to ask a question fatal to his peace of mind:

> "'Suppose that all your objects in life were realized; that all the changes in institutions and opinions which you are looking forward to, could be completely effected at this very instant: would this be a great joy and happiness to you?" And an irrepressible self-consciousness distinctly answered "No!" At this my heart sank within me: the whole foundation on which my life was constructed fell down.'[1]

In his blank dejection, which he compares with the mood of Coleridge in the *Dejection* Ode, he realized that what should have been the emotional foundations of his life and interests had been worn away by analysis before they had been properly laid. Analytic habits, he remarks in retrospect, are 'a perpetual worm at the root both of the passions and of the virtues; and, above all, fearfully undermine all desires, and all pleasures, which are the effects of association'. His education had failed to create in him a body of feelings strong enough 'to resist the dissolving influence of analysis', so that he found himself, at the beginning of adult life, 'with a well-equipped ship and a rudder, but no sail'. There seemed 'no power in nature sufficient to begin the formation of my character anew, and create in a mind now irretrievably analytic, fresh associations of pleasure with any of the objects of human desire'. The quality of his nervous prostration (a state in which he questioned whether he could continue to

[1] *Ibid.*, p. 113.

live for as long as a year) can be surmised from the symptom that, whereas music had always been one of his joys, and now became a chief consolation, he now began to be 'seriously tormented by the thought of the exhaustibility of musical combinations'.

Deliverance came through Wordsworth, who, as the poet of Despondency Corrected, was peculiarly fitted to minister to a mind thus diseased. If Mill could have then read *The Prelude*, he would have recognized, in Wordsworth's account of his dark night of the soul, and the ensuing dayspring, an experience similar to his own, though quite differently caused. Mill was not the only overwrought nineteenth century intellectual to feel Wordsworth's healing power, but none has acknowledged his debt more memorably.

> 'What made Wordsworth's poems a medicine for my state of mind was that they expressed, not mere outward beauty, but states of feeling, and of thought coloured by feeling, under the excitement of beauty. They seemed to be the very culture of the feelings, which I was in quest of.'[1]

Mill tells us (and we can well believe it) that this crisis left certain marked effects upon his opinions and character. First, although he never abandoned the theory that 'happiness' is the test of conduct and the end of life, he was now convinced that 'this end was only to be attained by not making it the direct end'. 'Ask yourself whether you are happy, and you cease to be so'. Aim at something else, then, at something other than your own happiness—the happiness of others, the improvement of mankind, or 'some art of pursuit'—and you will 'find happiness by the way'. Secondly, he now began to allow due weight, amongst the conditions of well-being, to 'the internal culture of the individual', and ceased to attach 'exclusive importance to the ordering of outward circumstances', and to speculative training. 'The cultivation of the feelings became one of the cardinal points in my ethical and philosophical creed'. What Wordsworth says of 'Nature' may be applied to his own action upon Mill:

[1] *Ibid.*, p. 125.

> '*Nature's self*
> *By all varieties of human love*
> *Assisted, led me back through opening day*
> *To those sweet counsels between head and heart*
> *Whence grew that genuine knowledge, fraught with peace.*'
>
> [*Prelude*, B text, xi, 350.]

Soon after, the influences of European thought, and 'especially those of the reaction of the nineteenth century against the eighteenth', began to stream in upon him—from Coleridge and the Coleridgeans (Sterling and Maurice), from Goethe, from Carlyle's early articles, and from the Saint-Simonians and Comte. He learned that truth is more complex and many-sided than he had previously dreamt; that governments and institutions can have only a limited action, because they are themselves the products of the social power-balance; that any political theory must presuppose a workable philosophy of history. Nevertheless he never joined, as a belligerent, in the reaction against the eighteenth century, but watched the fight between it and the nineteenth from afar, striving to unite in his own consciousness the half-truths for which they respectively stood.

II. Logic: 'Ethology' and Sociology

But, if we are to see Mill in his true proportions, we must recognize that, in spite of his open-mindedness, his deepest presuppositions were rooted in the eighteenth century subsoil. The main direction of his striving had been predetermined by the previous revolutionary age: it was towards the improvement of the human lot by the removal of ancient prejudice and established dogmatism. The sense of inveterate error to be exploded, of mouldering Bastilles of tyranny and injustice to be stormed, gives a revolutionary animus and ring to his writings, even though he is acknowledging the wisdom of received opinions, or deploring the later aftermaths of the very movement for which he stands. Like Comte and Marx, he was a 'reformer of thought for the sake of action'[1]; unlike either, he always conceived of the 'action' as lying within the framework of parliamentary democracy. From Comte he learned 'the law of the three stages', which became the basis of his philosophy of history; he learned, that is, that there are certain necessary stages in social evolution, and that these follow each other in a fixed order. Comte alone, he held, had given us the clue to history by discovering 'the law of the successive transformations of human opinion'. Western civilization had passed through the 'theological' and 'metaphysical', and was now entering upon the 'positive' stage. With Comte he believed that this last transition had produced in the modern world a distinctive intellectual anarchy; old received opinions had lost prestige, and no new ones had yet gained authority. He derived from Comte and the Saint-Simonians the distinction between 'natural' and 'critical' (or 'transitional') states of society: 'natural', when power and capacity co-exist in the governing class, 'critical', when this organic coherence has been disturbed, as it now has. Already in *The Spirit of the Age* we find him in possession of some of these leading ideas; they are there obviously relevant as Reform Bill propaganda, it is true, but they are shown to have wider applications. Governing classes, he tells us, exert influence either by wisdom and virtue, by sacerdotal power, or by wealth and position, or by a combination of these. Until the Reformation all three influences were operative: energy, intelligence, religious prestige and wealth all worked in alliance. The Church even acted as the vanguard of civilizing advance, in so far as it put merit above rank, and distant ideals above present concerns. By the time of the Reformation, however, it had lost its intellectual lead, and in succeeding centuries it was either violently overthrown (in the 'progressive' countries), or else it triumphed at the expense of intellectual 'progress'. Mill remarks, though without explaining the circumstance, that Christianity has been the only 'natural' religious order compatible with 'progress', Hinduism and Islam having remained 'stationary'. Today (1831), the 'natural' order,

---

[1] T. Whittaker, *Reason: a Philosophical Essay* (Cambridge 1934), ch. iii, 'Comte and Mill'—a valuable summary.

prolonged since the Reformation by the admitted ability and prestige of the landed class, has collapsed. Wealth and influence are no longer synonymous with wisdom and leadership. The aristocracy, which might indeed have continued to lead, has thrown away its own chances, and nothing remains but a transfer of power where it rightly belongs. Power must be lodged with the able and the energetic, and such men now exist outside the ruling classes. Mill believed in the possibility of indefinite progress and perfectibility, but assumed that the masses would never be able to do better than choose the best leaders (hence, no doubt, Carlyle's approval of this essay).

The *System of Logic*, Mill's first major work, appeared in 1843, though he had been engaged upon it for ten years. It is neither within my purpose nor my capacity to analyse or criticize this famous book; I shall merely show its relevance to our present discussion. The *Logic* would never have become, as Leslie Stephen [1] says it did become, 'a sacred scripture for Liberal intellectuals', if it had merely been what its title suggests. Like all Mill's works, as I have hinted, it was a book with a tendency; its purpose was 'to provide a logical armoury for all assailants of established dogmatism'. What constitutes 'scientific proof' in the investigation of Nature? how do we know when a proposition is 'true'? In answering these questions Mill keeps ever in mind, as his hypothetical opposition, the 'intuitionist' party—assumed to be the sinister philosophical interest of the time—those, that is, who explain knowledge by *a priori* methods. Mill will base all knowledge, even mathematical certainty, upon 'experience'. The 'necessary' character ascribed to mathematical truths is an illusion; in 'causation' too, there is no metaphysical 'tie', but merely invariable succession; 'real kinds' in Nature are clusters of accidental attributes. Mill, as Leslie Stephen comments, 'is so resolved to leave nothing for the mind to do, that he supposes a primitive mind which is not even able to distinguish "is not" from "is". It is hard [he adds] to understand how such a "mind", if it were a "mind", could ever acquire any "experience" at all.' [2]

---
[1] *The English Utilitarians* (1900), vol. iii, p. 76.   [2] *Ibid.*, p. 106.

But Mill saw 'intuitionism', as Hobbes had seen 'separated essences', as the philosophical smoke-screen masking the enemy's position; for Hobbes, it concealed the pretensions of sacerdotalism, for Mill, those of all who in his day resisted 'reform'.

For our present purposes the most significant portion of the *Logic* is Book vi,[1] 'The Logic of the Moral Sciences', where Mill applies his principles to ethics, politics and history. Can there be such a thing as moral *science* at all? a 'science' of human nature? of the formation of character? of society, and of history? Can we, that is to say, arrive, in these spheres, at fixed laws and scientific proofs and predictions? The nettle of liberty-and-necessity must clearly be grasped at the outset of any attempt to constitute a 'science' of ethics or politics. Our volitions and actions, Mill argues, are the invariable effects of *causes*: 'given the motives which are present to an individual's mind, and given likewise the character and disposition of the individual, the manner in which he will act may unerringly be inferred'. The upholders of 'free will' feel that this doctrine is derogatory to human dignity, and claim that it is refuted by our consciousness of freedom ('Sir, we *know* our will is free, and there's an end on't'). But the degrading thing is not the view that 'our volitions and actions are the invariable consequents of our antecedent states of mind'; what is objectionable is the notion of some magical constraint—'necessity'—exercised by cause over effect, and the consequent by-passing of 'states of mind' in reckoning up 'causes'. Human actions 'are never ruled by any one motive with such absolute sway, that there is no room for the influence of any other'. The Owenites say that character is formed *for* us (by environment), and not *by* us: 'but this is a grand error'. Man has, 'to a certain extent, a power to alter his character. Its being, in the ultimate resort, formed for him, is not inconsistent with its being formed *by* him as one of the intermediate agents.' This is the valuable truth that the free-will teachers have preserved—not that effects are ever uncaused, or that different effects can flow from the same causes, but that

[1] 1875 ed., vol. ii.

man can elect to be determined by one cause rather than by another. A drunkard, let us say, becomes temperate; how can this be? His intemperance had been the invariable effect of fixed causes, i.e. the temptation working upon an idle and thirsty condition. After his conversion his new temperance is equally the effect of causes, but of different causes; the temptation passes him harmlessly by, because instead of meeting an absorbent substance, it now strikes armour and glances off it. Therein lay the man's freedom, that he could change the previous sequence, not by overthrowing causation, but by introducing a new term into its series. Mill asserts here, what he also says in *Utilitarianism*, that although our volitions are 'originally' determined by desire of 'pleasure', we come by habit to will the means without thinking of the end: the debauchee still seeks excess when it has ceased to be pleasant, and the 'moral hero' seeks virtue in spite of its painfulness. We only have a 'confirmed character' when our purposes have become independent of the pleasure or pain from which they arose.

There is, then, he believes, or there can be, a science of human nature. But it will not be an exact science, like Astronomy; it will be an inexact one, like 'Tidology'. There can be such a science in so far as approximate truths (empirical 'knowledge of mankind') can be shown as corollaries of universal laws of human nature. Mill will keep clear of metaphysics; he will not ask what 'Things' or 'Mind' are 'in themselves'. We cannot yet be certain (as Comte claims to be) that states of mind and associations are all 'really' physiological. We can thus talk intelligibly, in the meantime, of 'laws of mind'; the laws of association, for example, have been largely though not conclusively proved. The *science of the formation of human character* is for Mill of supreme importance; it is that to which all other sciences lead up, and he coins for it the name of 'ethology'. Men have not all one character, but there exist universal laws of the formation of character—not empirical laws ('old age is cautious', 'all men are liars', etc.), but the causal laws which give such observations whatever truth they have. In this complex investigation, where it is impossible to isolate our subject or to take in all relevant factors, the direct experimental method is not applicable. We must *deduce* the laws of ethology from the general laws of mind, and then correct them by observation.

It is typical of Mill's eighteenth century affinity that for him the primary thing—the point of departure and the final end—is always the individual, whereas with Comte society precedes the individual. Nevertheless Mill has read Comte to much purpose, and devotes an important section to 'Social Science': 'a thing of yesterday', as he calls it, yet a science in which general laws are attainable for our guidance. First he dismisses as misleading two older methods of social investigation, the 'Chemical' and the 'Geometrical'. The former was associated for him with a misguided 'parroting after Bacon', that is, with a crude empiricism uninformed and unchecked by general laws of human nature. He shows that in sociology we cannot, as in chemistry, make artificial experiments, and that the whole field is too complex for this technique; in politics many causes, and not one only, produce the effects. The Geometric method (associated with the names of Hobbes, Bentham and James Mill), on the other hand, errs by assuming that all the phenomena can be deduced from one single property of human nature—as 'fear' in Hobbes, or 'worldly interests' in Bentham[1], and by not allowing for the actual conflict of forces. In the ensuing criticisms of Benthamite 'political economy' we have a good example of the way in which Mill often transcends without rejecting his master's teaching. The 'interest-philosophy of the Bentham school' assumes, he says, (i) that human beings are governed in all their actions by their worldly interests, (ii) that the actions of average rulers are determined solely by self-interest, (iii) that rulers will govern in accordance with the interest of the governed when their own selfish interests coincide therewith, and (iv) that no rulers are so situated unless they are accountable to the governed. But these propositions are not universally true,

---

[1] It is interesting to note that it was Macaulay's attack (*Edinburgh Review*, 1829) on James Mill's *Government* which convinced J. S. M. that both his father's geometric deductive method and Macaulay's own chemical method were incomplete.

he replies. Men, and rulers, are swayed by the sense of duty, by philanthropy, by tradition, public opinion, class-feeling, habitual sentiments and the like. We do need the check of 'accountability', but it is a pity that the theory of Parliamentary Reform should be mistaken for a complete theory of society.

Sociology, then, Mill concludes (with Comte), must follow the inverse deductive method, i.e. it must generalize from history, but 'verify' its generalizations by deduction from the laws of human nature. Its task is immensely complex, for it must consider *all* the relevant causes and then compound them. Yet Mill cannot give up 'the dismal science' without a struggle. He has just shown that self-interest is not the universal motive, and that all previous sociologies have been over-simplified. Yet, he goes on to remark, it *is* true that certain sets of social effects are *mainly* due to particular causes, and so may be treated separately, as organs of the body can. Thus the science of Political Economy exists in its own right, in so far as it is concerned with those phenomena which do arise from the desire of wealth—the desire of wealth checked (he adds, remembering his catechism) by laziness, self-indulgence and the pressure of population. So many phenomena do thus arise (though not all), that it is worth while to reason as if it had full sway —to reason thus once and for all, and then allow for the modifying circumstances. Political Economy makes deliberate and conscious abstraction of the wealth-motive from all others; 'not that any political economist was ever so absurd as to suppose that mankind are really thus constituted, but because this is the mode in which science must necessarily proceed'. This, says the economist, is how men would act supposing that they were solely influenced by the profit-motive—and how nearly this is so, after all! Political Economy, Mill says, will fail to explain or predict real events, in so far as other causes really do operate. For instance, an English or American economist may easily err by assuming as normal an intensity of competition which in fact only exists in Britain and the U.S.A.; he may not have heard that there are other men (say, for instance, Italians, or Tahitians?) who care more about ease or vanity than pecuniary gain. Was ever science more oddly vindicated? First Mill explodes the geometric method, then as a dutiful son and disciple he puts it together again—murmuring that this is how science 'must necessarily proceed'; it must proceed, in fact, by constructing a false picture first in order to put it right later on.

Mill returns to surer ground when he comes to deal with the science of history, or the methods of historical interpretation. 'States of society', what are they, and how are they produced? The problem is 'to find the laws according to which any state of society produces the state which succeeds it and takes its place'. This enquiry opens up 'the great and vexed question of the progressiveness of man and society'. Is social evolution an 'orbit', or a 'trajectory'? Mill believes that there is 'progressiveness'; this does not necessarily imply 'improvement', though he believes that there is a tendency that way too. The new historical school in France has tried to establish a law of progress; Comte alone, however, has seen the need to connect empirical generalizations from history with the laws of human nature. In this sphere there is a bewildering interplay of cause and effect: circumstances produce character, but character reacts upon circumstances. 'What we now are and do, is in a very small degree the result of the universal circumstances of the human race, or even of our own circumstances acting through the original qualities of our species, but mainly of the qualities produced in us by the whole previous history of humanity.' But, in this vast and complex process of social dynamics, perhaps some one element preponderates? Yes! and Mill's answer is the reverse of Marx's (did he ever read Marx, one wonders?)—Opinions, Belief and Knowledge: these are the determining causes of social change. All changes have been preceded by a change in knowledge or belief. 'Polytheism, Judaism, Christianity, Protestantism, the critical philosophy of modern Europe and its positive science'—these have been the determinants. What we must seek, therefore, is *'the law of the successive transformation of human opinions'*,[1]

[1] *Op. cit.*, p. 527 (my italics).

and Comte alone has so far attempted to formulate this. Mill considers Comte's *loi des trois états* to be a generalization of high scientific value, showing the concurrence of historical evidence with *a priori* human probabilities. The notion of a 'Science of History' (Mill adds here in this later edition) has recently been popularized in England by Buckle, who in his *History of Civilization* [1] has ascribed all progress to 'advance in scientific knowledge', minimized the importance of individuals ('great men') and exalted 'the spirit of the age' and 'general causes'. On this Mill remarks that (once again) we must not confuse Causation with Fatalism by fancying that individuals or governments cannot modify general laws. Mill had been the friend of Carlyle, and he differed from Buckle and Macaulay on the importance of 'great men'. All the same, he admits, 'we cannot foresee the advent of great men', and, as 'general causes' tend to increase in importance, never again can we expect individuals to count for so much.

That he expected individuals always to count for a great deal, however, can be seen throughout his writings, and nowhere more clearly than in the last section of the *Logic*, which deals with the conduct of life. What are 'proper objects of approbation'? When we begin to speak of 'ought' instead of 'is', we must have some standard by which to determine the goodness or badness of objects of desire. This is not the place, Mill says, to justify his opinion on this subject; he will merely state his conviction that 'conduciveness to happiness' is the ultimate principle of teleology. As in *Utilitarianism*, Mill admits that this may not always mean happiness to the noble individual; but what is 'nobility'? why is it noble?

> 'The character itself should be, to the individual, a paramount end, simply because the existence of this ideal nobleness of character, or of a near approach to it, in any abundance, would go further than all things else towards making human life happy; both in the comparatively humble sense, of pleasure and freedom from pain, and in the higher meaning, of rendering life, not what it now is

[1] Vol. i, 1857; vol. ii, 1861.

almost universally, puerile and insignificant—but such as human beings with highly developed faculties can care to have.'

III. *The Principles of Political Economy* (1848-49)

Here again I shall only glance at a few significant aspects. In this famous work Mill, as usual, is trying to reconcile incompatibles; this time, the premises of Ricardo and Malthus are to be squared with his own passion for human amelioration. How are the best ends of socialism to be gained without abandoning the values of individualism and *laissez-faire*? The historical setting of this book was the recent triumph of Free Trade, and the widening estrangement between the philosophical radicals and the classes they claimed to lead and represent. Chartists, evangelical promoters of factory acts, and the many who loathed the New Poor Law (1834), all alike suspected them of being cold, hard-hearted Gradgrinds and Malthusians. Mill, as a political economist, has been called a 'hopeful Malthusian': why was he hopeful? He believed neither in the providence of God nor in the beneficence of Nature; in average humanity, too, he had no great faith. Man was improvident, and Nature niggardly. He held, with Malthus, that the human race, left to itself, could double itself in one generation, and that the resulting pressure of population upon means of subsistence would lead, if unchecked, to misery, disease and starvation. He held, too, that profits tend towards a minimum, and that there is a law of diminishing returns from land. Deep beneath all political devices and remedies there lay, for Mill, these ineluctable economic facts. We were ever steadily approaching, and indeed now upon the verge of, what he called 'The Stationary State'[1]—the state when there is no longer any piling up of capital, when capital no longer overflows into the 'backward' countries of the world, and when the 'opening of markets' in these and the food-producing lands defeats itself by stimulating the birth-rate and the needs of those very countries. It all reads disconcertingly

---

[1] *Political Economy* (6th ed., 1865), vol. ii, bk. iv, ch. 6.

like a prophecy of the world's present plight. To account for
Mill's hopefulness in face of this sombre vision we need
only remember that he was writing one hundred years ago,
and that he had been brought up in the radical, reforming
tradition. 'Improvement' *must* take place, for this is the very
meaning of existence. But not necessarily 'progress', in the
sense of ever-accumulating capital, ever-expanding trade
and ever-mounting numbers; Mill must be given great
credit for seeing this clearly. He knew that 'progress' in that
sense, if left to itself, must 'end in shallows and miseries':
a belief which, he pleaded, was no wicked invention of
Malthus, but a law recognized by his predecessors and only
to be combated on Malthusian principles. It is the misfortune of Mill, of his uncomfortable position between two
worlds, that he is continually being hit by the boomerang
of his own ideas. Mill's presuppositions were those which,
in the age just past and gone, had indeed been the spearhead
of revolutionary change. He, supposing them still to be
such, finds himself compelled, at every turn, to retreat and
prepare defensive positions. Thus, in this classic work on
political economy, written (as we have seen) on the assumption that men all want to become richer and richer, and that
they must not be interfered with while so doing, Mill first
finds himself checked by the ghost of Malthus (all this will
end in shallows and miseries), and then, with a volte-face
which shows that he was greater than he knew, he asks the
startling questions: Do we *want* to get richer and richer?
May not the 'stationary state' be 'a very considerable improvement on our present condition'? Why desire continual
increases of production, accumulation and population?—
these are not in themselves ultimate ends. 'I confess', he
says (in a passage which might come from *Culture and
Anarchy*), that 'I am not charmed with the ideal of life held
out by those who think the normal state of human beings is
that of struggling to get on'. In the stationary state, when
men have ceased to be engrossed by this material struggle,
there will be more room for improving the art of living, and
'much more likelihood of its being improved'. The true
purpose of mechanical inventions will then at length appear:

not to increase wealth, but to abridge labour, and create leisure for cultivating the graces of life:

> 'Hitherto it is questionable if all the mechanical inventions yet made have lightened the toil of any human being. They have enabled a greater population to live the same life of drudgery and imprisonment, and an increased number of manufacturers and others to make fortunes. They have increased the comforts of the middle classes. But they have not yet begun to effect those great changes in human destiny, which it is in their nature and in their futurity to accomplish.'[1]

But Mill, with his surprising and endearing many-sidedness, produces another (and a Wordsworthian) reason for preferring the stationary state to the Brave New World of the progress-worshippers: let us call a halt to the increase of population—why? because

> 'it is not good for man to be kept perforce at all times in the presence of his species. A world from which solitude is extirpated, is a very poor ideal. Solitude, in the sense of being often alone, is essential to any depth of meditation or of character; and solitude in the presence of natural beauty and grandeur, is the cradle of thoughts and aspirations which are not only good for the individual, but which society could ill do without. Nor is there much satisfaction in contemplating the world with nothing left to the spontaneous activity of nature; with every rood of land brought into cultivation, which is capable of growing food for human beings; every flowery waste or natural pasture ploughed up, all quadrupeds or birds which are not domesticated for man's use exterminated as his rival for food, every hedgerow or superfluous tree rooted out, and scarcely a place left where a wild shrub or flower could grow without being eradicated as a weed in the name of improved agriculture. If the earth must lose that part of its pleasantness which it owes to things that the unlimited increase of wealth and population would extirpate from it, for the mere purpose of enabling it to support a larger, but not a better or a happier population, I sincerely hope, for the sake of posterity, that they will be content to be stationary, long before necessity compels them to it.'[2]

[1] *Ibid.*, p. 332.   [2] *Ibid.*, p. 331.

JOHN STUART MILL

What a piece of work is Mill! The steam-engine radical, frightened at his own progress, whistling for the flowery meadows, his power-loom prose booming out the sentiments of Rousseau or D. H. Lawrence! Seldom can mortal man have affirmed in accents less poetical, how gracious, how benign is solitude. A joyless knowledge of the sources of joy pervades all Mill's work, and his prose is grey with it. Yet the knowledge is his, and present-day advocates of National Parks and Nature-Preserves (all honour to them) should recognize him as a forerunner.

But the Malthusian spectre walks again: is this not mere Utopian dreaming? What if, the stationary state once reached, the population went on increasing just the same? Has Mill, with his belief in the niggardliness of Nature and the fecklessness of man, any right to suppose otherwise? 'Only when', he has said,

> 'in addition to just institutions, the increase of mankind shall be under the deliberate guidance of judicious foresight, can the conquests made from the powers of nature by the intellect and energy of scientific discoverers, become the common property of the species, and the means of improving and elevating the common lot.'

Will men, then, ever 'be content to be stationary' in this respect, 'before necessity compels them to it'? Whereas Malthus had thought not, Mill was hopeful. Not for nothing had he been steeped, from the dawn of life, in the hope and expectation of unlimited betterment. The 'existing habits' of mankind *can* be improved, by education and an enhanced standard of living. They can be improved by State intervention—and here, by another typical paradox, the arch-individualist comes in sight of Socialism. Once again the boomerang strikes him; he bends his head to dodge it, and proceeds, in patient dejection, to examine how much State action can be allowed without giving up the individualist essentials.

Production of wealth must not be tampered with, but the State may do much to ensure its better distribution—'of which one indispensable means is a stricter restraint on population. Levelling institutions, either of a just or of an unjust kind, cannot alone accomplish it; they may lower the heights of society, but they cannot, of themselves, permanently raise the depths.' He seems to have expected that the 'stricter restraint' would spontaneously be applied by the people as education enriched their lives and as improved conditions enhanced their self-respect. And so, there must above all be national education, enforced and financed, though not provided, by the State. There must be laws 'favouring equality of fortunes so far as is consistent with the just claim of the individual to the fruits, whether great or small, of his or her own industry'; for example, there should be a limit to what can be acquired by gift or inheritance, though a limit not stringent enough to exclude 'a moderate independence'. If, in this way, there were to be no more enormous fortunes (except those earned and acquired in one lifetime), many more people might be exempt from 'coarser toils', and have leisure for 'the graces'. To relieve the existing pressure of population there should be emigration; there should also be home-colonization, leading to that peasant-proprietorship which in France had so successfully produced frugality and Malthusian restraint: 'obedience to Malthus makes the prosperous French peasant, disobedience, the pauperized English labourer'.[1] There should be laws restraining imprudent marriages, and alleviation for 'displaced' workers; the government may own canals and railways, and may even nationalize land and take 'unearned increment'. Factory legislation Mill could not bring himself to approve, but he recommended the protection of child-labourers. All these measures of State Socialism, he held, would be much nearer to realization in the 'stationary state' than now, and all these he approved. It is thus true to say that Mill has provisionally abandoned *laissez-faire*; he wants (as Leslie Stephen puts it) 'a huge dead-lift', an interference by government, though he still hopes that this will be an interference to end interference. He believed to the last in private property, and above all in *competition*. He conceded to the Socialists that co-operative associations may be good, but

[1] Leslie Stephen, *op. cit.*, p. 192.

'I utterly dissent from the most conspicuous and vehement part of their teaching, their declamations against competition. . . . They forget that wherever competition is not, monopoly is; and that monopoly, in all its forms, is the taxation of the industrious for the support of indolence, if not of plunder.'

Competition admittedly has its evils, but it prevents greater evils, it stimulates individual faculties:

'It is the common error of Socialists to overlook the natural indolence of mankind. . . . Competition may not be the best conceivable stimulus, but it is at present a necessary one, and no one can foresee the time when it will not be indispensable to progress.' [1]

iv. *On Liberty* (1859)

'The grand, leading principle, towards which every argument in these pages directly converges, is the absolute and essential importance of human development in its richest variety.'

In taking, for his most famous Essay, this motto from Wilhelm von Humboldt, Mill is defining the sense in which he proposes to discuss 'Liberty'. The argument follows on from where we have just left off: he is going to discuss in more detail, but also with more philosophical breadth, 'the nature and limits of the power which can be legitimately exercised by society over the individual'. Once again we find Mill wrestling with paradoxes, and defending his principles against their own consequences. Indeed, this Essay is the palmary instance of that posture in him, for the menace here is the very liberal-democratic state which he and his party had toiled to create. Mill was discovering (without so formulating it) the truth of the 'dialectical' principle, that a historical 'moment' tends to generate its own negation; out of the very liberty for which he had striven had proceeded a new sort of tyranny. The old *laissez-faire* liberty had produced an order in which only the privileged few were really free; the rest of mankind were free only to sell their labour or starve. To remedy this, the principle of 'equality' had

---

[1] *Political Economy, loc. cit.*, pp. 376-7.

been invoked, and the franchise had been in wider (not yet 'widest') commonalty spread. To remedy the yet remaining evils of free competition Mill had been prepared, as we saw, to admit a considerable measure of State Socialism. But all this meant more and more legislation, more and more interference with the individual; could it be that liberty and equality were incompatible? In working for equality, were we sacrificing something still more valuable? What Mill would have thought of our present-day 'democracy' one trembles to imagine; it is sufficiently remarkable to find him, already in 1859, aware of the impending tyranny of 'collective mediocrity'. 'The tendency of all the changes taking place in the world', he says, 'is to strengthen society, and diminish the power of the individual.' And this tendency profoundly disturbed him, for the most deeply seated of his *unconscious* beliefs (on the *conscious* level he sometimes denied it) was that the 'natural' was better than the contrived, and that the individual was a 'natural' unit, while society was 'artificial'. I believe that there was a conflict between Mill's unspoken and his explicit assumptions on the 'natural', for if 'Nature' were all that he says of her in his posthumous Essay of that title (see below, pp. 177 ff.), he would have no right to defend the individual as part of the natural order. This latent respect for Nature, this predisposition to 'let be', was part of Mill's eighteenth century inheritance. The Essay *On Liberty*, although written in the heart of the Victorian age, still has about it the ring of mental fight, the heroic tone of 1789. One might have supposed that in 1859 no new *Areopagitica* was called for, but Mill was far from seeing the matter in that light. To him, mid-Victorian England seemed 'not a place of mental freedom', and, as we have seen, he feared that other freedoms were about to perish. *On Liberty*, then, is a veritable *Areopagitica*, and its strenuous tone explicable, because Mill felt himself to be attacking two kinds of tyranny in succession: in the first part, that of intellectual torpor and intolerance; in the second, the monstrous offspring of the democratic Frankenstein.

The sap runs freely and strongly throughout the first section, which deals with liberty of thought and discussion.

'Discussion' was indeed the breath of life to Mill, who as a youth had formed a debating circle which met twice a week from 8.30 a.m. until 10. He craved for the free play of mind upon all subjects, but found that in England it was considered ill-bred to discuss serious topics in society; France was much more congenial in this respect. His secluded upbringing, and his father's ascendant influence, had implanted deep within him the feeling that English thought, like English society, universities and religion, was still in the grip of sinister conservatism; he could therefore see himself as an eighteenth century 'philosophe' attacking the infamous old Goliath. For Mill, the 'great' moments in history were those when ideas and assumptions were being thoroughly overhauled, when discussion most mightily raged, and 'the yoke of authority was broken': he specifies the Reformation, the late eighteenth century in France, and the 'Goethian and Fichtean period' in Germany, as epochs when Europe was mentally awake. One gathers that he would have been prepared to add to these the early centuries of Christianity, when the faith was still fighting for existence, and when its adherents were consequently aware of what they were fighting for. But these impulses are now wellnigh spent; there is in England now 'a tacit convention that principles are not to be disputed', and there has descended upon us the 'deep slumber of a decided opinion'.

> 'A state of things in which a large portion of the most active and inquiring intellects find it advisable to keep the general principles and grounds of their convictions within their own breasts, and attempt, in what they address to the public, to fit as much as they can of their own conclusions to premises which they have internally renounced, cannot send forth the open, fearless characters, and logical, consistent intellects who once adorned the thinking world.'[1]

In face of the continued pressure of an older civilization, with its social inequalities and privileges, its traditional religion and morality, Mill and the middle-class radicals could still feel themselves to be in the vanguard of human

[1] *Liberty*, p. 93 (Everyman ed.).

advance, and still feel that their interests were those of the masses of mankind (though the masses had a way of not quite seeing this).

I will briefly rehearse the argument. If we try to suppress opinions: (i) The opinion to be suppressed *may* be true. Were not Socrates and Christ put to death as heretics, blasphemers and corrupters of morality? Did not Marcus Aurelius, a better 'Christian' than nearly all so-called Christian rulers, persecute Christianity? It is a fallacy to suppose that 'Truth' as such has any special survival-value; 'history teems with instances of truth put down by persecution'.

(ii) Even though the alleged heresy be indeed an error, and the orthodox opinion true, yet if the orthodox never hear their views questioned, they themselves will not understand on what grounds they hold them. 'He who knows only his own side of the case, knows little of that'; absence of discussion weakens belief. Creeds are operative when they are being affirmed against opposition, and mere formal husks when they have long been accepted. The doctrines of the Sermon on the Mount are considered sacred, but they now produce little effect 'beyond what is caused by mere listening to words so amiable and bland'; the real allegiance of the modern Christian is paid to worldly interests: he believes his doctrines 'just up to the point at which it is usual to act upon them'.

(iii) The conflicting doctrines may share the truth between them, and in this case it may be that the minority-opinion contains just that part of it which is ignored by the majority. One-sidedness is an inherent defect of the human mind itself, and revolutions and improvements in opinion are not simple replacements of error by truth, but rather the rise of one part of truth and the obscuration of another—the new fragment being simply 'more adapted to the needs of the time, than that which it displaces'. We have noticed how Mill saw in the contrasted world-views of the eighteenth and nineteenth centuries a type of this one-sidedness, and with this in mind he here says that the 'paradoxes of Rousseau' burst, 'like a bombshell', in the midst of eighteenth century opinion, 'forcing its elements to recombine in a better form and with additional ingredients'. In the great practical concerns of life, above all in politics, 'truth' is a 'reconciling and combining of opposites', and if one of two opinions has a better claim to be countenanced it is that which at the moment happens to be in a minority. An interesting part of this discussion, for our present purpose, occurs where Mill considers Christian ethics, which are reputed to contain no half-truth, but the whole truth, in matters of conduct. Here he clearly feels that he is vindicating a minority view against an all-but unanimous prejudice. After distinguishing between Gospel Christianity, which never purported to teach a complete ethical system, and ecclesiastical Christianity, which did, he declares

> 'that it is, in many important points, incomplete and one-sided, and that unless ideas and feelings, not sanctioned by it, had contributed to the formation of European life and character, human affairs would have been in a worse condition than they now are.' [1]

What 'ideas and feelings'? Magnanimity, he replies: high-mindedness, sense of personal dignity, sense of honour, energetic pursuit of good, sense of duty to mankind without thought of heavenly reward, sense of duty to the State; in a word, the pagan virtues, and their modern counterparts as represented in the ideals of chivalry and the 'gentleman'. These and such-like secular standards must be combined with those of Christianity to produce the moral regeneration of mankind. One may suppose that this is the kind of sentiment which James Mill had advised his son not to express, but which, now that the latter is actually burning his boats, he glories in avowing.

Nothing in Mill is more profound or of more lasting value than this first section. Yet if his grave ghost should revisit this troubled world of a hundred years later, we should have to pose it with another problem about minority opinion: what, we should ask, if the whole *raison-d'être* of a given minority should be its determination to force its views at all cost upon the majority, and its readiness to imprison and murder all who will not submit? Shall that minority be

[1] *Ibid.*, p. 108.

tolerated, lest its suppression may mean the loss of some neglected fragment of truth? Perhaps even Mill would have hesitated here; he might, however, have said: suppress the party by all means, but enquire what hideous maladjustment has made its appearance possible, and remedy *that*.

The argument of the second section (which I have partly anticipated, and will therefore treat more summarily) is: given intellectual liberty, men must also be free to plan their own lives as they think fit; liberty in living must go with liberty in thinking—provided always that the individual does not make himself a nuisance to other people. It is here that Mill examines, on the principles already explained, the limits of the power of the State over the individual, the ruling assumption being the characteristic one, that 'leaving people to themselves is always better, *ceteris paribus*, than controlling them'. In order to draw his boundary line Mill makes a distinction between self-regarding and public actions; individuals must be unhampered in all that affects themselves only, but the State may intervene to prevent anti-social behaviour. The distinction is hard to maintain, though Mill's 'salutary jealousy of social interference' [1] will find a response in those today who dislike State regimentation and dread its continual and mounting encroachments. Mill would have occupied stronger ground here if he had been a Christian; he could then have given precise meaning to what was evidently his thought, that for the soul's health there must be spiritual sanctuaries, as well as Nature-Preserves, where the governmental writ does not run. Mill, as I have suggested, is here faced with some highly unwelcome results of the very movement for which he had always stood; democracy, or the rule of the average mediocre man, has now triumphed, and from this very 'liberty' is proceeding a new bondage: 'society has now fairly got the better of individuality'. 'The general tendency of things throughout the world is to render mediocrity the ascendant power among mankind.' [2] Genius, and originality of thought or conduct, 'can only breathe freely in an atmosphere of freedom', and this freedom is vanishing from our

[1] Cf. J. MacCunn, *Six Radical Thinkers* (1907), p. 82.
[2] *Liberty*, p. 123.

modern mass-civilization. 'The only power deserving the name is that of masses, and of governments which make themselves the organ of the tendencies and instincts of masses'—that is (in England), of the middle-class or 'collective mediocrity'. Mill is driven, like Carlyle, to fly for rescue to 'the highly-gifted and instructed One or Few' to guide the 'Sovereign Many'—though he explicitly discountenances 'the sort of "hero-worship" which applauds the strong man of genius for forcibly seizing on the government of the world and making it do his bidding in spite of itself'. No, there must be no Führers; the wise and the noble must only 'point out the way'. Unfortunately, 'energetic characters on any large scale are becoming merely traditional', and we are daily approaching an almost Chinese uniformity. Mill would not have found the 'energetic characters' of a hundred years later at all to his taste, and he would have been amazed to find that their aim was precisely to produce such uniformities, and to produce them by methods of 'interference' which would have reduced him to suicide. I will conclude by quoting his memorable warning against the evils of standardization:

> 'The circumstances which surround different classes and individuals, and shape their characters, are daily becoming more assimilated. Formerly, different ranks, different neighbourhoods, different trades and professions, lived in what might be called different worlds; at present to a great degree in the same. Comparatively speaking, they now read the same things, listen to the same things, see the same things, go to the same places, have their hopes and fears directed to the same objects, have the same rights and liberties, and the same means of asserting them. Great as are the differences of position which remain, they are nothing to those which have ceased. And the assimilation is still proceeding. All the political changes of the age promote it, since they all tend to raise the low and to lower the high. Every extension of education promotes it, because education brings people under common influences, and gives them access to the general stock of facts and sentiments. Improvement in the means of communication promotes it, by bringing the inhabitants of distant places into personal contact, and keeping

up a rapid flow of changes of residence between one place and another. The increase of commerce and manufactures promotes it, by diffusing more widely the advantages of easy circumstances, and by opening all objects of ambition, even the highest, to general competition, whereby the desire of rising becomes no longer the character of a particular class, but of all classes. A more powerful agency than even all these, in bringing about a general similarity among mankind, is the complete establishment, in this and other free countries, of the ascendancy of public opinion in the State. . . .

'The combination of all these causes forms so great a mass of influences hostile to Individuality, that it is not easy to see how it can stand its ground. It will do so with increasing difficulty, unless the intelligent part of the public can be made to feel its value. If the claims of Individuality are ever to be asserted, the time is now, while much is wanting to complete the enforced assimilation.'

The 'time is now' 1949, not 1859, and the assimilation has gone incalculably further—too far for remedy, Mill would perhaps have thought. However, if anything is 'still wanting to complete it' (as we must hope), his words are many times more urgent than ever.

v. *Utilitarianism* (1861-63)

Our previous discussion of Bentham's *Deontology* must serve to excuse us from any exhaustive account of this Essay. Mill, in treating this, the central theme of his life and thought, is once more 'inly rack'd', and vexed by contraries. He is squeezing hard at the old Utilitarian orange to make it yield what it never contained, and he only obtains the juice he needs by a sleight of hand of which he appears unaware. Or, as has been said without metaphor, he destroys the simplicity of Benthamism without giving up its principle.[1] No wonder Mill was 'joyless'; there can be few spiritual postures more uncomfortable than that of watching, open-eyed, one's own thought-world destroying itself and yet of being unable to shift into a new one. His aim in this Essay

[1] Whittaker, *op. cit.*, ch. iii.

is to show that Utilitarianism will yield a morality as lofty as any 'transcendental' or religious system. The view that 'actions are right in proportion as they tend to promote happiness, wrong as they tend to promote the reverse of happiness', excites intense dislike, he admits, in those who think that life has a 'nobler' end than pleasure. In order to answer this objection Mill makes his famous qualitative distinction between the 'sorts' of pleasure—performs, in fact, with seeming innocence, the conjuring trick which produces 'ought' out of 'is'. '*Some kinds of pleasures are more desirable and valuable than others*' (my italics). What can make them so, except their being greater in 'amount'? Of two pleasures, he replies, that is the more valuable to which all who have experience of both give decided preference, and which they are prepared to purchase even at the cost of discomfort. Now those who are thus experienced have a marked preference for the pleasures of the intellect over those of the senses, and they believe that the quality of their happiness outweighs all consideration of quantity:

> 'It is better to be a human being dissatisfied than a pig satisfied; better to be Socrates dissatisfied than a fool satisfied. And if the fool, or the pig, are of a different opinion, it is because they only know their own side of the question. The other party to the comparison knows both sides.'[1]

From this judgment about the quality of pleasures by the only competent critics there can be no appeal; the most *desirable* pleasures are simply those which are in fact most *desired* by the best judges. At this point Mill is deflected by the Carlylean objection that happiness is unattainable, and that we must learn renunciation (*entsagen*). At the thought of this, all the indoctrinated optimism in Mill, all his philanthropy and humanity-religion, come to the surface, and he gives us a passage which, quite apart from its context, must still move and challenge all statesmen and all who care for their fellow-man. Happiness—not indeed rapture, but a steady burning of its flame—is already the lot of some, and 'the present wretched education, and wretched social arrange-

[1] *Utilitarianism* (Everyman ed.), p. 9.

ments, are the only real hindrance to its being attainable by almost all'. No one, he continues,

> 'whose opinion deserves a moment's consideration can doubt that most of the great positive evils of the world are in themselves removable, and will, if human affairs continue to improve, be in the end reduced within narrow limits. Poverty, in any sense implying suffering, may be completely extinguished by the wisdom of society, combined with the good sense and providence of individuals. Even that most intractable of enemies, disease, may be indefinitely reduced in dimensions by good physical and moral education, and proper control of noxious influences; while the progress of science holds out a promise for the future of still more direct conquests over this detestable foe. . . . As for vicissitudes of fortune, and other disappointments connected with worldly circumstances, these are principally the effect either of gross imprudence, of ill-regulated desires, or of bad or imperfect social institutions. *All the grand sources, in short, of human suffering are in a great degree, many of them almost entirely, conquerable by human care and effort;* and though their removal is grievously slow—though a long succession of generations will perish in the breach before the conquest is completed, and this world becomes all that, if will and knowledge were not wanting, it might easily be made—yet every mind sufficiently intelligent and generous to bear a part, however small and unconspicuous, in the endeavour, will draw a noble enjoyment from the contest itself, which he would not for any bribe in the form of selfish indulgence consent to be without.' [1]

Not only, then, could the general happiness be indefinitely extended, but in helping to extend it the noble individual may find, now and for long henceforth, the happiness of a Socrates. Such nobility might, indeed, procure him only the 'happiness' of martyrdom—it would be worth while were it so, for Utilitarianism seeks the happiness of the greatest number, not of the noble few—but in fact and in experience things are not as bad as that. All honour, of course, to those who have forgone personal enjoyments in order to minister to the world's welfare; a man who sacrifices them for any

---

[1] *Op. cit.*, p. 14 (my italics).

other purpose is a mere Stylites on a pillar, and deserves no admiration. As long as the world is in its present imperfect state, Mill fully grants, 'the readiness to make such a sacrifice is the highest virtue which can be found in man'. But he looks forward to a society so conditioned that the very distinction between personal and general happiness shall have disappeared. Utilitarianism, then (and this is the drift of his argument), demands nothing less than the morality of Jesus Christ: to do as you would be done by, and to love your neighbour as yourself.

Let us stand a little aside and contemplate Mill's position. Whence, let us first ask, the *obligation* to seek the general good rather than my own, or *as* my own? I may not happen to care much about the happiness of others: in that case, no 'framing of society' so as to produce an artificial identity of these interests will alter my inward quality as a moral being. Or, more broadly let us ask—do we, do we men in fact, care more for the general good or for our own? Both Bentham and Mill agree that we are 'naturally' selfish; very well then, the problem is how, out of selfish individuals, to elicit unselfish action. The Utilitarian can only answer: 'You desire your own happiness? I'll tell you how best to attain it—by promoting the happiness of others. You'll find that this makes you surprisingly happy. Try it and see. Those who have already tried it know that it is so.' But this still leaves one's happiness (though of the 'higher' kind) as the real object of pursuit, as the theoretic sanction of altruism. Even if we admit that the idea of a pleasure is the only motive that can allure us, it remains doubtful whether the mere promise, by a moral expert, of a more refined form of pleasure, will effect the required transition from egoism to altruism. This transition is at the core of the ethical problem; it cannot be slurred over as if it were easy. Human nature does not rise to such baits; it is moved much rather (so experience suggests) by commands, and still more by *love*. As soon as love enters the picture, the scene is transformed; the object of endeavour now becomes something outside self altogether, something which demands service for its own sake, and not for the sake of the accruing pleasure.

The loved object, whether God, person or society, requires of us a devotion in which we indeed find joy, but we do not love *on account of* the joy; we find the joy because we love. The Utilitarian principle begins at the wrong end: it makes an objective out of what is only a concomitant. The strange thing is that Mill actually learned this lesson during his mental crisis; he learned, at least, that the deliberate pursuit of happiness defeats itself: that happiness must be coaxed by a stratagem, and not carried by direct attack. Yet this discovery did not shake his inherited (or inculcated) conviction that happiness is the end of conduct and the test of right. One might have supposed that the discovery would have suggested grave doubts about the validity of happiness as a *summum bonum*: what? this most desirable object, this final end and aim, to whose attainment all else is subordinate, has it, then, one special characteristic distinguishing it from other possible aims, that it must *not* be sought for its own sake? Surely then, one might suppose, it cannot *be* the *summum bonum*? 'Ah, but', Mill replies, 'it is the happiness of others that you must seek, not your own; my melancholy [so he might continue] was due to my never having really been altruistic; I had sought my own happiness in that of others, and so the happiness of others failed awhile to give me pleasure.' It will be noticed that in these imputed words I have made Mill use the classic Utilitarian argument to deny itself: seek your own happiness in that of others, but if you do you won't be happy!—to this hopeless contradiction are we remorselessly led. It seems to follow that we must not seek our own happiness at all; that we must seek the general happiness without reference to our own. Mill virtually admits this, yet he cannot frankly surrender the implication that our own happiness is even then the true motive-force; he can admit no theoretic sanction for altruism except that it *does* produce the highest happiness. Nevertheless, in so far as he virtually abandoned his own position he had left Bentham behind, and crossed the frontier into religion. He stopped, indeed, at the command to love our neighbour as ourselves, and never admitted the dependence of this obligation on the first commandment—to love God with heart, soul, mind and strength. But he knew that altruism must be taught as a religion, and not dangled before one's eyes as a more enchanting kind of pleasure.

It must be taught as a religion, but as the Religion of Humanity, not as Christianity. The morality 'which education and opinion have consecrated is the only one which presents itself to the mind with the feeling of being *in itself* obligatory'; therefore, we may hope that some day, if our solidarity with mankind be taught as a religion, and the whole force of education and opinion directed towards fostering it, 'the feeling of unity with our fellow-creatures shall be (what it cannot be denied Christ intended it to be) as deeply rooted in our character, and to our own consciousness as completely a part of our nature, as the horror of crime is to an ordinarily well brought up young person'. At this stage virtue would have become, what Mill admits it should be even now, a *habit*; virtuous acts, that is, should be performed without conscious reference to their pleasurableness. Once again he seems to have given his case away. To say that we ought to acquire virtuous habits without conscious regard to pleasure is to say all that a non-Utilitarian moralist could urge; Mill saves his position, however, by the subterfuge that virtue is only happy-making conduct masquerading as something else. However, now that the argument has led up to the need for a religion, it seems ungracious to criticize Mill for offering us the wrong one; the remarkable thing is that he should offer us any religion at all. Further discussion at this point would no longer be about Utilitarianism; it would turn into a comparison between Christianity and the Religion of Humanity, or at least, between religion and humanism. This is to be considered in the next section, so here it must suffice to add one last comment. If I have been properly brought up, then, on Mill's principles, I may have the feeling that I must do what will make my fellows happy, but this sense of obligation will be conceived, not as a duty to God, but as a duty to mankind. One is reluctant to unsettle anybody's simple faith, but the sceptical Christian may feel bound to ask: is human nature really such as to be able to feel this overwhelming duty to make others happy—or, if to feel it, then to face all the ardours, discomforts, fatigues, isolations, committee-meetings and other martyrdoms of a life so devoted—to do all this, without the incentive known as 'love of God'? Such people there undoubtedly are—Mill was one of them—and they deserve all homage and praise. But they are rare, and I suspect that most even of these are really moved by energies springing from a source which was formerly religious, either in themselves or in their fathers or forefathers, and which is still religious in them also, except in name. It has been said that even if the character of the Deity were utilitarian—that is, as approving or willing what makes happy—yet the character of man is not so. We cannot love our fellows much unless we love God more.

VI. *Three Essays on Religion:*

1. NATURE
2. THE UTILITY OF RELIGION } 1850-58
3. THEISM, 1868-70

These three Essays appeared posthumously (1874), and Helen Taylor, in introducing them, explains that the first two were written before Mill could have read Darwin and Maine, and that the third, which was 'the last considerable work which he completed', represents, though in an unrevised form, 'the carefully balanced result of the deliberations of a lifetime'. From every point of view the Essays are of quite outstanding importance and interest; from that of the present discussion they are of palmary significance, because they reveal, with unmistakable clarity and even pathos, the final impotence of Mill's system of thought. Thomas Hardy once said that if there had really been a God, he believed he would have found Him; Mill, who might have said the same, is here seen in the last contortions of his life-long research, seeking for God with his earnest, exemplary face turned persistently in the wrong direction, and even finding a ghostly image which was sufficiently God-like to alarm one of his agnostic disciples (John Morley). All through his life, like some ungifted Moses, he had tried to strike water out of dry rocks—altruism out of self-love, liberty out of bondage—and now here, in culminating frustration, he tries to draw faith out of reason. The rod taps and taps; the rock yields no drop; while—hidden from his short-sighted eyes—the spring bubbles up close at his back. If any proof were needed of St Paul's proposition that by wisdom (reasoning) no man finds God, here is an admirable one. Yet Mill's strength was perfected in weakness, for, precisely by overworking his intellectual machine, he showed that he was not finally enslaved to it.

It were to be expected that in these Essays, where Mill comes to grips with all that Bentham and James Mill had taught him to regard as unprovable, fictitious and transcendental, the effect of his upbringing would be strikingly evident. His aversion from orthodox and organized Christianity was deeply rooted in the hard, eighteenth century subsoil of his mind. He speaks here throughout with that wintry, passionless precision which is the very expression of his face in the well-known portrait. Much as he may have learned from Coleridge and Comte in the field of historical philosophy, he seems, in writing of religion, to have advanced little beyond Hume; Romanticism, with all its deepened apprehension of the numinous, not to mention the Oxford Movement, with its recovery of faith, are as though they had never been. Religion, treated as though it were a collection of propositions, is brought before the old critical tribunals, and found wanting by the old 'scientific' tests. Orthodox religion is here rejected, partly indeed for moral reasons, partly because the Church is supposed to be the home of social privilege and mental darkness, but chiefly because it is not intellectually demonstrable.

I. NATURE

In the first Essay it is Mill's purpose to examine how far the old watchword of *naturam sequi*, which had been reaffirmed with new conviction by Rousseau, Wordsworth and the *laissez-faire* economists, is valid as an ethical principle. What 'nature' is it that we are invited to follow? First we must examine the meaning of this highly ambiguous term. Mill distinguishes two main meanings: (i) 'all the powers existing in either the outer or the inner world and everything which takes place by means of those powers'; and (ii) 'what takes place without the agency, or without the voluntary and intentional agency, of man'. Now human action, he argues, cannot help conforming to Nature in the first sense, while on the other hand its very aim and object, its *raison d'être*, is to alter and improve Nature in the second sense. If the 'artificial', that is, all the arts and techniques of civilization, is not better than the 'natural', why do we cultivate the garden? why dig, plough, build, or wear clothes? Though this is generally admitted, and within certain limits always acted upon, there yet remains a stubborn, unanalysed notion that Nature is God's work, and therefore perfect—a model for us to imitate; a notion, moreover, that it is impious to interfere with it, or attempt to control it—at any rate in new and unfamiliar ways. I have already stated my impression that Mill himself, in his plea for wild, uncultivated tracts, and still more in his passion for individual liberty and his suspicion of the State, was unconsciously influenced by this notion (as most men were then, and some still are). Yet religion itself, he goes on, teaches 'that the paramount duty of mankind upon earth is to amend himself', and

> 'all but monkish quietists have annexed to this in their inmost minds (though seldom willing to enunciate the obligation with the same clearness) the additional religious duty of amending the world, and not solely the human part of it but the material; the order of physical nature.'[1]

It is the old dilemma of *Candide*: 'the best of all possible worlds' versus 'we must cultivate the garden'.

Next Mill turns his lack-lustre eye upon the aforesaid order of physical Nature, and finds that although the spectacle is vast, even sublime and awe-inspiring, yet it is non-moral through and through. What strikes every unflinching

---

[1] *Three Essays*, 1874, p. 26.

observer, he says, is the 'perfect and absolute recklessness' of natural forces:

> 'Nearly all the things which men are hanged or imprisoned for doing to one another, are nature's every day performances'—

killing her creatures, as she does, by storm, earthquake, hunger, cold or disease, and that with 'the most supercilious disregard both of mercy and of justice, emptying her shafts upon the best and noblest indifferently with the meanest and worst'. Mill rises in these paragraphs to unusual heights of rancorous eloquence; here, under cover of an attack on 'Nature', he could give vent at once to his moral passion, his pessimism and his contempt for those who would have us reverence all these evils as a 'mystery'. The conclusion is that 'it cannot be religious or moral to guide our actions by the analogy of the course of nature'. What, then, are the theological implications of all this? Either that God wills misery, or that He is not omnipotent:

> 'Not even on the most distorted and contracted theory of good which ever was framed by religious or philosophical fanaticism, can the government of Nature be made to resemble the work of a being at once good and omnipotent.'

Mill now turns the attack upon the 'Rousseauist' theory of the natural goodness of man. Some hold that the impulsive, instinctive elements in human nature—those parts of it, that is, in which deliberate choice and contrivance are least influential, are the most 'natural', and therefore the most divine. Natural, perhaps, and so much the less divine:

> 'The result is the vein of sentiment so common in the modern world . . . which exalts instinct at the expense of reason.'

Mill counters this by asserting that 'nearly every respectable attribute of humanity is the result, not of instinct, but of victory over instinct'; the virtues are 'repugnant to the untutored feelings of human nature'. Take the simple case of cleanliness: 'can anything be more entirely artificial?' Children, and the lower classes of most countries (presumably the most 'natural' of mortals) 'seem to be actually fond of dirt'. Or take the social virtues: selfishness is the 'natural' thing; self-control and altruism have to be learnt and acquired. 'Savages are always liars': veracity too, then, comes by training. It is only through cultivation that virtue becomes second nature, stronger even than the first. True, the germs of virtue must have been present from the start, but left to themselves they would have been smothered by the weeds which grow so rankly and luxuriantly—so much more 'natural' are the vicious tares than the virtuous wheat (yet Mill frowns upon the Christians for believing that man is by nature wicked). We must, then, amend our own natures as resolutely as we must amend outward circumstances. 'Conformity to nature' has 'no connexion whatever with right or wrong'; the scheme of Nature was evidently not the work of a good and omnipotent utilitarian Creator, aiming at the good of human or other sentient beings:

> 'Whatsoever, in nature, gives indication of beneficent design, proves this beneficence to be armed only with limited power; and the duty of man is to co-operate with the beneficent powers, not by imitating but by perpetually striving to amend the course of nature—and bringing that part of it over which we can exercise control, more nearly into conformity with a high standard of justice and goodness.'[1]

Out of the innumerable possible comments suggested by all this, I will make only two. The first is that man, with his moral standards whereby he judges Nature, is himself a product of Nature, and any picture which denigrates her by abstracting man and setting him up in antithesis to her is necessarily a falsification. The true, the *whole* portrait, includes morality because it includes man. The alternative view, namely, that man is a supernatural intruder, though it might leave Mill's picture intact, would so change the perspectives that it would no longer be true for him.

The second comment (I am purposely avoiding theology here) is that when all has been said, and rightly said, about altering, amending and improving Nature, there still remains a sediment of truth in the old idea that she is to be rever-

[1] *Ibid.*, p. 65.

enced. Else why should Mill long for a few 'flowery wastes', a few undomesticated quadrupeds and birds—in a word, a few evidences of 'the spontaneous activity of nature'[1], in his 'stationary' Utopia? Why should he hold that 'leaving people to themselves is always better, *ceteris paribus*, than controlling them'[2]? It has been shown again and again that the contriving mind may go astray, may murder to dissect; that instinct may be wise where intellect is foolish; that in conscious meddling we may destroy the sources of life itself. In using our prerogatives as Nature's grown-up children, we must not disfigure our parent; or, to change the metaphor, we may conquer her, but feel our captive's charms.

2. THE UTILITY OF RELIGION

'The duty of man is to co-operate with the beneficent powers ... by perpetually striving', etc.: but the question next arises, may not religion be needed in order to instil into us the sense of this urgent necessity? Without it, shall we greatly care to strive perpetually, with so severe, so earnest an air, to realize these lofty ideals of justice and goodness? Whence come the ideals themselves? In the second Essay, then, Mill sets himself to consider the 'utility' of religion.

Formerly, we used to hear a great deal about the 'truth' of religion; now, in this 'age of weak beliefs', the ground has been shifted to its 'usefulness'. Perhaps religion is false, but then perhaps it is still useful. Nowadays men's beliefs are mostly the product of wishful thinking, and not of testing the evidence. It is time to consider

> 'whether all this straining to prop up beliefs which require so great an expense of intellectual toil and ingenuity to keep them standing, yields any sufficient return in human well being'.

Religion, of course, 'may be morally useful without being intellectually sustainable'; can its moral usefulness be made available without its dogmas? First, Mill urges that morality, of which we stand in such admitted need, has traditionally been taught as part of religion, and religion has thus enjoyed

[1] Cf. above, p. 160. [2] Cf. above, p. 168.

all the credit for it. But is this a necessary connexion? Authority, education and public opinion are all-powerful influences; almost any desired result can be obtained by means of them, without supernatural sanctions. Early religious teaching, he concludes, 'has owed its power over mankind rather to its being early than to its being religious'. Primitive men, indeed, would believe no scientific or moral truth unless they deemed it supernaturally imparted or attested, but with more advanced intellects it is otherwise. Shall we now give up the most undoubted moral truths because we believe them to have 'no higher origin than wise and noble human hearts'? No doubt Mill here remembered Comte: remembered that we are now in the third, the 'positive' stage of development, and that theology is superseded 'for all minds at the level of their age'.[1] Christianity—in the sense of the moral precepts of Jesus—holds up a noble and lofty ideal, and we shall not give this up simply because we have outgrown Christian doctrine.

Religion, and poetry, are both natural, if pathetic, attempts to penetrate the unknown by means of imagination; religion is the outcome of our craving for certain knowledge of what we can never certainly know. But we can gain all the elevated sentiment, all the inspiration we need, by trying to idealize and perfect *this earthly life*. Man (he repeats the old slogan) is capable of indefinite improvement, and we shall find enough, and more than enough, to engage our highest powers in working towards this end. While immersed in the task, we may indeed legitimately support ourselves by the idea that (note the juxtapositions) 'Socrates, or Howard, or Washington, or Antoninus, or Christ, would have sympathized with us'; this has been and still may be a wonderful incentive to high endeavour.

> 'The essence of religion is the strong and earnest direction of the emotions and desires towards an ideal object, recognized as one of the highest excellence, and as rightfully paramount over all selfish objects of desire. This condition is fulfilled by the Religion of Humanity in as eminent a degree, and in as high a sense, as by the

[1] Quoted Whittaker, *op. cit.*, ch. iii.

supernatural religions even in their best manifestations, and far more so than in any of their others.'[1]

And it is a *better* religion than all others, for, first, it is disinterested, i.e. it does not rely upon future rewards, and secondly, it is free from the main intellectual difficulty of orthodoxy—that of ascribing perfection to the author of 'so clumsily made and capriciously governed a creation as this planet, and the life of its inhabitants'.

> 'The Author of the Sermon on the Mount is assuredly a far more benignant Being than the author of Nature. But unfortunately, the believer in the christian revelation is obliged to believe that the same being is the author of both.'

Thirdly, it is free from what Mill regards as the *moral* difficulties of the faith: for instance, the belief that salvation depends upon certain conditions which are still unknown to the greater part of humanity, or the belief that God could make a Hell. Only one form of supernatural belief will fit the facts, in Mill's view—the Manichaean doctrine, that Nature and Life are the product, not of omnipotent goodness, but of 'a struggle between contriving goodness and an intractable material'. A man may legitimately believe this if he will (Mill's father did so); in that case, he will feel himself to be 'a fellow-labourer with the Highest'.

What of religion's promise of a future life? Well, as the 'condition of mankind becomes improved', as Mill cannot but think it must, and as men grow more and more unselfish (a man who could believe this has greater faith than most Christians!), they will come to 'care less and less for this flattering expectation':

> 'When mankind cease to need a future existence as a consolation for the sufferings of the present, it will have lost its chief value to them.'

Mankind, even now, 'can perfectly well do without the belief in a heaven'. Mill goes even further, and, like Butler's Erewhonians, conjectures that in a better condition of human

[1] *Three Essays*, p. 109.

life 'not annihilation but immortality may be the burdensome idea'.

3. THEISM

In this, the last and most important of these Essays, Mill asks what foundation there may be for the doctrines of religion 'considered as scientific theorems'—considered, that is, as what they are not and never can be. It is now taken for granted, he begins, that the canons of historical and scientific explanation are applicable over the whole field of experience; what place, then, is there for religious beliefs within this framework? 'We are looking at the subject', he truthfully remarks, 'not from the point of view of reverence, but from that of science'—in other words, in order to 'look at the subject', we will begin by turning our backs towards it. Mill's approach vitiates his argument from the outset, since the fear of the Lord is the beginning of wisdom, and the scientific understanding cannot analyse or replace the insights of religious experience upon which faith is founded. So he proceeds to tap and tap at the unyielding rock. I need not summarize in any detail his refutations of the various arguments for theism. Experience, he argues, does not support the necessity of a First Cause. Matter, or Force, have a better claim to have had 'no beginning' than Mind or Will, both of which in our experience *have* a beginning. Nor does the 'general consent of mankind' give us anything reliable to go upon, nor the argument from 'consciousness', in its Cartesian or Kantian forms. It does not follow that what is desirable is therefore true. When he comes to the argument from design in Nature, however, Mill pauses; he has now reached a type of argument with which he feels at home, one which is truly scientific, grounded upon experience. One would have supposed that Nature had already furnished Mill with a tolerably complete demonstration of atheism; but no, that deeper stratum of veneration for her, which underlay his censures, now crops to the surface. Mill had read Darwin since he wrote the former Essay, and he now finds, after all, that the 'adaptations' in Nature 'afford a large balance of probability in favour of creation by intelligence'. 'Natural selection' and 'the survival of the fittest' he regards as plausible 'recent speculations', though their adequacy to account for 'such truly admirable combinations as some of those in Nature' may long remain doubtful. Darwin's theory, even if admitted, 'would be in no way whatever inconsistent with Creation. But it must be acknowledged that it would greatly attenuate the evidence for it.'

There are then signs everywhere of wisdom and contrivance, even some evidence that the Creator desired the pleasure of His creatures. But Mill returns to his former plea: the evidence points only to a Being of great but limited power; 'any idea of God more captivating than this comes only from human wishes, or from the teaching of either real or imaginary Revelation'. As for Revelation, he affirms with Hume that miracles have no claim to the character of historical facts, and are 'wholly invalid as evidences of any revelation'. Yet Mill's admiration for Christ as a moral teacher constrains him here to make a statement which in its guarded hesitancy contrasts almost ludicrously with the Christian creed, and yet which, coming from Mill, represents an astonishing concession, and no doubt seemed to the more inflexible amongst his followers a sign of weakening powers. There is nothing in the supposition of Christ's divine mission, he says (here are the terrific words)—

'nothing so inherently impossible or absolutely incredible in this supposition as to preclude anyone from hoping that it may perhaps be true.' [1]

Thus at last, at the end of his long career, Mill gives us back an attenuated vestige of religious hope. Man does need, he grants, whatever help he can get from imagination without running counter to fact, and it is wise to make the most of any tenable probability or possibility. The belief in the existence of 'a Being who realizes our own best ideas of perfection'—a belief not utterly without evidence in Nature— 'gives an increase of force to those feelings beyond what they can receive from reference to a merely ideal conception'. As long as we recognize the *power* of the Creator to be limited (he insists upon this), we may legitimately believe

[1] *Three Essays*, p. 240 (my italics).

that His *goodness* is complete. So much for Theism; and now, what of Christianity? Mill has this to say in its favour, that 'it is Christ, rather than God, whom Christianity has held up to believers as the pattern of perfection for humanity. . . . And whatever else may be taken away from us by rational criticism, Christ is still left; a unique figure. . . .' The Christian reader may well feel that in the following utterance Mill's incomprehension becomes almost sublime in its perversity; yet let him—remembering what has led up to it—restrain his ironic sense when he reads that

> '*Religion cannot be said to have made a bad choice in pitching on this man* as the ideal representative and guide of humanity. . . . When to this we add that . . . it remains a possibility that Christ actually was what he supposed himself to be—not God, . . . but a man charged with a special, express and unique commission from God to lead mankind to truth and virtue'—[1]

then, what? Well, such impressions are well fitted to fortify 'that real, though purely human religion, which sometimes calls itself the Religion of Humanity, and sometimes that of Duty'. This 'religion', Mill is sure, is destined, 'with or without supernatural sanctions', to be the religion of the future. But meanwhile the faint supernatural hints he has allowed us may still 'contribute not a little' to give this 'true' religion 'its due ascendancy over the human mind'.

[1] *Ibid.*, p. 255 (my italics).

CHAPTER VII

AUGUSTE COMTE

1. The *Philosophie Positive*

WHO now reads Auguste Comte? Yet this is how G. H. Lewes salutes the *Philosophie Positive* (1830-42):

'A new era has dawned. For the first time in history an explanation of the World, Society and Man is presented which is thoroughly homogeneous, and at the same time thoroughly in accordance with accurate knowledge.'[1]

Never since Bacon's Great Instauration had any thinker announced the final triumph of truth over error in such ringing tones of jubilation as we hear in Comte, and in the acclamation of his disciples. 'A new era has dawned'; the mists of ignorance and delusion have dispersed, and the sun of Truth will henceforth pour upon us, in an endless day of the spirit, its unimpeded light. Why then has the Comtean sun been so soon and so thoroughly eclipsed? A number of causes might be suggested: the verbosity and boring redundancy of his works, his conceit, his excessive love of 'system' —leading in his later phases to something like monomania, and his reactionary propensities, which antagonized his own admirers. Above all he was eclipsed by Marx, who also spoke as one having authority, and whose doctrines, unlike Comte's, could serve immediately as the platform of a political party. Comte was a far more comprehensive thinker than Marx, but he left unanswered the great immediate question 'where do we go from *here*?', and so his colossal effort proved an Icarus-flight. Of his *Politique*, for instance, Lewes can write that there are no traces of insanity in it, as some had thought, and that he can now read it without disapproval as a Utopia. For the purposes of our present studies, however, the very causes which made Comte suspect to Mill, to

[1] *History of Philosophy from Thales to Comte* (5th ed., 1880), vol. ii, p. 690.

Lewes or to John Morley are those which render him a figure of salient and symbolic interest. For he alone, of those whose initial momentum came from the French Revolution, could ride with equal confidence the ensuing wave of reaction, and then, rising above the contemporary confusion, could reconcile conflicting tendencies in a new synthesis, combining much that was best in the past and in the present. He alone, of all the world-betterers and clean-sweepers, saw clearly that the new world must have a religion, and, since according to his philosophy the old one was necessarily dead, set himself to found a new one. It was this attempt above all which ruined his prestige; the materialists and infidels thought him crazy, and the orthodox thought him a blasphemous impostor. Nevertheless it is precisely this attempt (whatever we may think of the Positive 'Religion' as such) which makes it possible to regard Comte as the central figure of his century—of the century whose special problem was the reconciling of destruction with reconstruction, negation with affirmation, science with religion, the head with the heart, the past with the present, order with progress. My account of him will pretend to no completeness; it is intended mainly as an introduction to the study of some English writers (George Eliot in particular) who were either actually influenced by him, or whose intellectual trend was in the same direction. Comte is, in a sense, the century in epitome, so that to study him is to find the clue to much that the *Zeitgeist*, in a less systematic way, was doing through other minds and in other countries.

Comte may be regarded as a nineteenth century Schoolman, and his system as a *Summa* based, not on dogmatic theology, but on dogmatic science. He aimed at a systematic unification of all known truth on the basis of scientific method, and his proudest claim was to have completed the synthesis by extending this method to the fields of History, Politics and Morals, and thereby creating the new science of *Sociology*. First he constructs a hierarchy of the sciences in a dependent series, beginning with Mathematics, and proceeding through Astronomy, Physics and Chemistry to Biology (ending with Cerebral Physiology), and so on to

Sociology. His claim to have made Sociology for the first time a 'positive' science brings us to his most celebrated 'discovery', the *Loi des Trois États*, or the law of the three necessary stages in the evolution of human opinion, and so of society: he calls this 'my discovery of the law of human development'. The three stages, as mentioned above, are the Theological, the Metaphysical and the Positive. In the Theological, natural phenomena are ascribed to the volitions of supernatural beings, political events are attributed to providential superintendence, and governors are held to rule by divine right. In the Metaphysical stage, supernatural power is superseded by abstract 'principles' or 'forces'; 'Nature' replaces 'God'; political power is now based on natural right and popular sovereignty. In the Positive stage, the metaphysical entities have followed the gods into twilight. Forswearing as fruitless all enquiries into first or final causes, men now explain all facts in relation simply to each other, and in relation to more general facts, and social phenomena are studied in exactly the same way as those of chemistry or physics. J. H. Bridges illustrates the three stages as follows:

> 'Take the phenomenon of the sleep produced by opium. The Arabs are content to attribute it to the "will of God". Molière's medical student accounts for it by a *soporific principle* contained in the opium. The modern physiologist knows that he cannot account for it at all. He can simply observe, analyse and experiment upon the phenomena attending the action of the drug, and classify it with other agents analogous in character.'[1]

It was the aim of the Positive Philosophy to hasten the advent of the third stage in Europe by bringing Sociology within the same homogeneous system as the sciences which had already become positive (including Biology, which itself had only just reached that stage).

> 'This, then, is the Positive Philosophy', says G. H. Lewes, 'the extension to *all* investigations of those methods which have been proved successful in the physical sciences—*the transformation of Science into Philosophy*—the condensation of all knowledge into a

---

[1] Quoted by J. Morley in *Encycl. Brit.*, art. on Comte (11th ed.).

homogeneous body of doctrine, capable of supplying a Faith and consequently a Polity.'[1]

Positivism must rule the future; there can be no doubt of that. It is true that the quest for first and final causes is abandoned, but it was always a hopeless quest; 'it is no use asking for better bread than can be made of wheat'[2], and philosophy must simply give up such pretensions. The theological and metaphysical modes of thought are 'unfit for modern use'.

But Comte, like Marx in this respect, is no mere systematic 'explainer' of phenomena; he wants above all to *change* the world. Far more than Mill, he is a 'reformer of thought for the sake of action'. 'The theological base of the old "organic" order as it stood having been irrevocably destroyed by criticism, the problem is to find for the new order a positive base that shall be indestructible by criticism because it is perfectly rational.'[3] Applying to social development the conception of an unvarying law of consequences (derived from the physical sciences), Comte sees in the contemporary situation an intellectual and moral anarchy caused by the destruction of the 'theological' by the 'metaphysical'. This crisis can only be ended by a mighty constructive effort, in a word, by the emergence of Positivism. Of this transitional chaos the type-example, for Comte, was the French Revolution, but in his view the 'metaphysical' (or 'critical') phase began with Protestantism, and had been corroding the 'theological' ever since. His insight seems to me to appear conspicuously in his exposure of the transitory (shall we say 'dialectical') character of the Revolutionary programme. The Revolution appealed to principles which were necessarily invoked in order to destroy the old régime, but which, erected into dogmas, have themselves become obstructive to true progress. For example, there was (i) 'Liberty': yes! liberty from theological fetters certainly, but not liberty now and henceforth to think and do as we like! What is now needed is *control*: control by the few select minds (cf. Mill's 'highly gifted and instructed One or Few'), which alone can

---

[1] *Op. cit.*, p. 733 (second italics mine).
[2] *Ibid.*   [3] Whittaker, *op. cit.*, p. 40.

grasp the true laws of sociology. There was (ii) 'Nationality': this principle was necessary enough as an inspiration to the peoples engaged in the struggle against Napoleon, but its persistent survival has dragged Europe into reaction and international chaos. Or (iii) 'Popular Sovereignty': an advance on 'divine right' admittedly, but it leads now to 'careerism' and corruption. Moreover, being in antagonism to a bad old order, the Revolution represented all political authority as bad, and tried to reduce it to a mere police-force. (iv) 'Freedom of Enquiry': admirable—how else could my present work have been produced? But 'social order must ever be incompatible with a perpetual discussion of the foundations of society'[1]—a remark which indicates a point of cleavage between Comte and Mill. (v) 'Equality': but men are *not* equal.

At present, then, we are living uncomfortably wedged between two decaying systems (for the 'theological' has only been scotched, not destroyed); during their unconscionably protracted decline they maintain an uneasy equilibrium by mutual antagonism, the reactionary party idealizing the past and the revolutionaries despising it. The historic rôle of the 'metaphysical' doctrine was

> 'to break up a system which, having directed the early growth of the human mind and society, tended to protract that infantile period: and thus, the political triumph of the metaphysical school was a necessary preparation for the advent of the positive school, for which the task is exclusively reserved of *terminating the revolutionary period by the formation of a system uniting Order with Progress.*'[2]

The Positive Philosophy will transcend the old antithesis; it will unite past and present into a harmonious whole, recognizing 'the fundamental law of continuous human development', and seeing 'the existing evolution as the necessary result of

> the gradual series of former transformations, by simply extending

---

[1] For this whole passage cf. Harriet Martineau's translation of the *Philosophie* (1875 ed.), vol. ii, bk. 6, i.
[2] *Ibid.*, p. 9 (my italics).

to social phenomena the spirit which governs the treatment of all other natural phenomena.'

Comte's desire to terminate anarchy and build a New Order may seem to classify him, for good or ill, as a forerunner of the anti-liberal doctrines of our own time. In a broad sense this is true, but his 'Utopia', as we shall see, resembled the mediaeval order rather than any of our modern dictatorships. His call for the surrender of the 'vagabond liberty of individual minds' has, to English ears, an unpleasantly authoritarian ring; we can picture Mill's disapproval when he read that

> 'the requisite convergence of the best minds cannot be obtained without the voluntary renunciation, on the part of most of them, of their sovereign rights of free enquiry, which they will doubtless be willing to abdicate, as soon as they have found organs worthy to exercise appropriately their vain provisional supremacy.'[1]

It was, in fact, Comte's passion for unity and system, his desire to direct all social forces to some one end, that Mill instinctively suspected.[2] Indeed, to pass from Comte to Mill is to leave the Continental Autobahn for the winding English lanes. We notice, without surprise, that Comte disapproved of England; this intellectual Napoleon found, to his annoyance, that England remained outside the Continental System, and almost upset his classifications. He had to invent a new sub-stage to account for England; we have never, in this island, shown the correct antithesis between the theological and metaphysical phases: we have only had, instead, The British Constitution. Comte's scathing language on this theme expresses his disgust at our non-compliance with his clear-cut sequences; the British Constitution is only an accidental product of peculiar insular-Protestant conditions, and is inapplicable to any European state. He hated Protestantism as much as England, and for similar reasons: both stood for a compromise which, in so far as it worked

---

[1] *Ibid.*, pp. 25-6.
[2] See his letter to Gustave d'Eichtal, Oct. 8, 1829, quoted von Hayek, *op. cit.* (Introd.).

successfully, spoilt the symmetry of his historical theory. England, he says elsewhere, is worse than Venice in its national selfishness and organized hypocrisy; what a good thing, he adds, that Protestantism was not universally adopted! for then it might have been deemed a satisfactory solution of the issue.[1]

All previous attempts at Sociology, from Aristotle to Condorcet, had left it a pseudo-science, bearing the same relation to true science as alchemy to chemistry; it was a mere blend of theological-metaphysical notions and 'absolutes'. Statesmen and politicians still imagine that social phenomena can be modified at will as by some philosopher's stone:

> 'Banished for ever from all other classes of speculation, in principle at least, the old philosophies now prevail in social science alone; and it is from this domain that they have to be excluded, by the conception of the social movement being subject to invariable natural laws, instead of to any will whatever.' [2]

Political action may help processes already at work, but no more; it cannot alter the main trends, which are fixed by natural laws. Statesmen who think they are 'altering' these trends are themselves only puppets of the Immanent Will (Comte would have been horrified by Hardy's phrase, yet it is hard to see how his 'invariable natural laws' differ from such a 'metaphysical' notion). 'Great men' are far less important than 'Trends'—hence the frequency with which several hit on the same discovery at about the same time; it would have been made by someone else if none of them had lived. Comte thought it indisputable that 'development' ('social dynamics') has been accompanied by 'improvement', and cites Lamarck's authority for the effect of continual exercise in producing, in any animal, and especially in Man, an organic improvement transmissible to offspring. He also thought it indisputable (alas, the nineteenth century!) that 'the gradual development of humanity favours a growing preponderance of the noblest tendencies of our nature'.

---
[1] *Catechism of Positive Religion*, trans. by Richard Congreve (1858), Conclusion.
[2] H. Martineau, *op. cit.*, p. 70.

11. The *Politique Positive* and 'The Religion of Humanity'

During the ten years between the completion of the *Cours de Philosophie Positive* (1842) and the appearance of the first volume of the *Système de Politique Positive* (1852), Comte underwent what has been called a 'mental revolution'. Certainly he was then transformed from a philosopher into a pontiff; but it is probable that the 'break' has been exaggerated by those of his admirers who disliked the transition. There was in fact no real break; the elements of his 'polity' and 'religion' are present already in his earlier writings. Two great emotional crises at this time unquestionably gave to his later thinking an authority and conviction it might otherwise have lacked: in 1842 he was separated from his wife, with whom he had been unhappy from the year of their marriage (1825), and in 1845 he met and fell Dantesquely in love with Clotilde de Vaux, 'a lady whose husband had been sentenced to the galleys for life'. We know little of her beyond what he has told us, but that is all we need to know. His language about her far exceeds in exaltation, though it inevitably recalls, that of Mill about Mrs Taylor (who is described in the *Autobiography* as 'greatly the superior' of both Carlyle and Mill himself—'more a poet than he, and more a thinker than I'). Clotilde was the 'incomparable angel' who, after his long years of intellectual strain and unsatisfied affection, at last brought him 'new birth'. 'Above all women that I have read of in the past, have seen in the present, or can conceive in the future', she was Beatrice to his Dante (his own parallel). However, he is anxious to show that this *vita nuova* completed, without contradicting, all his previous efforts. Speaking of the unity and continuity of his career,[1] he says that his object throughout has been to elaborate 'a sound Philosophy, capable of supplying the foundation of true Religion'—this has been, indeed, 'the exceptional part assigned to me by the evolution of Humanity'. In his 'first life' he had to lay the speculative founda-

[1] Pref. to vol. i of the *Politique* (1851), trans. by J. H. Bridges, 1875.

tions, and show the superiority of Positivism over all theology, but in his new life, and in the present treatise,

> 'where the moral excellence of true Religion is illustrated, Feeling takes the first place. *The disastrous revolt of Reason against Feeling will never be terminated till the new Western priesthood can fully satisfy the claims of modern Intellect. But this being done, moral requirements at once reassume the place that belongs to them*; since in the construction of a really complete synthesis, Love is naturally the one universal principle' [my italics].

This 'proved religion' shows itself 'capable of superseding Revealed Religion at all points.' (We may note in passing, as an indication of Comte's exalted mood, that this Preface is dated—in accordance with the Positivist Calendar— '23 Aristotle, 63': i.e. 63 years since 1788, = 20 March 1851).

Comte was granted only one *annus mirabilis*: in a twelve-month Clotilde died. But his chaste and devout affection lived on, and 'the remainder of his life was a perpetual hymn to her memory'. He settled down to a daily routine of monastic simplicity and concentration, rising each morning at 5 for prayer, and devoting the day, until 7 p.m., to meditation and writing, with intervals for the reading of the *Imitation of Christ*, Dante and Homer. In the evenings, from 7 till 9, and on Sunday afternoons, he would receive visitors; on Wednesday afternoons he visited the tomb of Clotilde. The days were rounded off with prayer, and bed at 10.

> 'Love, then, is our principle; Order our basis; and Progress our end.'

Comte's religion has been described as 'Catholicism minus Christianity', or alternatively, 'Catholicism plus Science', and these phrases may serve to emphasize the synthetic and unifying power of Comte's mind, whereby he was able, much more fully than Mill or Carlyle, to reconcile the conflicting forces of his century, blending 'progress' with 'order', science with religion, and 'the march of mind' with the spirit of the Middle Ages. Condorcet and De Maistre coalesce in Comte. As revolutionary he proclaims the death of the old theological and metaphysical régimes; as counter-revolutionary he sees that, though errors must be swept away, there was in the old order 'something more noble and beautiful than that which seemed to be taking its place'.[1] The Middle Ages had the right structure and aims, but false beliefs; the modern world has the right beliefs but no structure or sense of direction: the solution is, then, to unite the new truth with the old order. This is what Comte attempts to do in the *Politique*, and in the foundation of the Religion of Humanity.[2]

First, having allowed the intellect the most all-embracing freedom and scope in the philosophical field, he now acknowledges the supremacy of the affections over the 'head'; 'greater distinctness', as he puts it, 'is given to the truth that the affective element predominates in our nature'. Positivism now turns to the task of devising 'a system which regulates the whole course of our private and public existence, by bringing Feeling, Reason and Activity into permanent harmony'. The positive spirit could not organize practical life 'until the science of Sociology had been formed; and this was done by my discovery of the law of historical development'. In future, the grand principle will be the subordination of all thought, all intellect, to the moral principle; men of science will become philosophers, and philosophers 'Priests'. Life thus becomes 'a continuous and intense act of worship'. The grand aims, to which all effort is now to be directed, are the amelioration of the order of Nature where that order is at once most imperfect and most modifiable, i.e. human society; and the triumph of social feeling (altruism) over self-love: 'Live for Others' becomes the great, the only really human, maxim. In the Middle Ages Christianity and Chivalry attempted these tasks: moral progress *was* then the aim, and Politics *were* subordinate to Morals; the Positive Religion which supersedes Christianity, however, comprises all that was wise and true in the 'partial' or 'special'

---

[1] Whittaker, *op. cit.*, p. 63.

[2] The ensuing summary is based on (*a*) ch. vi of the *General View of Positivism*, prefixed to vol. i of the *Politique* (1851), trans. by Bridges; (*b*) *The Catechism of Positive Religion*, trans. by Richard Congreve (1858).

religions, without the associated errors and superstitions. It recognizes that natural laws, unlike the Fate of polytheism, the divine will of theism, or the 'necessity' of metaphysics, are modifiable by man; man is indeed at once the product and the changer of his environment. He changes the real by developing it in accordance with its own laws.

But (asks the Lady of the Priest in the Catechism), does the Positive Religion, perhaps, puff up the intellect and dry up the heart? No, my daughter, the Priest (Comte) replies; on the contrary, it appeals to the heart through *the great conception of Humanity*, or the *Great Being*. By this grand idea 'the conception of God will be entirely superseded'; here at last is the true object of worship, recognizable as real, yet demanding as much reverence and devoted service as any theological fiction. Hitherto men have worshipped imaginary beings, vainly endeavouring 'to see without them what had no existence but within'. Positivism, on the other hand, offers a new Divinity which, instead of subsisting in 'solemn inaction' like the old Supreme Being, is alive and present and dynamic, and which, moreover, depends for its very existence upon the *love* of its worshippers. 'Humanity' differs from all previous gods in its very need of our service, in the pathos of its appeal to us to preserve it and make it more god-like; in the Positive Religion alone, 'the object of worship is a Being whose nature is relative, modifiable and perfectible'. It is in this way that by the new worship we are at the same time producing Progress, which is 'the development of Order under the influence of Love'. Positivism is superior to all former religions because it has an object which is 'real', because it satisfies the intellect as well as the heart, and because, instead of separating the life of action from the life of faith, it unifies them. Unlike Catholicism, it admits the existence of disinterested affection as a genuine fact of human nature; the triumph of altruism over egoism will really be possible when Positive education is brought into play, and when Industry—the modern counterpart of the military caste—has been disciplined as the military have always been. Subordinating all things to morality, it will embrace the Arts, as well as Philosophy and Politics.

Free from its theological fetters, Art will be able to follow spontaneously its natural vocation of 'idealising real life', and poetry will become the soul of worship. 'The poet is now called to his true mission, which is to give beauty and grandeur to human life, by inspiring a deeper sense of our relation to Humanity.'

But while emphasizing the superiority of Positivism, Comte is anxious to show that it is the true successor of Catholicism; his admiration for the mediaeval effort is profound, and his hope is 'to renew that attempt upon a sounder basis, and with surer prospects of success'. Catholicism became hostile to the progress it had itself initiated, and the intellect fell into disharmony with the heart. Positivism overcomes this by its new Priesthood, who are to be the intellectual leaders as well as the moral guides of the new order, and by the consecration of science 'as the source from which the universal religion receives its principles'. Positivism accepts the mediaeval distinction between Temporal and Spiritual power, and the new Spiritual Power, the scientific Priesthood, will be kept distinct and separate from all political powers; it will exercise its influence over society mainly through the systematic control of education, as well as by the organization and maintenance of public worship and festivals. Its authority and prestige will be upheld—and here we come to a highly characteristic part of Comte's teaching—by the influence of *Women*. At the break-up of the Middle Ages, the advance of pure intellect and the preoccupation with practical and material ends led to neglect of morality and a decline in love; throughout the period of modern anarchy, however, women have unconsciously preserved the best mediaeval traditions, and so have helped to save moral culture. With women, the 'consecration of the rational and imaginative faculties to the service of feeling has always existed spontaneously', and now that the subordination of intellect to heart has become the grand ruling principle, women will assume their rightful place of honour and veneration, lending their incomparable influence over private life to the support of the priestly educators. 'Humanity' itself, on the new symbolic Flag of Positivism, will be depicted as a young mother, carrying her infant son; the worship of the Virgin Mary may thus prove another connecting link between Catholicism and Positivism—the Virgin coming to be regarded as the personification of Humanity.

In the new order, human effort replaces 'Providence'; accepting the truths of science, Positivism teaches that 'we must look to our own unremitting activity for the only providence by which the rigour of our destiny can be alleviated'. Heaven will not help us, so we must help ourselves. The new human Providence has four main sub-sections: Women are the Moral Providence, the Priesthood the Intellectual Providence, the Patriciate (capitalists) the Material, and the Proletariat the General. 'The people represent the activity of the Supreme Being, as women represent its sympathy, and philosophers its intellect.' In an ideal order the spiritual power would suffice, and rank would correspond to merit; this ideal must ever be kept in view. But at present the social functions of rank and wealth must be recognized: 'that function is not to be destroyed, but to be improved and regulated'. The capitalists or Patriciate (and this is naturally pounced upon by Marxist critics when 'unmasking' Comte) are 'the nutritive reservoirs, the social efficiency of which mainly depends on their being concentrated in few hands'. Only moral suasion must temper 'their foolish and immoral pride'; if they resist, the spiritual power will condemn them, and this excommunication, when supported by the workers of each city and 'the women of every family', would be 'difficult to withstand'. Education will develop the realization that property involves social obligations not to be repudiated, and that labour is service, not to be fobbed off with money-payments and without 'gratitude'. The philosopher-priests, like the workers, are to have 'as little to do with wealth as with government'; they will form a married but propertyless caste, not even inheriting wealth from their own families—though they will receive sufficient remuneration on a fixed scale: £120 for 'aspirants', £240 for 'vicars', £480 for 'priests', and £2400 for The High Priest (i.e. Comte and all succeeding popes). Women, as a virtual priesthood, will also renounce property, together with inheritance and dowries; they must have no jobs or career away from The Home.

All these arrangements presuppose the reduction of the over-sized nation-states which arose after the collapse of the admirable mediaeval order—an order which he conceives as a voluntary union, founded on a common faith and a common priesthood, between nations which possessed quite as much independence as they needed or desired. Europe, he forecasts, will become a vast confederation of small republics: France will break up into 17 before the end of the nineteenth century; Ireland, and even Scotland and Wales, will separate from England (thus *one* item of the prophecy has not been falsified). This proliferation of small states will restore true patriotism by linking the family sentiment with love of 'country'. The old revolutionists expected us to rise without a break from primitive self-love to universal benevolence, but this soon degenerates into a 'vague and barren philanthropy': it is the home affections which most effectively temper the pride of intellect, and the positive polity and worship aim to develop these feelings. The new Western Republic, or federation, will have a common religious basis, a common priesthood, a common currency, weights and measures, but no political unity—though its spiritual centre will naturally tend to be Paris; no one power will possess or seek hegemony. After the establishment of the Republic in France, the Positivist International Council will send out missionaries to rope in first the West, then Russia, then the Mohammedans, the Hindoos and even negroes.

The cult of 'Sociolatry' (Comte's own term) is expressed and symbolized, and its necessary emotions fostered, by the private and public worship of the Religion of Humanity. Private worship (the foundation of Sociolatry) is based on 'the adoration of the best types we can find to personify Humanity', that is, on the worship of Woman as the domestic goddess: the 'Guardian Angels' being Mother (veneration), Wife (attachment) and Daughter (Kindness). We virtually adore our own family circle (the feminine part of it *par excellence*), and if our own family happens to be composed of 'bad elements' we must simply 're-create it subjectively'. (On hearing this, the 'Lady' in the *Positive Catechism* says 'These remarks complete the subject'.) There is prayer on waking, at midday, and on retiring to rest—that is, invocation of the angels. Prayer, as he wisely says, should not be 'asking for things': 'in prayer we identify ourselves more and more with the Being we adore'; in praying we should be loving, thinking and acting all at once. We may 'aid our effusions', especially at midday, with 'a judicious choice of passages from the poets'—and 'none but great poets are of use': the others do more harm than good. There are the nine 'social sacraments': *Presentation* (baptism); *Initiation* at the age of fourteen (confirmation), when the child passes into the hands of the priests to have its heart strengthened against its intellect; *Admission* at twenty-one, when he is authorized to serve Humanity; *Destination* at twenty-eight (choice of career, or ordination); *Marriage* (for men not before 28, for women 21); *Maturity*, lasting twenty-one years; *Retirement*, at sixty-three; *Transformation* (extreme unction, but without the loneliness of the Catholics' 'horrible ceremony'); and *Incorporation*, seven years after death (canonization). Positivist marriage involves 'eternal widowhood'—there are no second marriages, and divorce is allowed only in cases like Clotilde's.

The Public Worship is based on the new Positivist Calendar which replaces the Church Calendar. In this worship Humanity (symbolized by Mother and Child) is adored in a series of four-week Festivals dedicated to the various fundamental social relationships—marriage, Paternal and Filial, Fraternal, Master and Servant, etc.—and to the successive stages in the evolution of man: Fetichism, Polytheism and Monotheism (the latter subdivided into theocratic, catholic, Mohammedan and metaphysical). Amongst the long list of Positivist 'saints' St Paul appears, but not Christ. The Arts are called in to give the utmost ritual grandeur to these Static and Dynamic Festivals which will celebrate social order and progress.

By all these and many other means of grace the grand conceptions of solidarity (living for others) and continuity (living in the past and in the future) are kept ever-present before all minds, and the victory of the sympathetic feelings is assured. Comte assumes that science has settled the age-old controversy about human nature (its 'goodness' or 'depravity') by *demonstrating* the real existence of the altruistic instincts. Whereas theology always spoke as though we had none but bad passions, and no instincts of sympathy and benevolence, Gall the phrenologist has shown that there is an 'organ' of benevolence in the brain; moreover, the 'imaginary conflict between nature and grace' is now (phrenologically) superseded by the 'real' opposition between the posterior part of the brain—the seat of our personal instincts—and its anterior region, the seat both of our sympathetic impulses and of our intellectual faculties. 'Such is the indestructible basis on which, as founder of Positive religion, I proceeded to construct my systematic theory of the brain and the soul'.

And now (as Comte says at the end of the *Catechism*) 'Humanity definitively occupies the place of God', but—he graciously adds—'she does not forget the services which the idea of God provisionally rendered'.

It is proper to mention, if only to forestall the malicious, that Comte was for three months of his life insane, following gross overwork and the shock of his unhappy marriage. But he had no other such collapse, and his work—even the *Politique*—is not the work of a madman, unless it be madness to be always serious, always on the stretch, and never to be visited by one qualm of irony or one glint of humour. He was a joyless, self-intoxicated doctrinaire, no doubt; he moved inexorably along mental tramlines, and so could never deviate from his own groove enough to ask the fundamental, the damaging questions: *can* science be itself a philosophy? *can* we dispense with metaphysical enquiry? *can* we go on worshipping ourselves? Yet the scope and nobility of his system, the profundity of his historical generalizations, and the wisdom of many of his doctrines, are undeniable, and we are still awaiting the *Summa* he adumbrates. We may fitly conclude this sketch by recalling, as a message of special importance for our time, his hope that Positivism, by linking

AUGUSTE COMTE

the social system with the sciences, would revitalize science itself and abolish barren specialization:

> 'Special studies carried on without regard for the encyclopaedic principles which determine the relative value of knowledge, and its bearing on human life, will soon be condemned by all men of right feeling and good sense.'

CHAPTER VIII

GEORGE ELIOT: HENNELL, STRAUSS AND FEUERBACH

1. Introductory

F. W. H. MYERS, in an oft-quoted passage, has recorded a conversation with George Eliot at Cambridge in 1873, and I venture, on account of its high relevance, to quote it once again as a text for this chapter:

'I remember how, at Cambridge, I walked with her once in the Fellows' Garden of Trinity, on an evening of rainy May; and she, stirred somewhat beyond her wont, and taking as her text the three words which have been used so often as the inspiring trumpet-calls of men,—the words *God, Immortality, Duty,*—pronounced, with terrible earnestness, how inconceivable was the *first,* how unbelievable the *second,* and yet how peremptory and absolute the *third.* Never, perhaps, have sterner accents affirmed the sovereignty of impersonal and unrecompensing Law. I listened, and night fell; her grave, majestic countenance turned towards me like a Sibyl's in the gloom; it was as though she withdrew from my grasp, one by one, the two scrolls of promise, and left me the third scroll only, awful with inevitable fates. And when we stood at length and parted, amid that columnar circuit of the forest-trees, beneath the last twilight of starless skies, I seemed to be gazing, like Titus at Jerusalem, on vacant seats and empty halls,—on a sanctuary with no Presence to hallow it, and heaven left lonely of a God.'[1]

In the present book, which attempts to follow some of the main currents of thought and belief in nineteenth century England, George Eliot must needs occupy a central place. Probably no English writer of the time, and certainly no novelist, more fully epitomizes the century; her development is a paradigm, her intellectual biography a graph, of

[1] *Essays—Modern* (1883), pp. 268-9.

GEORGE ELIOT: HENNELL, STRAUSS, FEUERBACH

its most decided trend. Starting from evangelical Christianity, the curve passes through doubt to a reinterpreted Christ and a religion of humanity: beginning with God, it ends in Duty. George Eliot's representative quality is due largely to her unique position, amongst imaginative writers, as a focus for the best (and the worst) that was being said and thought in her time, in Europe as well as at home. No one was more thoroughly abreast of the newest thought, the latest French or German theory, the last interpretations of dogma, the most up-to-date results in anthropology, medicine, biology or sociology; it is she who first translates Strauss's *Life of Jesus* and Feuerbach's *Essence of Christianity*; if a Mackay writes *The Progress of the Intellect* (1850), it is Miss Evans who must review it for the *Westminster*. She was the first English writer to bring an intellect of that calibre to the service of fiction, and the wonder perhaps is that this preponderant cerebration did not devour her creative instinct more completely than it did. But as with Wordsworth, whom she greatly reverenced and in some ways resembled, the heart in her was kept alive by the recollection of her early life, and of the scenes and people associated with the feelings of childhood. In a sense her early novels are her *Prelude*, that is, the means by which she pierced below the hard crust formed by the years of translating, reviewing and mental overforcing, to the quickening beds of heartfelt memory which lay beneath. Having achieved this recovery of time past, she was then able to see in truer perspective the relations between advancing intellect and backward-yearning affections. From the very outset, however, she showed the instinct—which was deeply imbedded in the consciousness of the century as a whole—to see both sides of any question: to tolerate the ordinary while admiring the ideal, to cling to the old while accepting the new, to retain the core of traditions while mentally criticizing their forms. She succeeded, better than J. S. Mill, in uniting what he described as the two main streams of the nineteenth century mind—its two kinds of one-sidedness—the Benthamite, which stands outside and tests all received opinions, and the Coleridgean, which tries from within to discover what is true in them. We see this action and reaction going on both in her own life and in the novels. From the latter let us here take two preliminary examples—the first, significantly enough, from the very opening of her first fiction:

'Shepperton Church was a very different looking building five-and-twenty years ago. To be sure, its substantial stone tower looks at you through its intelligent eye, the clock, with the friendly expression of former days; but in everything else what changes! Now there is a wide span of slated roof flanking the old steeple; the windows are tall and symmetrical, the outer doors are resplendent with oak-graining, the inner doors reverentially noiseless with a garment of red baize; and the walls, you are convinced, no lichen will ever again effect a settlement upon—they are smooth and innutrient as the summit of the Rev. Amos Barton's head, after ten years of baldness and supererogatory soap. Pass through the baize doors and you will see the nave filled with well-shaped benches, understood to be free seats; while in certain eligible corners, less directly under the fire of the clergyman's eye, there are pews reserved for the Shepperton gentility. Ample galleries are supported on iron pillars, and in one of them stands the crowning glory, the very clasp or aigrette of Shepperton church-adornment—namely, an organ, not very much out of repair, on which a collector of small rents, differentiated by the force of circumstances into an organist, will accompany the alacrity of your departure after the blessing, by a sacred minuet or an easy "Gloria".

'Immense improvement! says the well-regulated mind, which unintermittingly rejoices in the New Police, the Tithe Commutation Act, the penny post, and all guarantees of human advancement, and has no moments when conservative-reforming intellect does a little Toryism by the sly, revelling in regret that dear, old, brown, crumbling, picturesque inefficiency is everywhere giving place to spick-and-span new-painted, new-varnished efficiency, which will yield endless diagrams, plans, elevations, and sections, but alas! no picture. Mine, I fear, is not a well-regulated mind: it has an occasional tenderness for old abuses; it lingers with a certain fondness over the days of nasal clerks and top-booted parsons, and has a sigh for the departed shades of vulgar errors.'[1]

[1] *Scenes of Clerical Life*, p. 1.

GEORGE ELIOT: HENNELL, STRAUSS, FEUERBACH

The second illustration is from *The Mill on the Floss*:

> 'Very commonplace, even ugly, that furniture of our early home might look if it were put up to auction; an improved taste in upholstery scorns it; and is not the striving after something better and better in our surroundings, the grand characteristic that distinguishes man from the brute . . . ? But Heaven knows where that striving might lead us, if our affections had not a trick of twining round those old inferior things—if the loves and sanctities of our life had no deep immovable roots in memory.'[1]

In what follows I hope to suggest that this 'conservative-reforming' impulse was the leading *motif* of her life: that her lifelong quest, as it was Comte's and the century's, was for a reconcilement between these opposites, a synthesis (as Comte would say) between the Static and Dynamic principles, between Order and Progress, Tradition and Enlightenment, the heart and the head. In the foregoing chapter I have considered Comte as at once a symbol and a producer of the intellectual climate of the mid-century—of that climate in which, after emerging from her provincial-evangelical chrysalis, George Eliot lived and moved. Though Comte made his impact upon her in due time (mainly, at first, through G. H. Lewes), this was not until the shape of her mind had already been formed in other moulds. I want now to consider three of these early formative influences, in the order in which they affected her: Charles Hennell, D. F. Strauss and Ludwig Feuerbach.

II. Charles Hennell's *Inquiry Concerning the Origin of Christianity* (1838)

Readers of George Eliot's *Life* know how immediately and decisively the reading of Hennell's book in 1841 changed her outlook. It was through this book, and the associated influences of the congenial philosophic circle at Rosehill, that she first encountered the 'higher criticism'. She 'fell for' it as instantaneously as Robert Elsmere succumbed to

---

[1] Bk. ii, ch. i (p. 173 in World's Classics ed.).

the arguments of Wendover in Mrs Humphry Ward's novel. Up till then this Theresa of the Midland flats had been seeking, through evangelical strictness and renunciation, the fulfilment of her yearnings after spiritual grandeur: not looking for earthly bliss, 'but considering this life merely a pilgrimage'. This spiritual tone, which was acquired, not from her own home circle at Griff (her father was an old-fashioned Tory Churchman), but from her school teachers Miss Lewis and the Misses Franklin, showed itself in a tendency to self-abnegation, characteristically accompanied, however, by a longing for distinction in sanctity, a desire to render some signal service which should be commensurate with her inner sense of superiority. 'Oh to be doing some little toward the regeneration of this groaning, travailing creation!'[1] On her first visit to London (Aug. 1838) with her brother Isaac, she was 'not delighted with the stir of the great Babel', and refused to accompany him to any theatres, spending her evenings alone reading. We find her, at this time, highly enjoying Hannah More's letters: 'the contemplation of so blessed a character as hers', she tells Miss Lewis, 'is very salutary'.[2] 'I was once told', she goes on, 'that there was nothing out of myself to prevent my becoming as eminently holy as St Paul; and though I think that is too sweeping an assertion, yet it is very certain we are generally too low in our aims, more anxious for safety than sanctity, for place than purity.' (How revealing are those alliterations that insist on creeping in, even in so exalted a passage!) She begins to read the Life of Wilberforce, and finds a similarity,

> 'if I may compare myself with such a man, between his temptations, or rather *besetments*, and my own, that makes his experience very interesting to me. Oh that I might be made as useful in my lowly and obscure station as he was in the exalted one assigned to him! I feel myself to be a mere cumberer of the ground. May the Lord give me such an insight into what is truly good, that I may not rest with making Christianity a mere addendum to my pursuits, or with tacking it as a fringe to my garments! May I seek to be

[1] Cross's *Life*, vol. i, p. 91 (1885 ed.). [2] *Ibid.*, p. 41.

GEORGE ELIOT: HENNELL, STRAUSS, FEUERBACH

sanctified wholly! My nineteenth birthday will soon be here (the 22nd)—an awakening signal.'[1]

Just before the actual awakening signal arrived (from Hennell, however), her mind, she says, was

'an assemblage of disjointed specimens of history, ancient and modern; scraps of poetry picked up from Shakespeare, Cowper, Wordsworth, and Milton; newspaper topics; morsels of Addison and Bacon, Latin verbs, geometry, entomology, and chemistry; Reviews and metaphysics'—

all petrified by daily cares, household worries and vexations. Let us think of her, as we take leave of these early scenes, in the characteristic posture of attacking Mrs Somerville's *Connection of the Physical Sciences*, and at the same time 'boiling currant jelly . . . and I grieve to say I have not gone through it so cheerfully as the character of a Christian who professes to do *all*, even the most trifling, duty as the Lord demands'.[2]

Into this mental conglomerate Hennell's book descended like a bomb. Charles Christian Hennell (1809-1850) was the son of a Manchester Unitarian business man, and himself spent most of his short life in various commercial houses in London, devoting his leisure to science, theology, German, Italian and music. He, and his sisters Caroline, Sara and Mary, and his brother-in-law Charles Bray (of Rosehill, Coventry)—that is, Miss Evans's inmost circle of friends after 1841—form a remarkable little intellectual élite, whose appearance in the mid-century speaks well for the culture of provincial England at the time. The Hennells were Unitarians of the school of Priestley and Belsham, and when in 1836 Caroline married Charles Bray, there was probably some family anxiety lest her piety might be undermined by that notorious free-thinker and phrenologist. Nor was this alarm groundless, for on their honeymoon in Wales Charles Bray tried to convert her to his views, having brought with

---

[1] *Ibid.*, p. 43.
[2] *Ibid.*, pp. 69-70. The currant jelly, she says, has made her hand ' tremulous ': hence, no doubt, the defective construction of the above-quoted sentence.

him for that purpose 'Mirabeau's' (i.e. Holbach's) *System of Nature*, Volney's *Ruins of Empires*, 'and other light reading of that sort'.[1] But, as Bray tells us, he only succeeded in making her exceedingly uncomfortable, for, with her, 'religion was not a question of theological controversy or biblical criticism, but of deep feeling and cherished home associations, and of convictions instilled into her mind from childhood under the influence of one of the most cultivated and powerful Unitarian preachers of the day, the Rev. Robert Aspland'. Poor Caroline referred the question to her brother Charles, 'who had already gone very fully into the subject, and had come out completely convinced on the Unitarian stand-points'. Reluctantly, Hennell yielded to the importunity of his sister and brother-in-law, and embarked once more on the attempt to separate truth from fiction, history from miracle, in the Gospel records. It cannot be said that he came to pray and remained to scoff, for the resulting book was chiefly distinguished from its eighteenth century forerunners by the reverence of its tone. But his enquiry certainly led him to results very different from those he had expected, or from any which Caroline could have desired. The investigation of the four Gospels, he tells us in the Preface to the *Inquiry*, was

> 'pursued for some time with the expectation that, at least, the principal miraculous facts supposed to lie at the foundation of Christianity would be found to be impregnable, but it was continued with a gradually increasing conviction that the true account of the life of Jesus Christ, and of the spread of his religion, would be found to contain no deviation from the known laws of nature, nor to require, for their explanation, more than the operation of human motives and feelings, acted upon by the peculiar circumstances of the age and country whence the religion originated.'

Although his conclusions differ in some important points from those of the most recent biblical critics, Hennell shows a remarkable instinctive command of the technique of textual criticism—remarkable, above all, because when he wrote

---

[1] Bray's Autobiography: *Phases of Opinion and Experience During a Long Life*, pp. 48-9.

GEORGE ELIOT: HENNELL, STRAUSS, FEUERBACH

the book he knew next to nothing of what had already been done in Germany. He grasped the nature of the 'synoptic' problem (he did not even know this name for it), realizing, for example, that it meant trying to date each book, estimating the character and intention of each author, comparing passage with passage to discover which (if either) copied from which, and weighing the probabilities for and against the historicity of every incident in the narratives, with due regard to the moment and purpose of composition and the readers for whom the work was written. It may be said that the conclusion of any such enquiry is presupposed from the start, since in order to embark upon it at all a man must already have abandoned all notion of Scriptural infallibility. This is true, but it does not follow that the task will be carried out, as it was by Hennell, with a single-hearted desire for truth, and an almost total absence of the spirit of mere destructiveness or levity. Hennell's work has been done much more thoroughly by a host of later commentators, and his method has largely become a matter of common acceptance; it is therefore unnecessary to describe his book in any detail: a few traits will suffice to indicate its quality, and the source of its impressiveness for a reader like Marian Evans. His introductory historical sketch already involves the presupposition on which his later judgments will be founded, for the story of Israel, from the Captivity to the death of Jesus, is there related as a chapter of *secular* history. The framework for the career and Messiahship of Jesus is set in the political vicissitudes of the Hebrew race, and their mounting expectation of a supernatural deliverance. Jesus is represented as an Essene enthusiast and revolutionist of extraordinary power and virtue, who, convinced that he is capable of leadership, conceives the tremendous idea of assuming the rôle of the long-awaited Messiah, and achieving the restoration of the Hebrew theocracy, or Kingdom of Heaven. His moral purity, and the intensity of his communion with God, give him such authority, and such actual therapeutic power, that he cures epilepsy and other disorders by a word, a touch or a look, and consequently gains the reputation of a wonder-worker. He perhaps himself comes to believe that he has supernatural powers. He appoints twelve disciples, each to rule over one of the twelve tribes of Israel in the new Kingdom. His sway over the multitude grows so great that the authorities become alarmed, the Romans fearing another insurrection like that of Judas of Galilee, and the Hebrew priests and nobles dreading an infringement of their privileges. Jesus decides to put his Messiahship to the final test, and, dramatizing his actions in accordance with the prophecy of Zechariah, advances upon Jerusalem, seated upon an ass's colt. Boldly assuming the highest authority, he expels the money-changers from the Temple—the most audacious of his outward actions. But at this point his career is checked: he realizes that his attempt will be in vain; the Kingdom of Heaven will not be established under his earthly regency. It is too late to retreat, and besides, the nobility of his character, and the inward assurance of his divine mission and prophetic office, render any compromise unthinkable. He resolves to face the worst with heroic dignity, and to hope and proclaim that through his martyrdom the Kingdom of Heaven may be realized later, probably by supernatural aid. After his crucifixion Joseph of Arimathea, in concert with Nicodemus, arranges for the secret removal of the body of Jesus from the tomb in his garden, in order to distract the attention of the authorities from himself; and, to induce the disciples of Jesus to depart peacefully, he stations an agent at the tomb who informs them that Jesus has risen, and has gone into Galilee. The disciples, who had been sunk in disillusionment at the failure of their leader, are at first incredulous, but when they find that the body has really disappeared, they are filled with a new and enormous hope: Jesus, then, was the Messiah after all, and his return from Heaven with full power and dominion may be shortly expected.

There is no need to summarize Hennell's further reconstruction of the history of the early Church, or to trace his account of the gradual elevation of Jesus, by the accretions of imagination and myth, and by the infiltration of Greek philosophical conceptions, to the status of incarnate 'logos', and finally to that of God. Enough has been said to indicate

GEORGE ELIOT: HENNELL, STRAUSS, FEUERBACH

the spirit and method of his work. It may be asked, on what grounds did Hennell become convinced that his conjectural natural history of Christianity—for he admitted that many gaps had had to be filled by conjecture—was substantially correct? The answer is partly to be found in his examination of the Gospel narratives; these, he finds, were not the work of eye-witnesses (unless the aged John were really the author of the Fourth Gospel), but of persons who in their several ways were trying, at a distance of perhaps two generations from the events described, to confirm the faith of the infant Church. In so doing, and without any intention to deceive, they availed themselves of that floating body of legend and tradition which, in an unscientific age, and at a time when imaginations were superheated by Messianic hopes and exaltations, was bound to grow up round the memory of so exceptional, so extraordinary a prophet as Jesus. Though the first three Gospels contain much material in common, and were either partly taken one from another or from some common source, their mutual discrepancies are sufficient to show that the writers deliberately altered their narratives to heighten their effects—Matthew, for example, often modifying a story to make it correspond more exactly with an Old Testament prophecy. The Fourth Gospel attributes to Jesus long theological discourses in a style utterly different from his manner in the first three, and closely resembling in style and content the epistles which are also ascribed to John. These and many other discrepancies once noted, it becomes clear that historical accuracy, as now understood, is not to be looked for in the Gospels. The miraculous parts of the narratives therefore, against the truth of which there must in any case be the strongest antecedent presumption, and which as between the evangelists are discrepant enough to shake confidence, must be set down as products of pious imagination. This conclusion is reinforced in the later part of the book by a critique of the Old Testament prophecies, in which it is demonstrated that the so-called Messianic passages are explicable without reference to Jesus, though Jesus himself, and his followers, continually applied them to his career and actions. With reference to the book of Isaiah, for example, Hennell observes that 'instead of admitting the natural order of things—that Jesus had imbibed the views of a book which he had read—it was supposed that the author of the book had, by means of a divine spirit of foresight, anticipated the views of Jesus'.[1] But Hennell's conclusions, supported though they are by the most careful sifting of the material, and by the kind of insight which has since guided so many perfectly orthodox biblical scholars, yet rest ultimately on certain deep-seated presuppositions—those, in fact, of the 'scientific' and 'positive' century in which he lived. Supernatural and miraculous events are out of the order of Nature, but the operation of natural law is uniform and invariable, therefore miracles do not happen and never have happened. The earliest histories, both secular and religious, of all nations, have been full of mythological and legendary stories intermixed with genuine historical matter: why suppose that those of the Jews and Christians are exempted from this rule? The same canons of critical interpretation are applicable to all ancient literature, whether 'sacred' or 'secular'. Hennell makes very little explicit use of these presuppositions, though he refers to the first in an interesting footnote where he suggests that the recorded miracles really express a primitive, and now outgrown, conception of what is truly 'miraculous'. Science, he says, proves that disease and death are often the penalties annexed by natural law to the abuse of men's powers: now,

> 'It may be presumed that the different parts of the divine plans harmonize with each other, and, therefore, that the credentials given by the Deity would not consist in an infringement of his own laws.
>
> 'Christ, by raising the widow's son at Nain, removed the natural penalty of the youth's own ill-regulated conduct, or that of his fathers. But if he had taken that occasion to make known the connexion established between imprudence and suffering, by explaining the causes which led to that young man's premature death, he would have acted in accordance with the divine laws, he would have saved many widows' sons from the same fate, and would have

[1] *Inquiry* (1838 ed.), p. 259.

given a more permanent and convincing proof of his being a man sent from God.... If, on opening the book which records his claims as a divine messenger, we were to find, instead of these stories of such difficult verification, declarations of the causes of blindness, fever, and palsy, and warnings to mankind to abstain from the courses which lead to such evils, the book would carry with it an evidence increasing with the lapse of ages, since the possession of such knowledge by a person in the age, country and circumstances of Christ would be as miraculous as any of the works referred to: and all readers, on finding that the most advanced stages of human knowledge had been anticipated by the peasant of Galilee, must themselves exclaim, "Whence had this man this knowledge, having never learned?" and, "Rabbi, we know that thou art a teacher sent by God, for no man could have this wisdom unless God were with him".'[1]

Perhaps the most striking evidence of Hennell's insight, however, is his clear recognition that the Gospels, whatever their status as history, are statements of the genuine faith of the earliest Christians, and as such are of the highest value and significance. Far indeed from his thought is any deistical 'exposure' of the evangelists, any suggestion of wilful deceit or imposture. His whole drift is to show how 'naturally' and spontaneously the myths grew up, and he occasionally pauses to ponder wistfully on the beauty and pathos of the result. 'Fictions proceeding from such feelings', he writes,

> 'must be of a different character from those thrown out in the mere wantonness of imagination. Hence the appearance of simplicity, earnestness, and reality, which in the midst of palpable inconsistencies, pervade the evangelic histories, and render even their fictions unique.... In short, in the stories of the resurrection and ascension of Jesus we see traces of the sentiments awakened in some inhabitants of an eastern and imaginative clime, at an eventful period of their country's history, by the life, precepts, and sudden death of one of the most extraordinary persons in history.'[2]

How much more 'gratifying' were it, he sighs, to enter fully into the feelings of the disciples, and 'allow our wishes to

[1] *Ibid.*, pp. 192-3. [2] *Ibid.*, p. 152.

overcome distrust'! But no; truth constrains us, and we must console ourselves for the loss of the Resurrection by reflecting that

> 'the sublime views which it was in part the occasion of bringing forth, and the moral revolution which it contributed to promote, are in themselves deeply interesting facts, which have an important bearing on every inquiry concerning the ultimate destination of the human mind.'

We see in this train of thought how it was that Hennell, like other heroic rationalizers, could claim that the 'essence' of Christianity remained unaffected by the destruction of its miraculous foundations. There is an 'easy' transition from 'Christianity as a divine revelation to Christianity as the purest form yet existing of natural religion':

> 'Christianity, thus regarded as a system of elevated thought and feeling, will not be injured by being freed from those fables, and those views of local or temporary interest, which hung about its origin. It will, on the contrary, be placed on a surer basis; for it need no longer appeal for its support to the uncertain evidence of events which happened nearly two thousand years ago, a species of evidence necessarily attainable only by long and laborious research, impracticable to most men, and unsatisfactory and harassing even to those who have most means of pursuing it; but it will rest its claims on an evidence clearer, simpler, and always at hand,—the thoughts and feelings of the human mind itself. Thus, whatever in it is really true and excellent, will meet with a ready attestation in every breast, and, in the improvement of the human mind, find an ever-increasing evidence.'[1]

'Many of the finer thoughts and feelings of mankind find a vent in fiction, expressed either by painting, poetry or the poetic tale; and the perception of historical inaccuracy does not prevent our sharing the thoughts and feelings which have embodied themselves in this manner.'[2] True, the disappearance of the notion of miraculous revelation, and the reduction of our hope of Heaven to a mere speculation, will

---

[1] *Ibid.*, Preface, p. viii.   [2] *Ibid.*, p. 214.

leave a distressing blank in the hearts of many. But they will find a substitute in the privileges and duties of this earthly life, in the advance of science, in the strengthening of character by adversity, and by discovering 'in the Universe itself a Son which tells us of a Father, and in all the natural beauty and moral excellence which meet us in the world an ever-present Logos, which reveals the grace and truth of its invisible source'.[1]

And now, picture the effect of this intoxicating draught upon our ardent young 'wrestler for the truth', our Theresa of the Midland flats, our cygnet among the ducklings—who only a few short years before had been fain to diet herself on the husks of Hannah More and Wilberforce, and on scraps of poetry, metaphysics and science picked up in the intervals of boiling currant jelly! It can be described as a dreadful exhilaration, like that of Eve after eating the forbidden fruit; exhilaration, because here at last was the Truth which makes one free—Truth, self-evident, compelling, authoritative: but dread, because of the thought of one's father, one's home-circle, one's Church, and Miss Lewis. It is the story of Carlyle and his mother over again; indeed, it is a situation which recurs constantly in nineteenth century biography, not only where a provincial emerges into the wider world, but wherever the younger generation achieves 'emancipation' from home influence at the price of estrangement and sad disharmony. Casting about at random for another instance, one thinks of R. L. Stevenson after the *éclaircissement* with his father about beliefs: 'if I had foreseen', he writes, 'the real hell of everything since, I think I should have lied, as I have done so often before. . . . Of course, it is rougher than hell upon my father, but can I help it? They don't see either that my game is not the light-hearted scoffer; that I am not (as they call me) a careless infidel. . . . I lay in bed this morning awake . . . and heard my father go out for the papers; and then I lay and wished—O, if he would only *whistle* when he comes in again! But of course he did not. I have stopped that pipe.'[2]

---
[1] *Ibid.*, p. 370.
[2] *Letters of R. L. Stevenson* (1911 ed.), vol. i, pp. 53 and 70.

With Marian Evans the break was sharp and painful, but short-lived; she gave up going to church, and there was a three weeks' separation from her father. But here, as so often with her, the heart came quickly into play to balance the head; her affections had twined too closely round 'the old inferior things' for this to last, and the old relations were outwardly resumed. And only two years later she can write with singular but characteristic balance and detachment to Sara Hennell:

> 'The first impulse of a young and ingenuous mind is to withhold the slightest sanction from all that contains even a mixture of supposed error. When the soul is just liberated from the wretched giant's bed of dogmas on which it has been racked and stretched ever since it began to think, there is a feeling of exultation and strong hope'—and zeal for proselytizing sets in. 'But a year or two of reflexion, and the experience of our own miserable weakness, which will ill afford to part even with the crutch of superstition, must, I think, effect a change. Speculative truth begins to appear but a shadow of individual minds. Agreement between intellects seems unattainable, and we turn to the *truth of feeling* as the only universal bond of union. We find that the intellectual errors which we once fancied were a mere incrustation, have grown into the living body, and we cannot in the majority of cases wrench them away without destroying vitality.... If, then, we are debarred by such considerations from trying to reorganize opinions, are we to remain aloof from our fellow-creatures on occasions when we may fully sympathize with the feelings exercised, although our own have been melted into another mould?' [1]

Miss Evans's friendship with the Hennells led directly to the first great intellectual task of her life, the translation of Strauss's *Leben Jesu*. The connexion between Charles Hennell and Strauss, it is interesting to note, arose after the publication of the *Inquiry*, which was written in ignorance of the great German work published three years earlier (1835). A certain Dr Brabant of Devizes, a German scholar, read the *Inquiry* with lively interest, and noting its extraordinary affinity with the *Leben Jesu*, sent a copy to Strauss,

[1] Cross's *Life*, vol. i, pp. 121 ff.

of whom he was a personal friend. Strauss was so much impressed that he had the work translated into German, and published it with a prefatory note, from which, partly for the sake of the noble magnanimity of its tone, but also for its intrinsic interest, a few phrases must be quoted:

> 'Not sufficiently acquainted with German to read continuously a learned work in that language, the labours of our theologians were only accessible to him [Hennell] so far as they were written in Latin, or translated into English, or treated of in English writings or periodicals: especially he is unacquainted with what the Germans have effected in the criticism of the Gospels since Schleiermacher's work on Luke. . . . Only so much the more remarkable is it, however, that both in the principles and in the main results of his investigation, he is on the very track which has been entered on amongst us in recent years. . . . That at certain periods certain modes of thought lie as it were in the atmosphere . . . and come to light in the most remote places without perceptible media of communication, is shown, not only by the contents, but by the spirit, of Mr Hennell's work. No further traces of the ridicule and scorn which characterize his countrymen of the Deistical school; the subject is treated in the earnest and dignified tone of the truth-seeker, not with the rancour of a passionate polemic; we nowhere find him deriving religion from priestcraft, but from the tendencies and wants of human nature. . . . These elevated views, which the learned German of our day appropriates as the fruit of the religious and scientific advancement of his nation, this Englishman, to whom most of the means at our command were wanting, has been able to educe entirely from himself. . . . An Englishman, a merchant, a man of the world, he possesses, both by nature and by training, the practical insight, the sure tact, which lays hold on realities. The solution of problems over which the German flutters with many circuits of learned formulae, our English author often succeeds in seizing at one spring.'[1]

Dr Brabant's daughter had begun to translate Strauss into English, but on her (singularly appropriate) marriage to Hennell, the latter—with prudent regard for his own conjugal amenities—persuaded Marian Evans to shoulder the

[1] Quoted *ibid.*, p. 101.

task. She assumed it, and carried it through, but not without much groaning and sickness of heart. The fact was that Strauss, with all his vastly greater learning and philosophical depth, could do little for her that Hennell had not already done; she no longer needed him, so the translating was merely a 'soul-stupefying labour', a heavy duty to humanity, to be discharged with deep sighs and languishing of spirit.

III. Strauss's *Life of Jesus*

This book is one of the landmarks and turning-points of nineteenth century religious thought, and calls for notice in our present survey quite apart from its effects upon George Eliot. It differs from Hennell's work, not so much in its actual conclusions, as in the encyclopaedic range of its erudition and the philosophic profundity of its basis—in other words, it differs as a work of German scholarship normally did differ, in the nineteenth century, from its English counterpart. It not only sums up and epitomizes the work of a generation of Teutonic sifters of the text of Scripture, but also effects a synthesis between their results and those of a generation of German thinkers from Kant to Schelling. It is in truth a noble, a palmary effort of the nineteenth century mind, and it shares with other great achievements of that century this quality: that it can still challenge us, and compel us, in the name of honesty and self-respect, to declare in what way we think we have improved upon it, outgrown it, or transcended its standpoint. It is indeed a crucial difficulty in studying the last century that it continually embarrasses us, as a father often embarrasses a son, by stating with pertinence and superior knowledge positions which we had assumed, without having really examined them, to be obsolete or untenable. Remoter centuries, like more distant forbears, have not this disturbing quality; we are not implicated in their absurdities, and can regard them with complacency. The nineteenth century compels us to define our own position, and as this is difficult and often painful, we have (until recently) avoided its society like prodigal sons, or by-passed it with a superficial irony.

GEORGE ELIOT: HENNELL, STRAUSS, FEUERBACH

The *Life of Jesus* has this quality in full measure. The critical mind of Western man had of course been engaged, at least since the fourth century B.C., in explaining, allegorizing, restating or rejecting its religious beliefs; it had pre-eminently been so engaged since the sixteenth century A.D. The eighteenth century had been critical indeed, but its attacks were too superficial to have much lasting effect. The nineteenth century attack was far more damaging, because it was based on a much wider and deeper understanding of history and of human nature: because, in a sense, it was not a direct attack at all, but undercut religion by the more subtle corrosive of a profounder comprehension. The distinctive nineteenth century phenomenon is the devout sceptic, the sage who rejects traditional religion not because he is shallow or immoral, but because he is too earnest to accept it—because he understands and tolerates all forms of religion too well to adopt any one of them. Strauss characteristically separates himself at the outset both from the 'supernatural' and the 'rationalist' schools of biblical criticism. Early exegesis regarded the Scripture-narratives naïvely as supernatural history, divinely attested and guarded from error. Rationalist criticism, still regarding them as 'history', tries to find 'natural' explanations for all miracles and mysteries. His own qualification for his task, he explains (and this self-knowledge is typical of him and of his nation), is an 'internal liberation of the feelings and intellect from certain religious and dogmatical presuppositions'—those, in short, of supernaturalists and rationalists alike. If theologians, he adds, regard this absence of presupposition from his work as unchristian, he for his part regards 'the believing presuppositions of theirs as unscientific'. But in place of these older rejected presuppositions, Strauss has two other vital presuppositions derived from the *Zeitgeist*: (i) that though miracles did not happen, yet the belief in them arises from demonstrable facts of human nature, and (ii) that all primitive histories, whether sacred or profane, are to be treated alike. 'The author is well aware', he says in the Preface to the first edition, 'that the essence of the Christian faith is perfectly independent of his criticism.' The words recall Hennell's, yet the tone is different: Hennell is simply offering apologetic consolation; Strauss's Olympian calm, as we discover later, has behind it the philosophic weight of the Hegelian synthesis. 'The supernatural birth of Christ,' he goes on, 'his miracles, his resurrection and ascension, remain eternal truths, whatever doubts may be cast on their reality as historical facts. The certainty of this can alone give calmness and dignity to our criticism, and distinguish it from the naturalistic criticism of the last century, the design of which was, with the historical fact, to subvert also the religious truth, and which thus necessarily became frivolous.' Proceeding, then, from the second presupposition, Strauss lifts the curtain on a panoramic view of Western thought, pagan and Christian alike, and traces in outline the evolution of religious conceptions. Everywhere the same pattern recurs: everywhere, as experience widens and knowledge grows more scientific, early sacred records and myths have somehow to be reconciled with more advanced notions, and the process of 'interpretation' begins. And, 'as the progress of mental cultivation mainly consists in the recognition of a chain of causes and effects connecting natural phenomena with each other', we get the two-fold realizations: either that 'The divine cannot have so happened', or 'That which has so happened cannot have been divine'. Many of the forms of possible interpretation appear already in Greece: Plato's attitude to the myths representing the first position, and Euhemerus representing the second—i.e. 'yes, these things happened, but they were acts of great or notorious men since deified by popular imagination'. In Polybius we already meet with the 'eighteenth century' approach: 'these stories were deliberately invented by priests and rulers to awe men into subjection'. Turning to the Hebrews, we find in Philo the allegorical method so frequently used in later days: wherever the Scripture seems to offer an 'unworthy' delineation of the Deity, His actions, motives or commands, or of the deeds of His acknowledged servants, a 'higher sense' is to be given to the text. This method, and what Strauss calls the 'partial' method—that is when the interpreter shuts his eyes to his awareness of disagreement, and proffers his gloss as the 'original' meaning of the text—both arise at the stage when the cultured mind has grown dissatisfied with parts of the record, but has not yet given up the assumption that the record *must* be in some sense 'right'. Origen, with his apparatus of 'three senses', the literal, the moral and the mystical, is for the most part at this stage, though in a few passages he grows bolder: the Scriptures, he says (Strauss's quotation),

> 'contain many things which never came to pass, interwoven with the history; and he must be dull indeed who does not of his own accord observe that much which the Scriptures represent as having happened never actually occurred.' Or again: 'he who would study history with understanding . . . must weigh each separate detail, and consider what is worthy of credit and may be believed without further evidence; what, on the contrary, must be regarded as merely figurative', etc.

Strauss passes with a mental sigh over the 'tedious centuries of the Middle Ages'[1], and comes on to the naturalists and deists of the seventeenth and eighteenth centuries: Chubb, Woolston, Reimarus and the rest, and notes in them (as already mentioned) that spirit of destruction and levity which vitiated their conclusions; to leave us with a Moses who was an impostor, a Jesus who was a political agitator, and disciples who spread deliberate falsehoods, simply would not do. At last Strauss reaches his own era, and gives us a very valuable summary of the work of his predecessors, the German critics of the 'rationalist' and 'naturalist' schools. Eichhorn, for example, awoke to the important realization that 'actual divine interposition *or* deliberate fraud' is not the true antithesis; the supernatural, according to him, was the 'spontaneous illumination reflected from antiquity itself', and we must learn how 'to translate the language of a former age into that of today'. Even he, however, fell at times into crude rationalizing, as when he suggested that Eve's apple might have been a poisonous fruit which really did permanently impair the constitution of the human race; this interpretation, however, he later abandoned for a mythical one: the

[1] *Life of Jesus*, vol. i, p. 11 (Marian Evans's trans., 1846).

source of evil is man's inveterate desire for a better condition than that assigned to him. Paulus is classified by Strauss as a Christian Euhemerus: the Gospel events all 'happened' in a natural way, and their historical truth can be discovered beneath their miraculous coverings. Kant revived the old method of moral allegorizing: if the Psalmist speaks vindictively of his 'enemies' we must understand this of the 'passions', which are to be subjugated or annihilated. Strauss has now arrived in sight of the true method of interpretation, the method he is to exemplify: the *mythical*. Semler, Gabler, Schelling and G. Bauer are mentioned as forerunners: Vater and De Wette have shown that the 'naturalistic' approach is inapplicable to narratives based, not on the immediate testimony of eye-witnesses, but on tradition, and written long after the events described. We are now given the key to the problem: we must prepare ourselves to find that the Scriptural miracles are, not conscious fictions, not exaggerations of real occurrences, but *myths*, that is, imaginative symbols—standing not for matters of fact, but for facts of mind, experiences, states of feeling. It should be in no way startling to find that Judaism and Christianity have their myths: myth grows from the very heart of religious experience, and is of its essence, since religion (not theology) apprehends truth not as naked concept but through image and symbol. Myth expresses religious experience, philosophical ideas, and even historical events, in the concrete form most congenial to the mental habit of the time which gives it birth. Thus with genuine myth there is complete unconsciousness, spontaneity and necessity in the process of its formation. In the ancient world, in the world which generated Christianity, the religious tendency was so overwhelmingly preponderant, and the knowledge of natural laws so limited, that there was a disposition to see the hand of God everywhere. What makes it so hard for us now to seize this point of view is that 'after many centuries of tedious research' we have attained the conviction that

> 'all things are linked together by a chain of causes and effects, which suffers no interruption.... This conviction is so much a habit of

thought with the modern world, that in actual life, the belief in a supernatural manifestation, an immediate divine agency, is at once attributed to ignorance or imposture.'[1]

Strauss emphasizes—and the quality of his insight is here well displayed—that the modern separation between matter of fact and matter of feeling, between 'prose' and 'poetry', history and fiction, was in early times unknown. It was in this setting that the traditions, later embodied in the Gospels, originated and grew. Strauss, like Hennell, finds the more immediate source of the Christian myths in the prevailing mood of Messianic expectation; their materials already existed, and only had to be 'transferred' to Jesus.

The bulk of the work consists of an exhaustive examination, carried out with Teutonic thoroughness and learning, and guided by the standards and assumptions above indicated, of the four Gospels. But in the 'Concluding Dissertation' Strauss turns aside to survey his completed work, and estimate its meaning for the modern world. In a passage of unwonted eloquence he laments the pain and loss which his critique must inevitably inflict upon many, and even shrinks in horror from what may seem 'so fearful an act of desecration':

> 'The boundless store of truth and life which for eighteen centuries has been the aliment of humanity, seems irretrievably dissipated; the most sublime levelled with the dust, God divested of his grace, man of his dignity, and the tie between heaven and earth broken.'[2]

But wait—he has something in reserve—something of the highest importance: he will try to 're-establish dogmatically what has been destroyed critically'. The critic, 'in proportion as he is distinguished from the naturalistic theologian and the free-thinker,—*in proportion as his criticism is conceived in the spirit of the nineteenth century*' (my italics), is

> 'filled with veneration for every religion, and especially for the substance of the sublimest of all religions, the Christian, which he

[1] *Ibid.*, p. 71.   [2] *Ibid.*, vol. iii, p. 396 ff.

perceives to be identical with the deepest philosophic truth; and hence, after having in the course of his criticism exhibited only the differences between his conviction and the historical belief of the Christian, he will feel urged to place that identity in a fresh light.'

Now that Christianity has been shown to be mainly a 'mental' product rather than a piece of history, we need a critique of dogma as a sequel to our historical criticism. Strauss pleads that this task must form the subject of a separate work (he carried it out in his later book *Christian Dogmas in their Historical Development*), but he gives us a remarkably able and sympathetic summary of Christian dogmatic teaching from the beginnings to his own time. The climax is reached when he identifies the 'substance' of Christianity with the deepest philosophic truth, that is to say, when he finds in it a symbolic expression of Hegel's profoundest insights. The Absolute Idea splits dialectically into One and Many, Self and Other; it realizes itself in History; it comes to self-consciousness in Man. Man is the true 'Incarnation'; the world in him returns in reconcilement to God. For Christ, the one, the unique God-man, substitute Humanity, and you have the ultimate meaning of the great myth.

> 'Is not the idea of the unity of the divine and human natures a real one in a far higher sense, when I regard the whole race of mankind as its realization, than when I single out one man as such a realization? Is not an incarnation of God from eternity, a truer one than incarnation limited to a particular point of time?'

This, it has been said, was 'saving' Christianity by 'turning it into an unchristian doctrine'.[1] I must not enter upon the vast discussion here suggested, nor try to pose Strauss with such questions as—what was there about the 'historical Jesus' which caused the Messianic expectations to be transferred to *him* rather than to anyone else? Or, how can such a concept as that of eternal incarnation be turned into 'aliment' for the saving of sinful men? The interesting point,

[1] S. Hook, *From Hegel to Marx* (1936), p. 86.

with which I will end this discussion, is that Strauss faces up to all the implications of his outlook for Christian ministers who may adopt it, as he cannot but believe the most enlightened will. The dilemma of Robert Elsmere, which seemed so startling to readers of that novel—indeed, every aspect of the 'modernist's' plight down to the present day, is foreseen and discussed by Strauss. What shall the clergyman do when he has seen the light, learnt the secret? Renounce his Orders and become a professor? But this would be to desert the Church just when he has become the bearer of vital truth; moreover, as professor he could only address those most likely to be learning the truth in any case, or damage the Church still further by dissuading the best students from taking Orders. Stay in the Church, then, and preach the identity of Christianity and philosophy? But no one will understand him. Keep his best thoughts for a few initiates, and preach the old doctrines with mental reservations? But the sense of his own hypocrisy will probably suffocate him. Strauss does not pretend to solve the problem or to give authoritative advice to the Robert Elsmeres. He inclines to think that the enlightened clergyman should stay where he is, and attempt without violence to lead his listeners gradually in the right direction, avoiding hypocrisy by skirting dangerous ground, and always affirming those truths which are common to him and his hearers. It will be a difficult task, for example, to preach an Easter sermon without equivocation, but he may dwell upon the *meaning* of the resurrection, affirming the spiritual facts of rebirth and regeneration. Here Strauss brings his great undertaking to a close, with a final 'Time will show'.

iv. Feuerbach's *Essence of Christianity*

I am not attempting to rewrite George Eliot's life, nor even to sketch in any detail the stages of her spiritual development; the aim of this chapter is to present that development as representative of a main current in nineteenth century belief, and to isolate a few of the influences which controlled its direction. I shall therefore pass over the eight years which intervened between the translations of Strauss and of Feuerbach, merely mentioning that they included many important events—her father's death (1849), her stay at Geneva (June 1849 to March 1850), the removal to London and her appointment as assistant editor of the *Westminster Review* (1851), her immersion in the London ferment of 'advanced' thought, and the ensuing contacts with leading thinkers and writers: Lewes, Carlyle, Dickens, Harriet Martineau, Francis Newman, Professor Owen, Cobden, Herbert Spencer, Combe (the phrenologist) and the rest. It was during these years and through some of these contacts that Comte's writings first reached her. Harriet Martineau's two-volume translation of Comte's *Positive Philosophy* appeared in 1853, just at the time when George Eliot was at work on Feuerbach; and the combined testimonies of these two writers, who, quite independently and along different roads, had reached the same conclusion, must have convinced her that here, indeed, was an irresistible tide of truth pouring in on all sides, and reaching even the coasts of this provincial isle. It should be her task to widen the breach for its entry. The translation of Feuerbach's *Wesen des Christentums* was her last act before she left England with Lewes; its publication, and that decisive step, both took place in July 1854. M. Bourl'honne has even suggested, not without some warrant, that the spirit of Feuerbach, and especially his views on friendship and marriage, may have contributed something towards making her 'union' with Lewes possible.[1] Hennell and Strauss had widened her intellectual horizons and let in the light; Comte and Feuerbach, with their exaltation of love and their apotheosis of humanity, ministered to those heart's affections which in her were even stronger than the intellect.

Before speaking further of Feuerbach, however, I want to pause a moment to illustrate Miss Evans's outlook in the period between the two translations, and this can conveniently be done by glancing at her first article in the *Westminster*, a review of R. W. Mackay's *Progress of the Intellect* (1850).

---

[1] P. Bourl'honne, *George Eliot, Essai de Biographie Intellectuelle et Morale*, Paris, 1933.

GEORGE ELIOT: HENNELL, STRAUSS, FEUERBACH

Mackay was a disciple of Strauss and Baur, and in reviewing him she was in effect defining the position she had reached.

Such a book as Mackay's, she begins, is valuable in showing that each age has had a faith and a symbolism suited to its own stage of development. She praises the combination, in this writer, of erudition with panoramic breadth of view, comparing him in this respect with Cudworth and the modern Germans:

> 'England has been slow to use or to emulate the immense labours of Germany in the departments of mythology and biblical criticism; but when once she does so, the greater solidity and directness of the English mind ensure a superiority of treatment.'[1]

It is Mr Mackay's faith (and Miss Evans's) that

> 'divine revelation is not contained exclusively or pre-eminently in the facts and inspirations of any one age or nation, but is co-extensive with the history of human development, and is perpetually unfolding itself to our widened experience and investigation.'

The 'master-key' is the 'recognition of the presence of undeviating law in the material and moral world—of that invariability of sequence which is acknowledged to be the basis of physical science, but which is still perversely ignored in our social organization, our ethics and our religion'. Religion and science are correlative, and ultimately one: 'no object in nature, no subject of contemplation, is destitute of a religious tendency and meaning'. There is an *'ascensio mentis in Deum per scalas creatarum rerum'*; a superstructure of faith can be securely built only on the foundations of the known.

'The introduction of a truly philosophic spirit into the study of mythology' is a great step forward; we owe it chiefly to the Germans. How greatly it surpasses 'the superficial Lucian-like tone of ridicule adopted by many authors of the eighteenth century'! The idea that many parts of the Old Testament 'have a mythical character' has 'long been familiar to German critics', but is 'still startling to the English

[1] *Westminster Review*, vol. 54 (1851).

theological mind'. But the mythical theory (and here she speaks from experience)

> 'delivers the mind from a heavy burthen of contradiction and absurdity, and the religious sentiment from the admission of painful anomalies.'

Miss Evans concludes with a piece of advice to the theologians:

> 'Since these conclusions are denied by no competent critic uncommitted to the maintenance of certain tenets, it would be wise in our theological teachers, instead of struggling to retain a footing for themselves and their doctrine on the crumbling structure of dogmatic interpretation, to cherish those more liberal views of biblical criticism, which, admitting of a development of the Christian system corresponding to the wants and the culture of the age, would enable it to strike a firm root in man's moral nature, and to entwine itself with the growth of those new forms of social life to which we are tending.'

In January 1853 Miss Evans wrote to the Brays:

> 'I begin to feel for other people's wants and sorrows a little more than I used to do. *Heaven help us! said the old religion; the new one, from its very lack of that faith, will teach us all the more to help one another.*'[1]

No aphorism could more succinctly express the results of all her reading and thinking up to date; it was also the message of Feuerbach, whom she was then translating. Intellectual emancipation was well and fair, but it was not all: there were also the claims of the heart's sympathies, the summons to attend to 'other people's wants and sorrows'. Feuerbach contributed the necessary touch of prophetic warmth. Here was another version of the Religion of Humanity—not, like Comte's, chilly and over-systematic, but oracular, full of sacred rage. Feuerbach had studied at Berlin under Hegel, but had grown sick of his teaching: 'God was my first thought', he said, 'Reason my second; Man my third and last.' Hegelianism was the last refuge of the old theology;

---

[1] Cross, *op. cit.*, vol. i, p. 302 (my italics).

GEORGE ELIOT: HENNELL, STRAUSS, FEUERBACH

Christianity has now lost all meaning for our time, and a new religion is called for—a de-supernaturalized humanism. 'His work consists', said Marx, 'in the dissolution of the religious world into its secular basis.'[1] The following extract well illustrates this viewpoint, and explains why Marx took the interest in him that he did:

> 'It is a question today, you say, no longer of the existence or non-existence of God, but of the existence or non-existence of man; not whether God is a creature whose nature is the same as ours, but whether we human beings are to be equal among ourselves; not whether and how we can partake of the body of the Lord by eating bread, but whether we have enough bread for our own bodies; not whether we render unto God what is God's and unto Caesar what is Caesar's, but whether we finally render unto man what is man's; not whether we are Christians or heathens, theists or atheists, but whether we are or can become men, healthy in soul and body, free, active and full of vitality. *Concedo*, gentlemen! That is what I want, too. He who says no more of me than that I am an atheist, says and knows *nothing* of me. The question as to the existence or non-existence of God, the opposition between theism and atheism, belongs to the sixteenth and seventeenth centuries, but not to the nineteenth. I deny God. But that means for me that I deny the negation of man. In place of the illusory, fantastic, heavenly position of man which in actual life necessarily leads to the degradation of man, I substitute the tangible, actual, and consequently also the political and social position of mankind. The question concerning the existence or non-existence of God is for me nothing but the question concerning the existence or non-existence of man.'[2]

Feuerbach's work belongs to that powerful stream of tendency, flowing from Hegel to Marx, which was driving men deeper and deeper in upon themselves, and teaching them to discover in their own needs and longings as individuals, but above all as members of human society, the source and indeed the whole reality of the ideal worlds of thought and faith. Religion is simply a mirage, reflecting in shadow-pictures the real tensions and discontents of earthly life; in early

---
[1] *Theses on Feuerbach*, No. IV.
[2] Pref. to vol. i of *Sämmtliche Werke*, 1846; quoted by S. Hook, *op. cit.*

times, when men genuinely 'believed', it served its purpose, but now that it can only be upheld by sophistries, it is seen for what it is—a delusive spectre which beckons us away from the true sphere of our duty and service. Religion is sociology and anthropology masquerading as mystery and dogma. 'Consciousness of God is self-consciousness'; but man at first does not know this—he supposes God to be 'objective'. Hence

> 'the historical progress of religion consists in this: that what by an earlier religion was regarded as objective, is now recognized as subjective; that is, what was formerly contemplated and worshipped as God is now perceived to be something *human*.' 'The divine being is nothing else than the human being, or rather the human nature purified, freed from the limits of the individual man, made objective —i.e. contemplated and revered as another, a distinct being. All the attributes of the divine nature are, therefore, attributes of the human nature.'[1]

In religion man 'alienates' himself from himself, worships his own self-generated wraith, and then wonders why he languishes. We must drag him back from this enchantment, break its spell, and bring him home to himself. All our ideas are turned upside-down by this 'alienation': for instance, we think and speak about the 'attributes' of the 'Divine Being', whereas we should be thinking of the divinity of the attributes themselves: 'he alone is the true atheist to whom the predicates of the Divine Being—for example love, wisdom, justice, are nothing; not he to whom the subject of these predicates is nothing.' The human understanding suggests that God is impersonal and passionless: the moral sense, that He is morally perfect, but also inexorable. But this is not enough: man needs Love, Mercy and Forgiveness as well as Justice, so these must be attributed to God also. God must become Man, then! And so we come to the Incarnation, not by the usual theological road, but as a stage in the shaping or evolution of the idea of God. Feuerbach turns the dogma 'God became Man' into a statement of his own thesis: God

---

[1] *Essence of Christianity* (1854), pp. 12-14.

does become Man—not as a fact of history or of revelation, but as a fact of social psychology.

> 'Who then is our Saviour or Redeemer? God or Love? Love; for God as God has not saved us, but Love, which transcends the difference between the divine and human personality. As God has renounced himself out of love, so we, out of love, should renounce God; for if we do not sacrifice God to love, we sacrifice love to God, and, in spite of the predicate of love, we have the God—the evil being—of religious fanaticism.' [1]

There is a standing conflict between theology, the religion of the head, with its metaphysical descriptions of God as unconditioned, eternal, unchangeable, etc., and the (true) religion of the heart, which demands a loving, sympathizing—that is a human—God. 'In the Incarnation religion only confesses, what in reflection on itself, as theology, it will not admit; namely, that God is an altogether human being.' The 'love of God to man' is, being interpreted (or rather inverted, according to Feuerbach's principle), the love of *man* to man contemplated objectively. The statement 'God loves man' is an 'orientalism' for 'the highest is the love of man'. That which in truth is the 'essence of the fable' appears, to ordinary religious belief, only as the *moral* of the fable. And so Feuerbach, using the acid solution of his 'Copernican' revolutionary theory, develops the religious negative in reverse, reading black where you read white, and vice versa. 'God suffers' means 'it is divine to suffer for others'; the mystery of 'The Trinity', and the notion of the Holy Family, express the disconsolate void of the old ascetic Christian life, and its need for warmth and society; 'The Son' satisfies our need for mental images; Prayer, the turning to Omnipotent Goodness, means adoring our own heart, regarding our own feelings as absolute; Miracle is 'the sorcery of the imagination, which satisfies without contradiction all the wishes of the heart'; the Resurrection of Christ is 'the satisfied desire of man for an immediate certainty of his personal existence after death'; Justifying Grace is the completion of my sins or defects by my friend's merits; Heaven is 'life in unison

[1] *Ibid.*, p. 52.

with the feeling, with the idea, which the present life contradicts'. All this, and much more, leads Feuerbach to his second section entitled 'The False or Theological Essence of Religion', where he shows that 'God' is an ideal substitute for the real world, a wish-fulfilling symbol, which we worship, because we find that easier and more satisfying than improving the real world. 'God fills to me the place of my species, of my fellow-men'; I therefore turn away from them and the world to Him. This faith is only tenable, only justified, when it is supported by real, unsophisticated belief in miracles, or when it is lived out in genuine asceticism. The modern attempt to combine it with scientific culture, with belief in universal natural law, is an impossible hypocrisy. It is a perversity, he says (with insight) 'to adhere to the biblical and dogmatic Christ, and yet to thrust aside miracles. If the principle be retained, wherefore deny its necessary consequences?' But these modern confusions are a clear sign that it is time now to raise ourselves above the old religious standpoint altogether, and recognize that the social relationships of mankind are divine in themselves. Religion has sacrificed man to God; this must now cease. Christianity, it is true, contains both Faith and Love, but in Christianity Love is 'only the *morality*', Faith the true 'religion'. The sublimest of all Christian sayings is 'God is Love': but this should have been—'Love is God'.

> 'And we need only . . . invert the religious relations—regard that as an end which religion supposes to be a means—exalt that into the primary which in religion is subordinate . . .—at once we have destroyed the illusion, and **the unclouded light of truth streams in upon us.**'[1]

I will conclude this summary (as Feuerbach does the book itself) with his remarks on the Sacraments as symbols of the holiness of Life and of Nature:

> 'The sacrament of Baptism inspires us with thankfulness towards Nature'—because she furnishes us with that divinest of all purifying liquids—'the sacrament of bread and wine with thankfulness to-

---

[1] *Ibid.*, p. 271 (my italics).

wards man. Bread and wine typify to us the truth that Man is the true God and Saviour of man' (though here again we must remember our gratitude to 'holy Nature' for supplying the wheat and the vine). Eating and drinking are themselves religious acts: 'Oh! if thou shouldst ever experience [hunger and thirst], how wouldst thou bless and praise the natural qualities of bread and wine, which restore to thee thy humanity, thy intellect! It needs only that the ordinary course of things be interrupted in order to vindicate to common things an uncommon significance, *to life, as such, a religious import*. Therefore let bread be sacred for us, let wine be sacred, and also let water be sacred! Amen.'[1]

How far Feuerbach has moved towards Marxism will be appreciated from the foregoing examples: yet, as Marxists and some others are well aware, Marx himself was dissatisfied. Feuerbach had written as if demonstrating a truth was the same thing as making it prevail; he had no concern for revolutionary practice. I will quote now the whole of Marx's Fourth Thesis on Feuerbach:

'Feuerbach starts out from the fact of religious self-alienation, the duplication of the world into a religious-imaginary world and a real one. His work consists in the dissolution of the religious world into its secular basis. He overlooks the fact that after completing this work the chief thing still remains to be done. For the fact that the secular foundation lifts itself above itself and establishes itself in the clouds as an independent realm is only to be explained by the self-cleavage and self-contradictoriness of this secular basis. The latter must itself, therefore, first be understood in its contradiction, and then by the removal of the contradiction be revolutionized in practice. Thus, for instance, once the earthly family is discovered to be the secret of the holy family, the former must then itself be theoretically criticized and radically changed in practice.'

Feuerbach was right, then, in saying that the religious world is illusory, a compensation for the defects of the real world, but he did not go on to seek the origin of the illusions where it is to be found, in the class-tensions of society. His 'Man' is merely a collection of individuals 'naturally' held together,

[1] *Ibid.*, pp. 273-4.

not the balance of antagonist forces which society is in practice. Consequently, his religion of humanity has no cutting-edge. A Christian reader might well agree, but for different reasons. His comment, his question, might be: 'Spill your "sacredness", your "holiness", your "divineness", as freely as you will over men, vineyards, cornfields—everywhere! but tell us—whence do you acquire your sense of the "holy"? You do not make man holy, make him God, by just kneeling down and worshipping him. You may say that man ought to be holy, but that is to judge him by an ethical standard derived from outside him—from the real God whom you deny.'

CHAPTER IX

GEORGE ELIOT, CONCLUSION

WHOEVER has been reading George Eliot will recognize that with most of the underlying principles of Strauss, Comte and Feuerbach she was in agreement. The supersession of God by Humanity, of Faith by Love and Sympathy, the elimination of the supernatural, the elevation of the natural, the subordination of intellect to heart, thought to feeling—these may all be found in her novels as well as in her letters. Heaven will not help us, so we must help one another; this realization tinges our whole life with anguish, but it is the cross which the new elect must bear:

> 'The "highest calling and election" is to *do without opium*, and live through all our pain with conscious, clear-eyed endurance.'[1]

But her studies, as well as her own inmost propensities, inclined her to rely upon truth of feeling, and this engendered a wide tolerance and reverence for all religious forms which have expressed, and still express, the primary needs of the human heart. To her 'conservative-reforming intellect', the merely negative kinds of 'free-thinking' were hateful:

> 'I have a growing conviction,' she writes to Sara Hennell, while at work on *Scenes of Clerical Life*, 'that we may measure true moral and intellectual culture by the comprehension and veneration given to all forms of thought and feeling which have influenced large masses of mankind—and of all intolerance the intolerance calling itself philosophical is the most odious to me.'[2]

And again, to Charles Bray (July 5, 1859):

> 'people are, for the most part, so incapable of comprehending the state of mind which cares for that which is essentially human in all forms of belief, and desires to exhibit it under all forms with loving

[1] Cross, *op. cit.*, vol. ii, p. 283 (letter to Mme Bodichon, Dec. 26, 1860).
[2] *Ibid.*, vol. i, p. 432 (Feb. 24, 1857).

truthfulness. Freethinkers are scarcely wider than the orthodox in this matter,—they all want to see themselves and their own opinions held up as the true and the lovely.'[1]

Lord David Cecil will have it that George Eliot was 'not religious'; I cannot agree with him—or rather, I cannot agree that that is the least misleading way of saying what he means. 'Religious' seems to me to be just what she was, and many others of whom she is the type; the whole predicament she represents was that of the religious temperament cut off by the *Zeitgeist* from the traditional objects of veneration, and the traditional intellectual formulations.[2] She was not, of course, a 'practising Christian', but in her estrangement from the 'religion *about* Jesus' she was none the further from the 'religion *of* Jesus'. She knew the hunger and thirst after righteousness, and the need for renunciation—the need to lose one's life in order to gain it. And, though her religious consciousness was pre-eminently moral, it was not exclusively so; she also had the faculty of reverence, the capacity to acknowledge the reality of the unseen. When reading Darwin's *Origin of Species* she writes:

> 'to me the Development Theory, and all other explanations of processes by which things came to be, produce a feeble impression compared with the mystery that lies under the processes.'[3]

Hers was in fact the middle position of conservative-liberalism; it is a position not easy to sustain, and I do not think that George Eliot ever—at least not for any long period—recovered lasting heart's-ease. There could only be, for her, effort, striving, endurance, and that 'terrible earnestness' recorded by F. W. H. Myers.

> 'I have faith in the working out of higher possibilities than the Catholic or any other Church has presented', she writes in Comtist language, 'and those who have strength to wait and endure are bound to accept no formula which their whole souls—their intellect as well as their emotions—do not embrace with entire reverence.'

---

[1] *Ibid.*, vol. ii, p. 118.
[2] Cf. p. 105 above. Was Carlyle ' not religious ' ?
[3] Cross, *op. cit.*, vol. ii, p. 148 (letter to Mme Bodichon, Dec. 5, 1859).

—and then follows the phrase about *doing without opium*.[1] One of the clearest statements is this, taken from another letter to Mme Bodichon (written during the composition of *Romola*):

> 'Pray don't ever ask me again not to rob a man of his religious belief, as if you thought my mind tended to such robbery. I have too profound a conviction of the efficacy that lies in all sincere faith, and the spiritual blight that comes with no faith, to have any negative propagandism in me. In fact, I have very little sympathy with Freethinkers as a class, and have lost all interest in mere antagonism to religious doctrines. I care only to know, if possible, the lasting meaning that lies in all religious doctrine from the beginning till now.'[2]

It is a sentiment which would have been echoed by Coleridge, Carlyle, Maurice, Arnold, Sidgwick and many others. Her technique for retaining what she considered this 'lasting meaning', while rejecting what her intellect found unacceptable, was that of Strauss and the German 'higher criticism', and of Matthew Arnold and later modernists. Writing of Renan's *Vie de Jésus* she says:

> 'It seems to me the soul of Christianity lies not at all in the facts of an individual life, but in the ideas of which that life was the meeting-point and the new starting-point. We can never have a satisfactory basis for the history of the man Jesus, but that negation does not affect the Idea of the Christ either in its historical influence or its great symbolic meanings.'[3]

Or again:

> 'The divine will is simply so much as we have ascertained of the facts of existence which compel obedience at our peril.'[4]

Thirty years after the letter to Sara Hennell about religious conformity (cf. above, p. 218), her position is virtually unaltered: she would go to church constantly, she says, for the sake of fellowship in worshipping 'the highest good', were

---

[1] *Ibid.*, vol. ii, p. 283.   [2] *Ibid.*, p. 343 (Nov. 26, 1862).
[3] *Ibid.*, pp. 359-60 (to Mrs Peter Taylor, July 30, 1863).
[4] *Ibid.*, vol. iii, p. 48.

there no reasons against following this inclination. For those without definite religious convictions, church-going will be better than mere negation. My last extracts on this theme are from letters written to Mrs Ponsonby in 1874 and 1875:

> 'My books have for their main bearing a conclusion ... without which I could not have cared to write any representation of human life—namely, that the fellowship between man and man which has been the principle of development, social and moral, is not dependent on conceptions of what is not man: and that the idea of God, so far as it has been a high spiritual influence, is the ideal of a goodness entirely human (i.e. an exaltation of the human).'

Loss of belief in a future life, she goes on, does not rob us of our moral sense, our sense of duty, our sympathy; we retain our 'sense of quality in actions', just as we continue to appreciate colour even after becoming aware of the laws of the spectrum. We should consider our early religious experience as 'a portion of valid knowledge', and 'cherish its emotional results in relation to objects which are either substitutes or metamorphoses of the earlier'.

> 'And I think we must not take every great physicist—or other "ist"—for an apostle, but be ready to suspect him of some crudity concerning relations that lie outside his special studies, if his exposition strands us on results that seem to stultify the most ardent, massive experience of mankind, and hem up the best part of our feelings in stagnation.'[1]

This instinct for the understanding of all forms of thought and feeling, this quest for that which is essentially human in all varieties of belief, can of course be illustrated to any extent from the novels. 'Pity and fairness', she once wrote, 'embrace the utmost delicacies of the moral life', and this delicacy, together with her balanced regard for improvement and for old imperfect things, appears clearly in her treatment of contrasted types of churchmanship. Mr Gilfil's sermons (of which he kept a large heap, 'rather yellow and worn at the edges') certainly belonged to the class of the old and imperfect, but when his congregation, having dozed through

---

[1] *Ibid.*, pp. 245 and 253 (Dec. 10, 1874 and Jan. 30, 1875).

the sermon's 'agreeable monotony', 'made their way back through the miry lanes', they were 'perhaps as much the better for this simple weekly tribute to what they knew of good and right, as many a more wakeful and critical congregation of the present day'.[1] The same attitude appears in her treatment of Mr Irwine in *Adam Bede*, and in the contrast between him and Mr Ryde: 'Mrs Poyser used to say ... Mr Irwine was like a good meal o'victual, you were the better for him without thinking on it, and Mr Ryde was like a dose o'physic, he gripped you and worreted you, and after all he left you much the same.'[2] The contrast reappears, in *Middlemarch*, in Mr Farebrother and Mr Tyke: Mr Farebrother, the man of the world who plays for money, yet who has pity and fairness, fine human tact and ripe wisdom, and knows the secret of renunciation; Mr Tyke, protégé of Bulstrode, who is doctrinal and evangelical but non-human. It was George Eliot's constant objection to evangelicalism, that in its emphasis upon the will and acts of an implacable Deity it extinguished human love and service. She extended this objection to all general ethical maxims if followed without regard to their human results:

> 'There is no general doctrine', she says in *Middlemarch*, 'which is not capable of eating out our mortality if unchecked by the deep-seated habit of direct fellow-feeling with individual fellow-men.'[3]

Fred Vincy feels no remorse for his careless borrowings until he sees their actual effect upon the Garth family: 'Indeed we are most of us brought up in the notion that the highest motive for not doing a wrong is something irrespective of the beings who would suffer the wrong.'[4] 'We cannot be utterly blind to the results of duty, since that cannot be duty which is not already judged to be for human good.'[5] The whole analysis of Mr Bulstrode's self-justifications is meant to illustrate these principles.

---

[1] *Scenes of Clerical Life*, pp. 94-5 (World's Classics ed.).
[2] P. 200 (World's Classics ed.).
[3] *Middlemarch*, bk. vi, ch. 61 (New Cabinet ed., 1913, vol. iii, p. 133).
[4] *Ibid.*, vol. i, p. 379. [5] Cross, *op. cit.*, vol. iii, p. 48.

On the other hand, George Eliot admires the evangelical awakener if his gospel is really constructive, if it is informed with the spirit of love: it is enough to mention Mr Tryan in *Janet's Repentance*. She laughs at him indeed, or rather at some of the effects he produces in Milby—e.g. Miss Pratt's literary effort, which was 'Six Stanzas, addressed to the Rev. Edgar Tryan, printed on glazed paper with a neat border, and beginning "Forward, young wrestler for the truth!"' —nevertheless,

> 'Evangelicalism had brought into palpable existence and operation in Milby society that idea of duty, that recognition of something to be lived for beyond the mere satisfaction of self, which is to the moral life what the addition of a great central ganglion is to animal life.... Whatever might be the weaknesses of the ladies who pruned the luxuriance of their lace and ribbons, cut out garments for the poor, distributed tracts and quoted Scripture, and defined the true Gospel, they had learned this—that there was a divine work to be done in life, a rule of goodness higher than the opinion of their neighbours; and if the notion of a heaven in reserve for themselves was a little too prominent, yet the theory of fitness for that heaven consisted in purity of heart, in Christ-like compassion, in the subduing of selfish desires.... The first condition of human goodness is something to love; the second, something to reverence. And this latter precious gift was brought to Milby by Mr Tryan and evangelicalism.'[1]

Or there is her attitude to Methodism in *Adam Bede*:

> 'It is too possible that to some of my readers Methodism may mean nothing more than low-pitched gables up dingy streets, sleek grocers, sponging preachers, and hypocritical jargon—elements which are regarded as an exhaustive analysis of Methodism in many fashionable quarters.'

But the picture she would have us form of it is

> 'an amphitheatre of green hills, or the deep shade of broad-leaved sycamores, where a crowd of rough men and weary-hearted women drank in a faith which was a rudimentary culture, which linked

[1] *Scenes*, pp. 319-20.

their thoughts with the past, lifted their imagination above the sordid details of their own narrow lives, and suffused their souls with the sense of a pitying, loving, infinite Presence, sweet as summer to the houseless needy.'[1]

Romola's attitude to Savonarola may here be recalled: it is George Eliot's own attitude to dogmatic religion. In so far as he stands for the prophetic will and insight, for the determination to bring Florence back to God, and to die if need be in the attempt, Savonarola is grand and heroic in her eyes; such absolute devotion to the highest aims and standards awes and humbles her; she forgets his superstitious beliefs and sees only the saint; she returns to Tito at his command. But when Savonarola refuses to speak the word that will save her godfather's life, all is changed:

> "'Do you, then, know so well what will further the coming of God's Kingdom, father, that you will dare to despise the plea of mercy—of justice—of faithfulness to your own teaching? . . . Take care, father, lest your enemies have some reason when they say, that in your visions of what will further God's Kingdom you see only what will strengthen your own party."
>
> "'And that is true!" said Savonarola, with flashing eyes. Romola's voice had seemed to him in that moment the voice of his enemies. "The cause of my party *is* the cause of God's Kingdom."
>
> "'I do not believe it!" said Romola, her whole frame shaken with passionate repugnance. "God's Kingdom is something wider—else, let me stand outside it with the beings that I love."'[2]

In her grief and rage at finding him insensible to human appeal, she loses all that admiration which had made her hitherto 'unmindful of his aberrations, and attentive only to the grand curve of his orbit'. It is interesting, however, that George Eliot's passion for impartiality leads her, in a comment on the foregoing dialogue, to by-pass Romola and partially rejustify Savonarola:

> 'It was inevitable that she should judge the Frate unfairly on a question of individual suffering, at which *she* looked with the eyes of personal tenderness, and *he* with the eyes of theoretic conviction.

---

[1] *Adam Bede*, p. 38. [2] *Romola*, p. 508 (World's Classics).

In that declaration of his, that the cause of his party was the cause of God's Kingdom, she heard only the ring of egoism. Perhaps such words have rarely been uttered without that meaner ring in them; yet they are the implicit formula of all energetic belief. And if such energetic belief, pursuing a grand and remote end, is often in danger of becoming a demon-worship, in which the votary lets his son and daughter pass through the fire with a readiness that hardly looks like sacrifice: tender fellow-feeling for the nearest has its danger too, and is apt to be timid and sceptical towards the larger aims without which life cannot rise into religion.'[1]

Her typical view on the conflict between 'theoretic conviction' and human tenderness (already indicated in the extract from *Middlemarch* about 'general doctrine') is to be seen in a letter to Charles Bray:

'I dislike extremely a passage [in his book, *The Philosophy of Necessity*] in which you appear to consider the disregard of individuals as a lofty condition of mind. My own experience and development deepen every day my conviction that our moral progress may be measured by the degree in which we sympathize with individual suffering and individual joy.'[2]

To further this kind of 'moral progress' was her most consciously held aim as a novelist, just as it was Wordsworth's aim to widen his readers' sensibility, and make them more 'actively and securely virtuous'. Indeed, George Eliot carries on the Wordsworthian tradition in more ways than one.

'If art does not enlarge men's sympathies, it does nothing morally. I have had heart-cutting experience that *opinions* are a poor cement between human souls: and the only effect I ardently long to produce by my writings is, that those who read them should be better able to *imagine* and to *feel* the pains and the joys of those who differ from themselves in everything but the broad fact of being struggling, erring, human creatures.'[3]

Artistic power she defined as 'an instinctive perception of the varied states of which the human mind is susceptible, with

---

[1] *Romola*, p. 517. [2] Cross, *op. cit*, vol. i, p. 472 (Nov. 15, 1857).
[3] *Ibid.*, vol. ii, p. 118 (July 5, 1859).

ability to give them out anew in intensified expression'.[1] Connected with this outlook is her deliberate renunciation of the stock themes of traditional fiction and the stage-properties of 'romance', in favour of that imaginative penetration of the commonplace which she often achieves, and too often also rather embarrassingly *discusses* in the novels themselves. 'My artistic bent', she says (and this, in a letter to Blackwood, will make no reader wince)—

> 'is directed not at all to the presentation of eminently irreproachable characters, but to the presentation of mixed human beings in such a way as to call forth tolerant judgment, pity and sympathy.'[2]

It is when she breaks off her own narratives to justify her methods that, in spite of the interest and truth of the matter, the manner and tone make one writhe—as when, in *Amos Barton*, she archly rallies an imaginary lady reader (who thinks Mr Barton uninteresting) with a 'But, my dear madam'—most of your fellow-beings are 'of this insignificant stamp', yet they have their sublime promptings, their sacred joys, etc., and ends:

> 'Depend upon it, you would gain unspeakably if you would *learn with me* [my italics] to see some of the poetry and the pathos, the tragedy and the comedy, lying in the experience of a human soul that looks out through dull grey eyes, and that speaks in a voice of quite ordinary tones.'[3]

In her positive creative achievement, however, she abundantly shows the power attributed to Wordsworth by Coleridge, that of spreading the depth, height and atmosphere of the ideal world around situations, forms and incidents 'of which, for the common view, custom had bedimmed all the lustre, had dried up the sparkle and the dew-drops'. It was by confirming in her this conception of the novelist's aim, namely, the enlargement of sympathy by the imaginative

---

[1] *Ibid.*, vol. i, p. 174 (beginning of 1848).
[2] *Ibid.*, vol. i, p. 431 (Feb. 18, 1857).
[3] *Scenes*, p. 48. See also the passage in *Adam Bede* (pp. 193 ff.) where she compares her methods with those of the Dutch school of painting. It contains what is possibly the most irritating remark in George Eliot's whole work: 'But bless us, things may be lovable that are not altogether handsome, I hope?'

heightening of the real, that G. H. Lewes probably rendered his most valuable service to her. 'You must try and write a story'—full credit has been allowed him for that piece of wise encouragement, but what is less widely known is that Lewes had already, before their intimacy, written an essay on *The Lady Novelists* in the *Westminster* (July 1852), in which he outlined the theory that became hers—that fiction should be based on real experience, and that it should enable readers to share a profounder realization of the feelings and the plight of common humanity. He had even, in advance of his time, propounded a psycho-analytic theory of artistic creation, that it is a resolution of, and compensation for, the artist's inward conflicts and dissatisfactions, and that feminine art is the transposition on to the aesthetic plane of the specifically feminine forms of suffering. Lewes even anticipates the illustration of the oyster's secretion, since popularized by Housman: the poem is the pearl which insulates and glorifies the pain. In a second essay, *Realism in Art* (*Westminster*, Oct. 1858), published while *Adam Bede* was in preparation, he says that 'realism' should be considered as opposed, not to 'idealism' but to 'falsism'; the true business of art is intensification, not distortion or falsification of the real. The common appearances of daily life will furnish all we ought to ask.[1] No doubt Lewes was himself influenced here by Comte's views on the social function of the arts (cf. above, pp. 197-8).

The tension in George Eliot's mind between ideal and actual, action and reaction, ambition and renunciation, appears in her preoccupation with the theme of the 'egotistical sublime', her recurrent treatment of efforts after sanctity, great and signal service, or self-realization—efforts which are thwarted by circumstance, 'the gradual action of ordinary causes', the blight of the commonplace. We have noted the spiritual ambitiousness of her own evangelical youth—her emulation of Hannah More and St Paul, her anxiety 'to be doing some little [i.e. a very great deal] toward the regeneration of this groaning, travailing creation'. The content of this ambition was changed after her 'conversion'

[1] For these references I am indebted to Bourl'honne, *op. cit.*

(or perversion) to the Religion of Humanity, but it never left her; it remained in the form of that 'terrible earnestness' we have spoken of, that sense of the peremptoriness of Duty —of duty whose claims were all the more absolute because its 'divine' sanction had been destroyed. It remained, after she had found that her service must be rendered through fiction, in her haunting sense of responsibility to mankind in all that she wrote ('the high responsibilities of literature that undertakes to represent life'[1]). Of a spring trip to Italy in 1861 she writes: 'We must be for ever ashamed of ourselves if we don't work the better for it.' True, this was written to her publisher, but it illustrates the workings of her ever-accusing conscience: time must not be wasted, an account must be rendered, pleasure must be justified by its fruits. And soon after she adds:

> 'I will never write anything to which my whole heart, mind and conscience don't consent, so that I may feel that it was something —however small—which wanted to be done in this world, and that I am just the organ for that small bit of work.'[2]

After her provincial salad days were over, the thwarting, the frustration of which she was ever conscious, came not from outward circumstances but from her unconquerable self-distrust: 'Shall I ever write another book as true as "Adam Bede"? The weight of the future presses on me....'

> 'If it were possible that I should produce *better* work than I have yet done! At least there is a possibility that I may make greater efforts against indolence and the despondency that comes from too egoistic a dread of failure.... What moments of despair I passed through ... despair that life would ever be made precious to me by the consciousness that I lived to some good purpose! It was that sort of despair that sucked away the sap of half the hours which might have been filled by energetic youthful activity; and the same demon tries to get hold of me again whenever an old work is dismissed and a new one is being meditated.'[3]

---

[1] Cross, *op. cit.*, vol. ii, p. 293 (to Blackwood, March 30, 1861).
[2] *Ibid.*, p. 303.
[3] *Ibid.*, p. 306 (From Journal, June 16 and 19, 1861, written while composing *Romola*).

At those rather awful Sunday *salons* at The Priory in later years, she always tried to communicate, to each disciple who was summoned to her footstool, something precious and profound—some moral souvenir which could be taken away and treasured for life. M. Bourl'honne thinks that George Eliot never attained true humility, although she was constantly denouncing spiritual pride and indulging in a false self-abasement. But if so, she knew it herself, if we may take the biography of Maggie Tulliver to be in this respect (as it surely is) the transcript of her own experience. The setting is given in that chapter on the religion of the Dodsons ('A Variation of Protestantism unknown to Bossuet') whose like had never yet been seen in English fiction, and which displays to the full George Eliot's sociological insight as well as her special gift of sympathizing where yet she criticizes.

> 'The religion of the Dodsons consisted in revering whatever was customary and respectable: it was necessary to be baptized, else one could not be buried in the churchyard, and to take the sacrament before death as a security against more dimly understood perils; but it was of equal necessity to have the proper pall-bearers and well-cured hams at one's funeral, and to leave an unimpeachable will. A Dodson would not be taxed with the omission of anything that was becoming, or that belonged to that eternal fitness of things which was plainly indicated in the practice of the most substantial parishioners, and in the family traditions—such as, obedience to parents, faithfulness to kindred, industry, rigid honesty, thrift, the thorough scouring of wooden and copper utensils, the hoarding of coins likely to disappear from the currency, the production of first-rate commodities for the market, and the general preference for whatever was home-made. The Dodsons were a very proud race, and their pride lay in the utter frustration of all desire to tax them with a breach of traditional duty or propriety. A wholesome pride in many respects, since it identified honour with perfect integrity, thoroughness of work, and faithfulness to admitted rules: and society owes some worthy qualities in many of her members to mothers of the Dodson class, who made their butter and their fromenty well, and would have felt disgraced to make it otherwise. To be honest and poor was never a Dodson motto, still less to

seem rich though being poor; rather the family badge was to be honest and rich, and not only rich, but richer than was supposed.'

'Surely the most prosaic form of human life': 'you could not live among such people'? Let us see, she proceeds, how it affected Tom and Maggie Tulliver—'how it has acted on young natures in many generations, that in the onward tendency of human things have *risen above the mental level of the generation before them, to which they have been nevertheless tied by the strongest fibres of their hearts*' (my italics). Maggie, the predestined heretic from this religion, has to endure unspeakable yearnings. 'Stifled for want of an outlet towards something beautiful, great, or noble', she stumbles upon Thomas à Kempis, and experiences a sense of awakening, of revelation and of conversion. 'Forsake thyself, resign thyself, and thou shalt enjoy much inward peace'—then her melancholy, her chronic malaise, were the results of egoism? 'A strange thrill of awe passed through Maggie as she read, as if she had been wakened in the night by a strain of solemn music, telling of beings whose souls had been astir while hers was in stupor.' She sees for the first time 'the possibility of shifting the position from which she looked at the gratification of her own desires—of taking her stand out of herself, and looking at her own life as an insignificant part of a divinely-guided whole'. But what next?—

> 'With all the hurry of an imagination that could never rest in the present, she sat ... forming plans of self-humiliation and entire devotedness; and, in the ardour of first discovery, renunciation seemed to her the entrance into that satisfaction which she had so long been craving in vain. She had not perceived—how could she until she had lived longer?—the inmost truth of the old man's outpourings, that renunciation remains sorrow, though a sorrow borne willingly.'

Inevitably, then, she dramatizes herself, sees herself as heroic in her very renunciation:

> 'her own life was still a drama for her, in which she demanded of herself that her part should be played with intensity. And so it came to pass that she often lost the spirit of humility by being

excessive in the outward act; she often strove after too high a flight, and came down with her poor little half-fledged wings dabbled in the mud.'

The same pattern appears again in Dorothea Brooke, 'Theresa of the Midland flats' (the phrase I have already applied to her creator), whose sufferings likewise arose from 'a certain spiritual grandeur ill-matched with opportunity'. So too with Romola, with Lydgate and with Gwendolen, where thwarting circumstance assumes its most menacing shape—the incompatible marriage. The great souls in George Eliot are brought low, and come down to earth, with wings dabbled in the mud. Romola, it is true, attains a sort of ultimate deliverance, finds sanctity in service—but there is a note of fairy-tale unreality in those last chapters (just as there is, though in a different form, in the 'idyllic' *Silas Marner*); the destinies of Maggie, Lydgate, Dorothea and Gwendolen are nearer to her intuition. 'Doing without opium' truly involves much anguish, and one can understand why George Eliot once said 'it would be better if my life could be done for me, and I could look on'. Bourl'honne is right, I think, when he says that 'the inspiration of her work is clearly optimistic, the intention which animates it being to show the possibility of good and the power of the will; the work as it was achieved is no less clearly pessimistic, the general impression which emerges from it being the powerlessness of man against circumstances and the checkmate of the will'. The keenness of her unsatisfied yearnings was tempered in her later years, but the clear-eyed endurance had strained her to excess, and the final calm seems in part to be that of exhaustion.

CHAPTER X

MATTHEW ARNOLD

1. Introductory

'MY poems', wrote Matthew Arnold to his mother in 1869, 'represent, on the whole, the main movement of mind of the last quarter of a century, and thus they will probably have their day as people become conscious to themselves of what that movement of mind is, and interested in the literary productions which reflect it'. Not only his poems, but all his works have this representative character, and it is the main purpose of the present chapter to show this, and to show it (as befits the scope of this book) by examining chiefly his writings on politics and religion. I do not suggest that Matthew Arnold was 'a representative Englishman' of his time, in the sense that perhaps Macaulay or Dickens were representative. Indeed, he had several traits which are not supposed to be particularly 'English': many-sidedness, a European outlook, and—the quality which he praised in Joubert—'amenity'. He was, not the most brilliantly gifted nor the most forceful of the eminent Victorians, but the most intelligent: he *understood* best the 'main movement' of his own time, and the very qualities of detachment and flexibility which remove him from the ranks of the 'representative' make him for us the clearest and least distorting mirror of the age. Arnold's 'intelligence', moreover, was not of the kind which, in separation from virtues of the heart and of the spirit, can sometimes be sterile or negative. To adapt phrases of his own, he applied a fusion of sentiment and intellect to the main trends of the modern world, and he applied them with a sense of responsibility which was serious without solemnity, and earnest without portentousness. As a poet he can be ranked amongst the first four or five (shall we say?) of his time; as a literary critic he can hardly be given any but the first place. And what other Victorian can we name who, along with such distinction, is also an educational reformer, and a compelling writer of social, political and religious criticism? Indeed, in Arnold we encounter a new phenomenon, the 'literary' intelligence playing freely upon the great concerns of human life. He was the first to see and to proclaim the importance, for the modern world, of the qualities of mind and spirit which literary culture can give, and literary criticism has gained immensely from his expansion of its scope. 'Students' of literature today should not think of him, as it is to be feared they often do, as the author of a small volume of poems, and of *Essays in Criticism*, a man of letters who occasionally forgot himself to the extent of writing books about religion; this is to misconceive the true proportions of his work, to miss his centre of gravity. *Estote ergo vos perfecti!* was the motto of *Culture and Anarchy*, and it may very well stand as the motto of Arnold's whole message. His literary essays should be viewed, not as the main current from which his other writings are offshoots, but as tributary rills swelling the mainstream of his life's effort. And his main effort was that of a sage, a teacher, a moralist and a physician of the human spirit. Arnold was as conscious as George Eliot that his life had been thrown upon 'an iron time of doubts, disputes, distractions, fears', and in his poetry he often allows himself to mourn for the days

> 'when wits were fresh and clear,
> And life ran gaily as the sparkling Thames:
> Before this strange disease of modern life,
> With its sick hurry, its divided aims,
> Its heads o'ertaxed, its palsied hearts, was rife.'

> 'This tract which the river of Time
> Now flows through with us, is the plain:
> Gone is the calm of its earlier shore
> Border'd by cities and hoarse
> With a thousand cries is its stream.'

But to think of him as a mere 'escapist' on the strength of such passages (and they are recurrent) in his verse would be as great a mistake as to fancy that his prose is the work of a strayed reveller from the realms of gold. He may be 'a foil'd circuitous wanderer'—a wanderer

> 'between two worlds, one dead,
> The other powerless to be born',

but if in his verse he is often the elegist of the dead world (and of something dead or dying within himself), in his prose he assists the birth of the new with cheerful alacrity. It has sometimes been thought strange that the man who in verse could mourn so poignantly could yet, in his prose writings as in his daily life, be so urbane, sunny and debonair —could even, in his youth, indulge in a little Byronism and surface foppery, and be described, in his maturity, as 'an elegant Jeremiah'.[1] But we have, in these very contradictions, something of the secret of Arnold's power, and of his comparative invulnerability:

> 'Radiant, adorn'd outside, a hidden ground
> Of thought and of austerity within.'

He knew, and had 'felt along the heart', the deep malady of his time, and for that very reason could diagnose it and spend the greater part of his life in trying to cure it. Of the other critics and prophets of that generation, which could have written *Sohrab* or *Thyrsis*? of the other poets, which could have written *Culture and Anarchy* or *Literature and Dogma*? Arnold's social and religious criticism may be amateurish, but it has the poet's sensibility, and the critic's sanity and nimbleness, which are often lacking in the professionals. Similarly, his literary criticism derives its weight and authority from its connexion with his effort to see life steadily and see it whole.

I make no apology, then, for devoting most of the ensuing remarks to his religious writings; they are not only relevant to the purpose of the present book, but they are also the corner-stone of Arnold's work. Arnold is commonly thought of as the apostle of Culture and of Poetry, but to him religion was the highest form of culture and of poetry. The highest art, he says, the art of Pheidias, of Dante or of Michelangelo,

---

[1] 'Coupled, by a strange perversity of fate, with just that very one of the Hebrew prophets whose style I admire least.'—*Culture and Anarchy*, p. 3 (1869).

is an art 'which by its height, depth and gravity possesses religiousness.' Poetry passes into religion on its highest level, and religion must pass into poetry in order to penetrate and transform 'that poor inattentive and immoral creature, man'. *Estote ergo vos perfecti!*—'the full perfection of our humanity' —that was Arnold's lifelong quest, and he sought it with the earnestness imbibed from the Rugby of his father, with the passion of an Oxford Hellenist who had also felt the spell of Newman, and with the sensibility of a poet who lived, not in any ivory tower or palace of art, but at close quarters with the dismal and illiberal life of Philistine England. He sought it also—and this is what distinguishes him from the other Victorian prophets—with that serene detachment, that inward poise, which make *Culture and Anarchy* (in particular) a masterpiece of ridicule as well as a searching analysis of contemporary society. Even in his religious books there is 'mental laughter'; what appears in his poetry as lassitude or nostalgia is, in his prose, transformed into banter and delicate mockery. There is in him an occasional touch of affectation, even of vanity, and his mannered reiterations can be annoying when clearer definitions are what we want; but usually the tone is almost perfect in its amenity, and he never becomes effete or precious like Pater, strident like Carlyle, or hysterical like Ruskin.

ii. *Culture and Anarchy*

The particular 'anarchy' confronting Arnold during the composition of this 'Essay in Political and Social Criticism' (1867-69) was the anarchy, or the omens of it, associated with 'shooting Niagara', with the second Reform Bill, with trades-union disturbances, Fenian outrages, Reform League riots in Hyde Park, the campaign of John Bright, the Murphy riots at Birmingham and Manchester, and the like. But these were to him only symptoms of that deeper anarchy of the spirit to which he opposes the idea of 'Culture'. The old world was dead, killed by the French and Industrial Revolutions, and in the vast, sprawling democracy which had succeeded he could see no centre of control, no sense of direction, little in fact but the worship of Mammon and machinery, supported by a faith in the virtue of 'doing-as-one-likes', and a complacent belief in material progress. How to make order emerge from this chaos, how to restore purpose and idea to the social organism, how to maintain communications with the past and the future, these were the problems he set himself to solve. 'Things in England being what they are,' he wrote soon after the book was published, 'I am glad to work indirectly by literature rather than directly by politics.'[1] Arnold was convinced of the 'beneficent function' of literature, and speaks of the 'immense work' it has to do in the middle region between religion and science: 'I do hope that what influence I have may be of use in the troubled times which I see before us as a healing and reconciling influence.'[2]

Modern civilization has become 'mechanical and external, and tends constantly to become more so'. Now 'Culture', like religion, 'places human perfection in an *internal* condition, in the growth and predominance of our humanity proper, as distinguished from our animality'; 'not a having and a resting, but a growing and a becoming, is the character of perfection as culture conceives it; and here, too, it coincides with religion'.[3] 'Faith in machinery' is our besetting danger: faith in coal, railways, wealth and increasing population, as if these were 'precious ends in themselves'; faith, too, in our freedom to say and to do just what we like:

> 'But culture indefatigably tries, not to make what each raw person may like, the rule by which he fashions himself: but to draw ever nearer to a sense of what is indeed beautiful, graceful, and becoming, and to get the raw person to like that.'[4]

Culture does not mean, as 'that fine speaker and famous Liberal', Mr Bright, supposes, 'a smattering of the two dead languages of Greek and Latin'; it is 'a study of perfection'; it means 'getting to know, on all the matters which most

---

[1] *Letters*, ed. G. W. E. Russell (1901), vol. ii, p. 77 (Oct. 17, 1871).
[2] *Ibid.*, p. 41 (June 25, 1870).
[3] *Culture and Anarchy*, pp. 12-13 (references are to the first ed., 1869).
[4] *Ibid.*, p. 17.

concern us, the best which has been thought and said in the world, and through this knowledge, turning a stream of fresh thought upon our stock notions and habits'; it means trying to make 'reason and the will of God prevail'. So understood, it may help to stem 'the common tide of men's thoughts in a wealthy and industrial community'; it may at least 'save the future, as one may hope, from being vulgarized, even if it cannot save the present'.

Arnold next surveys the English scene, analysing the structure of our society, and the characteristic ideas of each class, in order to see whether any one of the three main classes can serve as an organ of culture, a nucleus of the new order. Everyone knows his classification of English society into Barbarians, Philistines and Populace; indeed, so many came to know it, and the other recurrent phrases—'sweetness and light', 'Hebraism and Hellenism', etc.—within a few years following the book's appearance, that Disraeli once congratulated Arnold on being 'the only living Englishman who had become a classic in his own lifetime'. 'The fact is', Arnold comments, 'that what I have done in establishing a number of current phrases . . . is just the sort of thing to strike him. He had told Lady Airlie before I came that he thought it a great thing to do, and when she answered that she thought it was rather a disadvantage, for people got hold of my phrases and then thought they knew all about my work, he answered—Never mind, it's a great achievement!'[1] To Carlyle, the aristocracy seemed the only possible centre of authority; to Mr Lowe, the middle classes: to the Reform League, the working class. But as for the 'Barbarians' (aristocracy), they have had their day; their fine qualities of high spirit, serenity and distinguished manners, valuable in more stable epochs, do not fit them for leadership in times of swift change. They are 'inaccessible to ideas', and so in a time like the present, 'a time for ideas, one gets, perhaps, in regarding an aristocracy, even more than the idea of serenity, the idea of futility and sterility'. So that when 'Mr Carlyle, a man of genius to whom we have all at one time or other been indebted for refreshment and stimulus', recommends

[1] *Letters*, vol. ii, p. 219 (Feb. 21, 1881).

the aristocracy for their 'dignity and politeness', culture reminds us that they possess one chief ingredient of perfection but not the other: beauty, but not intelligence; sweetness, but not light. Arnold had undergone the impact of Carlyle in his earlier days, just as he had felt the 'charm' of Newman, but his later allegiance was given to neither. Carlyle became for him a 'moral desperado'; he talks wearily of 'that regular Carlylean strain which we all know by heart and which the clear-headed among us have so utter a contempt for'[1]; and finally, on Carlyle's death, he tells M. Fontanès that he 'never much liked Carlyle. He seemed to me to be "carrying coals to Newcastle" . . .: preaching earnestness to a nation which had plenty of it by nature, but was less abundantly supplied with several other useful things'.[2] Certainly, if Carlyle was wrong about the aristocracy, he was still more perverse to preach 'earnestness' to the Philistines; it was to recommend 'several other useful things' to that very class that *Culture and Anarchy* was chiefly written. No: the Philistines are too smug, too self-satisfied and too 'Hebraic' to form the desired 'centre'; the Populace, too raw and too blind. The members of each of the three classes, as such, are intent merely upon exercising their birthright of 'doing as they like', which means, following the dictates of their 'ordinary selves'. But culture teaches us that we have a 'best self' as well as an 'ordinary self', and tries to develop in us that 'best self', at the expense of 'our old untransformed self'. And culture, accordingly, suggests the idea of *The State* as the organ and repository of the collective best self, and the true centre of authority in the new world.

For Arnold the key to the whole position was to be found in the Philistines, the great middle class—and especially its main stronghold, the Puritan or Dissenting connexion—now the most influential section of English society. And to them he devotes most of his attention, for he knew them well. Lay school inspectors (and school inspecting, it must never be forgotten, was Arnold's daily occupation for thirty years) at that time visited only the Nonconformist schools, and

[1] *Letters of M. A. to A. H. Clough*, ed. H. F. Lowry (1932), pp. 111 and 151.
[2] *Letters*, vol. ii, p. 222.

Arnold had perforce become terribly familiar with, though never at his ease in, Zion. About Puritanism he has said some of his hardest things, though he himself, like all the best Victorians, had the moral core of it within him. Puritanism, by which Arnold usually means Protestant Dissent, is of two types, the bitter and the smug: both of them thwarting to 'the full perfection of our humanity'. After the Renaissance, as he never tires of repeating, the spirit of England entered the prison-house of Puritanism, and had the key turned upon it there for two hundred years. Puritanism has plenty of fire and energy, plenty of conscience and sobriety; it has made England strong just where France is weak; but its ideal of perfection is narrow and incomplete. It has 'Hebraism', the principle of conduct, but not Hellenism, the principle of sweetness and light. To it we owe, indeed, our moral fibre, our instinct for honesty and purity —for 'conduct' in short, which, as Arnold insists elsewhere, comprises three-fourths of life. But conduct is only one item on the school report, albeit the most important; conduct alone is not enough; Thomas Arnold had intended Rugby to produce scholars as well as Christian gentlemen. As Arnold puts it, 'he who knows only his Bible knows little of that'; even a Quaker drawing-room, haunt of peace and purity, would be the better for a piano. Arnold attributes to the Hebraizing Philistines (an odd paradox, yet so it is: they are children of Israel but not children of light) the main defects of contemporary England: its parochialism, its provinciality, its vulgarity, its lack of centrality, its lack of contact with the great European movements, and even with its own most venerable traditions. Already, in that essay on *The Function of Criticism at the Present Time* which anticipates the main argument of *Culture and Anarchy* ('criticism' being there defined in terms almost identical with those later applied to 'culture'), Arnold had illustrated these defects in his happiest vein of irony: it is really, he had said, 'the strongest possible proof of the low ebb at which in England the critical spirit is, that while the critical hit in the religious literature of Germany is Dr Strauss's book, in that of France M. Renan's book, the book of Bishop Colenso is the critical hit of the religious literature of England'. And there was Miss Cobbe with her 'new religion', and the British College of Health, in the New Road:

> 'Everyone knows the British College of Health; it is that building with the lion and the statue of the Goddess Hygeia before it; at least I am sure about the lion, though I am not absolutely certain about the Goddess Hygeia. This building does credit, perhaps, to the resources of Dr Morrison and his disciples; but it falls a good deal short of one's idea of what a British College of Health ought to be. In England, where we hate public interference and love individual enterprise, we have a whole crop of places like the British College of Health; the grand name without the grand thing.'[1]

Taking the Pilgrim Fathers as archetypal patterns of Puritanism, Arnold remarks that, 'notwithstanding the mighty results' of their voyage,

> 'they and their standard of perfection are rightly judged when we figure to ourselves Shakspeare or Virgil,—souls in whom sweetness and light, and all that in human nature is most humane, were eminent,—accompanying them on their voyage, and think what intolerable company Shakspeare and Virgil would have found them!'[2]

In the same way he looks round at the Nonconformist religious organizations of contemporary England, the home of 'the Dissidence of Dissent and the Protestantism of the Protestant religion': 'look', he exclaims,

> 'at the life imaged in such a newspaper as the *Nonconformist*;— a life of jealousy of the establishment, disputes, tea-meetings, openings of chapels, sermons; and then think of it as an ideal of human life completing itself on all sides, and aspiring with all its organs after sweetness, light, and perfection!'

The Puritans, considering themselves to be in possession of the one thing needful, the *unum necessarium*, have felt free in

---

[1] *Essays in Criticism,* First Series (1916 ed.), p. 32.
[2] *Culture and Anarchy,* p. 29.

all else to follow the lead of their ordinary selves, have given full rein to their acquisitiveness and Mammonism, and have vulgarized and debased even the precious truths of which they have been the chief witness.

Against all this 'anarchy' Arnold opposes the idea of 'Culture', a term which comes in the end to stand for almost all that Arnold valued most deeply: religion and sound learning, 'criticism' and poetry, and—more specifically—the ideas of the State, the National Establishment and the University, the latter symbolized for him, of course, by Oxford. And it is significant that at this very point in the argument it is the thought of Oxford, and of Newman, that comes into his mind. In the midst of all the 'hardness and vulgarity of middle-class liberalism' and 'the hideous and grotesque illusions of middle-class Protestantism', Oxford, though it has 'not marched victoriously with the modern world', has 'told silently upon the mind of the country'; it has 'prepared currents of feeling which sap our adversaries' position when it seems gained'; it has kept up 'communications with the future'. Oxford, like the Grande Chartreuse, may be part of the dead or dying world, it may be the home of lost causes and impossible loyalties, and yet—

> 'steeped in sentiment as she lies, spreading her gardens to the moonlight, and whispering from her towers the last enchantments of the Middle Age, who will deny that Oxford, by her ineffable charm, keeps ever calling us nearer to the true goal of all of us, to the ideal, to perfection?'

Arnold's business is not to explain how 'the State' could ever become the organ of Culture and the best self of the nation, or how it could avoid being the organ of whatever class happened at the time to be in the ascendant. But he may be given credit for seeing clearly, at a time when State action of almost any kind was viewed with suspicion (especially by the Nonconformists), that the thing needed was more and more central planning, more enlightenment at the heart of the body politic, and above all, State education for the middle classes and the masses. Culture, he said, was no class perquisite to be enjoyed by the exclusive and privileged few;

it was the best friend of equality, because it could not securely subsist unless it permeated the whole mass. 'The men of culture', he writes, 'are the true apostles of equality'; culture, by turning a free play of ideas on to all stock notions, the inveterate prejudices of each class or sect, 'seeks to do away with classes' altogether. But the special task of Arnold as an educationalist was to urge the vital and immediate need of providing State secondary schools for the middle classes. They were the preponderant section of society, their strength was the nation's strength, their crudeness its crudeness: civilize and humanize the Philistines, therefore! His ideal, one feels, would have been government by a State closely resembling, though more modern in outlook than, Oxford, and the spread of culture over the whole country (in a phrase of Professor J. Dover Wilson) [1] 'by an indefinite multiplication of non-residential Rugby Schools under State supervision'.

Arnold's fundamental political belief was that 'moral causes govern the standing and the falling of States': that, as he told the Americans,

> 'in a democratic community like this, with its newness, its magnitude, its strength, its life of business, its sheer freedom and equality',

the danger lay in the absence of discipline, in hardness and materialism, and above all in the absence of any adequate ideal, or sense of purpose and direction. Aristocracy, as we saw, has served its turn, and democracy is the force of the future, but if we are to avoid the special dangers of democracy some substitute must be found for the standards (exquisite culture, high manners, grand style) hitherto set by the aristocracy. The greatest of these dangers is that which comes 'from the multitude being in power, with no adequate ideal to elevate or guide the multitude'. A nation, to be great, needs not only freedom for individuals: it is great

> 'when these numbers, this freedom, and this activity, are employed in the service of an ideal higher than that of the ordinary man,

[1] See the excellent Introduction to his edition of *Culture and Anarchy* (1932), p. xiii.

taken by himself. Our society is probably destined to become much more democratic; who or what will give a high tone to the nation then?'

Arnold put his faith in all that he meant by 'Culture'—which, as we have seen, included religion as well as education, the quest for perfection and light in all things. But his characteristic plea on the practical level was for State secondary schools on the lines of the French Lycées, not to replace Eton and Harrow and Rugby, but to give the middle and lower classes their share in the best culture of the nation. The middle classes, and pre-eminently the 'kernel of these classes, the Protestant Dissenters', have rightly enough suspected State action in the past, associating it with Conventicle Acts, Test Acts and the like. But they should realize that times have changed; the State can now be their truest friend. Abroad, the problem might be how to reduce the power of the State; here, it was the opposite.

In *Friendship's Garland* (1871), amid much that is of merely passing interest, and amid much somewhat tiresome archness and persiflage, the section headed 'My Countrymen' may be noted as valuable, and particularly the passage contrasting England's great moment, the year 1815, with her condition half a century later. At that moment, in 1815, England had the secret of the way things were moving; the stars were with her. Her aristocracy still led, and resistance to change—the *raison d'être* of all aristocracy—was then needed to check Napoleonism. Since then England has lost the aristocratic tone, and the middle class which now rules her destinies has no ideals except those of doing a roaring trade and being left to itself. Consequently England is now not much regarded on the Continent, and her lecturings of foreigners are treated with contempt. Nations can only be 'great' if they are 'bottomed on some vital idea or sentiment', and unless England 'gets *Geist*' (how it measures our distance from 1871 that the German 'Arminius' can serve as Arnold's mouthpiece for reason and all salutary truths!)—unless, that is, the middle class becomes more intelligent, and sees that the work to be done now is not that of 1815, but that of making human life more widely rational and just, she will sink to the position of 'a Holland'. Palmerston found England first in the world's estimation, and left her third (i.e. after France and the U.S.A.).

'Hardly a German newspaper can discuss territorial changes in Europe but it will add, after its remarks on the probable policy of France in that event: "England will probably make a fuss, but what England thinks is of no importance".'[1]

But some may say: what of it? the future is with America; America is outstripping us spiritually as well as materially, 'and if our race at last flowers to modern life there, and not here, does it so much matter?' To Arnold it does matter: he has 'a longing for this old and great country of ours to be always great in herself, not only in her progeny'.

> 'Yes, we arraign her; but she,
> The weary Titan, with deaf
> Ears, and labour-dimm'd eyes,
> Regarding neither to right
> Nor left, goes passively by,
> Staggering on to her goal;
> Bearing, on shoulders immense,
> Atlantean, the load,
> Wellnigh not to be borne,
> Of the too vast orb of her fate.'[2]

III. Arnold's Religious Writings

'*At the present moment two things about the Christian religion must surely be clear to anybody with eyes in his head. One is, that men cannot do without it; the other, that they cannot do with it as it is.*'

These words, taken from the Preface to *God and the Bible* (1875),[3] aptly sum up the whole drift and intention of Arnold's religious writings. In those sentences he takes up his characteristic position as 'middle-man', standing be-

---

[1] *Friendship's Garland* (1903 ed.), p. 118.
[2] *Ibid.*, Conclusion.
[3] Popular ed. (1906), p. viii (my italics).

tween and sharing the view both of the 'orthodox', who rightly hold that we cannot do without religion, and the free-thinking liberals, who rightly hold that we cannot do with it as it is. In these books of Arnold's the 'conservative-reforming' intellect of nineteenth century England finds its most complete and persuasive expression. Arnold is akin in spirit to the Cambridge Platonists of the seventeenth century, to Coleridge, and to his father Thomas Arnold; he is a child of the new era, and has felt the full strength of the modern spiritual east winds, but for him it ever remains as important to keep up communications with the past as with the future. To Arnold religion was always the thing that mattered most: all his efforts—in criticism, in politics, in education—really led up to it. It was therefore of vital importance to preserve it, to find a basis for it which should make it invulnerable to 'scientific' criticism and yet leave it ethically as powerful as before. In so far as this very problem is still before us today, I think these books of his are of continuing value. To grasp their significance it is necessary to remember several things—and first, that he was the son of Thomas Arnold. This meant that he had continually before him, as an object of reverential attachment and as an example, a man who combined the deepest religious convictions with an accessibility to the light of modern ideas which was rare indeed in English clergymen of his day. What chiefly weighed with him was his father's readiness to follow the lead of Coleridge and the Germans in entertaining more enlightened views on Scripture-interpretation:

> 'In papa's time the exploding of the old notions of literal inspiration in Scripture, and the introducing of a truer method of interpretation, were the changes for which, here in England, the moment had come. Stiff people could not receive this change, and my dear old Methodist friend, Mr Scott, used to say to the day of his death that papa and Coleridge might be excellent men, but that they had found and shown the rat-hole in the temple.'[1]

Religion must be perpetuated, but to be perpetuated it must be transformed far more radically than even his father would

---
[1] *Letters*, vol. ii, p. 23 (Nov. 13, 1869).

have allowed. And this brings us to the second point to be remembered: Arnold, from his own 'European' standpoint, saw that the undercutting of Christian 'foundations' by the *Zeitgeist* had proceeded much further than was dreamed by average believers in England. Such believers were apt, in their sheltered provincial backwater, to entertain serious illusions, and to imagine that they could 'save things which they cannot save'. A good medicine for such illusions

> 'would be the perusal of the criticisms which *Literature and Dogma* has encountered on the Continent. *Here in England that book passes, in general, for a book revolutionary and anti-religious.* In foreign circles of the liberal school it provokes a feeling of mingled astonishment and impatience; impatience, that religion should be set on new grounds when they had hoped that religion, the old ground having in the judgment of all rational persons given way, was going to ruin as fast as could fairly be expected; astonishment, that any man of liberal tendencies should not agree with them.'[1]

Some years after the books had been written, he said in a letter to his friend Sir M. Grant Duff—

> 'the central fact of the situation always remains for me this: that whereas the basis of things amidst all chance and change has even in Europe generally been for ever so long supernatural Christianity, and far more so in England than in Europe generally, this basis is certainly going—going amidst the full consciousness of the continentals that it is going, and amidst the provincial unconsciousness of the English that it is going.'[2]

Arnold's aim was not to awaken the English from their provincial unconsciousness: the time-spirit would soon do this in any case. His aim was to supply them with a new and true basis for their religion, so that when the inevitable awakening came, it should not lead them to reject Christianity itself along with their untenable traditional beliefs. 'The partisans of traditional religion in this country do not know, I think, how decisively the whole force of progressive and liberal opinion on the Continent has pronounced against

---

[1] Preface to *Last Essays on Church and Religion* (1903 ed.), p. vii (my italics).
[2] *Letters*, vol. ii, p. 234 (July 29, 1882).

the Christian religion.' And when that force reaches this country, as it surely will, 'liberal opinion' will follow suit, and will be inclined, unless something can be done in advance to prevent it, to abandon religion together with its pseudo-foundations. This brings us to the third point: to what particular audience did Arnold address himself? Not to those who were content, or 'striving to be content', with the received theology; to those who could still accept this he said 'For God's sake believe it, then!' Arnold was and still is attacked for robbing people of their simple faith, but in fact the robbery had already been perpetrated upon those he had in mind, and he was merely restoring to them—sometimes before they knew of their loss—something not so liable to be stolen. Nor were his arguments addressed to the frivolous and the insensible, nor to 'Liberal secularists', nor to Catholics—though some or all of these might, he thought, some day find his work useful to them. They were addressed to those who,

> 'won by the modern spirit to habits of intellectual seriousness, cannot receive what sets these habits at nought, and will not try to force themselves to do so, but who have stood near enough to the Christian religion to feel the attraction which a thing so very great, when one stands really near to it, cannot but exercise, and who have some familiarity with the Bible and some practice in using it.'[1]

He brands his own work as ephemeral by saying that it is addressed 'to one people and race, and to one sort of persons in it, and to one moment in its religious history'; whether the 'moment', however, was quite so transitory as he implies is open to question; *Literature and Dogma* has not lost all relevance even now. But he was certainly justified in claiming that, in due time, his work would be recognized for what it was: 'an attempt conservative, and an attempt religious'.[2] As I have already hinted, Arnold ('the founder of English Modernism', as he has been called) was trying to do for the nineteenth century what the Cambridge Platonists had done for the seventeenth. Whichcote, so Salter tells us, aimed

---

[1] Preface to *God and The Bible*, p. xxiii. [2] *Ibid.*, p. xxx.

'to preserve a spirit of sober piety and rational religion ... in opposition to the fanatic enthusiasm and senseless canting then in vogue', and Burnet testifies that he taught his hearers to consider 'the Christian Religion as a doctrine sent by God both to elevate and sweeten human nature'; Arnold would have accepted both these accounts as applicable to his own effort. Like Whichcote or John Smith, he wished to protect religion by planting it firmly on a basis of verifiable spiritual experience; like them again, and like Thomas Arnold, he wished to reunite the dissenting sects with the Church on a broad footing of comprehension; like them, he tried to show that religion had everything to gain, and only inessentials to lose, by welcoming the light of truth from every quarter.

The same leading ideas recur throughout *St Paul and Protestantism* (1870), *Literature and Dogma* (1873), *God and The Bible* (1875) and *Last Essays on Church and Religion* (1877). I propose to take *Literature and Dogma* as the central theme, referring to the other books when occasion arises.

Convinced that the human spirit cannot do without religion, and convinced no less that much that now passes for religion is unsound, and 'touched with the finger of death', Arnold proceeds to enquire how far religion rests upon unassailable facts of experience. If such facts can be found, then it is with these that we should start, and not with miracles which never happened, nor with theological formulae whose truth can never be demonstrated, and whose usefulness the human mind has outgrown. The title of the book already suggests its connexion with his work as a literary critic: the religious transformation he looked for could only be achieved by applying to the Bible and the creeds 'the qualities of flexibility, perceptiveness, and judgment, which are the best fruits of letters'. 'Culture', in fact, could yield a 'better apprehension' of religious truth than theological acumen or the 'vigorous and rigorous' theories of Tübingen professors. The distinction between 'Literature' and 'Dogma' corresponds to the distinction now current between 'emotive' and 'scientific' language: 'emotive' language being language used, not to describe or refer to a state of affairs, but to express or evoke a state of feeling; 'scientific', being language purporting to describe, with precision, objective facts. The language of the Bible is not, as is too often supposed, 'rigid, fixed and scientific', but 'fluid, passing and literary'; it is language *thrown out*, so to speak, at a not fully grasped object of the speaker's consciousness' —poetic language, not pretending to the precision of scientific or philosophical statement. The word 'God', for example, is for Arnold the chief and the most potent of emotive terms; its true function is to evoke in us the strongest possible sense of the authority of the moral law, of the reality of a power which 'makes for righteousness', and of our need to live in accordance with that law. If we try to turn it into a 'scientific' term, we at once get all the contradictions between the Absolute of metaphysics and the 'personal' God of traditional religion (the supernatural person conceived as a 'magnified and non-natural man'). Arnold habitually adopts a tone of puzzled humility in reference to metaphysics, speaking with Socratic self-abasement of his well-known incapacity for abstruse argument; at the same time he manages to imply that such arguments are mostly verbal juggling, having no value for the ordinary human being. But he comforts the 'plain man' by assuring him that he has really a better chance of reading the Bible successfully even than the Bishops of Winchester and Gloucester, who are so anxious, as Arnold mockingly reiterates, to 'do something for the honour of Our Lord's Godhead'. Arnold's satire normally sets up men of straw as symbolic bogies for attack, and what the Rev. W. Cattle or Mr Roebuck are for *Culture and Anarchy*, the said Bishops are for *Literature and Dogma*: they stand for sterile dogmatism, unrealized and unrelated to the *Zeitgeist* and to the facts of religious experience. However, 'the plain man' does need some help—not the help of theologians or metaphysicians, but the help of Culture; he needs to know something of the best that has been thought and said in the world; he needs literary experience— experience of how men have felt and expressed themselves in former times; he needs a historic sense; he needs the 'flexibility' of spirit which is the best fruit of literary training.

With such aids he may avoid that false approach to the Bible which seeks to extract dogma from poetry, or uses the text 'talismanically'; he may acquire that critical tact and insight which will enable him to discriminate between one text and another, to read between the lines, and to see what is vital for him and what is less so.

In the section entitled 'Religion Given' Arnold then examines the basis of Old Testament religion. Israel did not find out God by reasoning or by inference; he 'felt and experienced' what was revealed to him. What did he experience and feel? that which it is the glory of the Hebrew race to have known, that which is the firm foundation of all morality and all religion, that '*Righteousness tendeth to life*', that 'to righteousness belongs happiness'. 'O ye that love the Eternal, see that ye hate the thing which is evil'; 'to him that ordereth his conversation aright shall be shown the salvation of God.' This law, in whose fulfilment alone are true freedom and true happiness to be found, Israel—by no flight of metaphysical speculation, but merely by profound insight, conceived as the will and command of a power external to themselves, a power which they personified as 'God'. The essential faith of the Old Testament, then, for Arnold, is belief in 'the Eternal not ourselves that makes for righteousness'. The importance of realizing that religion is founded upon moral experience is, for Arnold, immense; his whole position, the whole force of his pleading, depend upon this. He desires for religion a basis of fact, which 'science'—that is, the positive modern spirit which accepts nothing unsure, nothing unverifiable—which 'science', in that sense, can and must accept. And of all 'facts' none is more inescapable, more completely attested by the universal experience of humanity, than that righteousness tendeth to life, that by transcending our lower, everyday selves and entering upon the life of the spirit, we do, experimentally, have life and have it more abundantly. 'Conduct', he says in the oft-quoted phrase, is the object of religion, and 'conduct is three-fourths of life'. Here, then, and not on any so-called 'proofs' from ontology, from prophecy or from miracle, let us begin to build our religion.

But come, 'this is mere moral babble', it will be said; to make it *religion*, a binding force and a power to transform and save us, we need something more. Precisely, says Arnold, we need *emotion*; religion is 'ethics heightened, enkindled, lit up by feeling;' it is 'not simply morality', but 'morality touched by emotion'.[1] 'Live as you were meant to live!' is morality; 'lay hold on eternal life', religion. The rules of morality were arrived at by experience—the experience that man is not a creature of the moment, but has in addition to his inferior, 'momentary' self, a best or whole self, and that attention to the needs of this best self brings liberty, and peace, and joy. These rules, however, only pass into religion when they become suffused with humble devotion, gratitude and love towards the divine lawgiver, who has attached to righteous living the peace which passeth understanding. 'Left to ourselves, we sink and perish; visited, we lift up our heads and live.'

But the religious consciousness of Israel, starting from these simple and profound insights, proceeded (as that of all other nations has done in the course of religious development) to superadd to them *Aberglaube*, or 'extra-beliefs'; it added, in particular, the expectation of a divine Messiah who should be the 'miraculous agent of Israel's new restoration'. And this leads us to Arnold's treatment of 'Religion New-Given', of the New Testament and Christianity. Jesus Christ, when he came, proved to be 'the last sort of Messiah whom the Jews expected'. The Jews had reached a conception of righteousness superior to that of all other peoples, but it was the mission of Jesus to correct and elevate that conception, and above all to furnish for righteousness the most powerful of sanctions. He taught the true 'method' and 'secret' of righteousness: the 'method' of *metanoia*, change of heart, rebirth, inwardness; the 'secret' of renunciation, losing one's life to gain it, assuming one's cross, dying to sin so as to rise again in the spirit. And, for the sanction, there was the most powerful of all motive-forces, love: love for Jesus himself, for his perfect selflessness, for his mildness and 'sweet reasonableness' (*epieikeia*), and the passionate

---

[1] *Literature and Dogma*, p. 21.

attachment ('faith') inspired by his ultimate sacrifice. Arnold's view of the Christian faith may be illustrated here by considering his interpretation of St Paul in *St Paul and Protestantism*. What was it that set Paul in motion? The core of his religious experience is to be found, not where Calvinism has placed it, in the formulae of predestination, election, justification and sanctification. The Calvinist scheme as set forth in the Westminster Confession, with its 'covenants, conditions, bargains and parties-contractors', 'could have proceeded from no one but the born Anglo-Saxon man of business, British or American'.[1] All this is to find in St Paul's eastern and figured language, just as it stands, the 'formal propositions of western dialectics'; 'what in St Paul is figure, and belongs to the sphere of feeling, Puritanism has transported into the sphere of intellect and made formula'. No, the impelling force with St Paul was 'the master-impulse of Hebraism,—*the desire for righteousness*'[2], the passion for a life wholly conformed to the will of God, wholly penetrated by its power. Paul found that through mere dutifulness and mere respect for divine law he could not achieve this. But the grand discovery of Paul, which has changed the course of history, was the discovery of a principle which by adding emotion to legal morality could make him more than conqueror over his divided self. 'The wish is there, but not the power of doing what is right' (I quote Moffatt's translation). 'I cannot be as good as I want to be, and I do wrong against my wishes.... So this is my experience of the Law: I want to do what is right, but wrong is all I can manage.... Miserable wretch that I am! Who will rescue me from this body of death? God will! Thanks be to him through Jesus Christ our Lord!'[3] Paul discovered *Christ*, and found there the needed dynamic; 'of such a mysterious power and its operation', says Arnold, 'some clear notion may be got by anybody who has ever had any overpowering attachment, or has been, according to the common expression, in love. Every one knows how being in love changes for the time a man's spiritual atmosphere, and makes animation and buoy-

---

[1] *St Paul and Protestantism* (1870), p. 19.
[2] *Ibid.*, p. 35.   [3] Romans vii, 18-25.

ancy where before there was flatness and dulness.'[1] When Paul had found Christ, 'the struggling stream of duty, which had not volume enough to bear him to his goal, was suddenly reinforced by the immense tidal wave of sympathy and emotion'[2], and 'to this new and potent influence Paul gave the name of *faith*'—'fast attachment to an unseen power of goodness', the faith that worketh through love. Paul's concern with Christ was 'as the clue to righteousness, not as the clue to transcendental ontology'; '"the law of the spirit of life in Christ Jesus", says Paul, "freed me from the law of sin and death".' This, then, was how faith 'justified', by enabling us to die to our multitudinous impulses, and live to the spirit; no longer tied by 'a set of mere mechanical commands and prohibitions, lifeless and unaiding', we identify ourselves with Christ, dying to sin with him, and rising with him to genuine life. Arnold finds that, although Paul certainly believed in the physical resurrection of Jesus, he yet constantly understood 'resurrection' also as a 'figure', and found its inmost meaning in that sense. It was indeed part of the 'astonishing greatness' of Paul that, living when and where he did, he yet grasped this spiritual notion, and made such signal religious use of it. Arnold has sometimes been taken to task for an alleged over-deference to 'science'; he was, as we have seen, anxious to separate from religion those elements which exposed it to scientific attack. But by 'science' he means simply the search for truth, or, more specifically, the modern spirit, in so far that spirit seeks to prove all things, and hold fast only that which is sure. An example of his use of the term occurs at this very point in *St Paul and Protestantism*:

'To popular religion, the real kingdom of God is the New Jerusalem with its jaspers and emeralds; righteousness and peace and joy are only the kingdom of God figuratively. The real sitting in heavenly places is the sitting on thrones in a land of pure delight after we are dead; serving the spirit of God is only sitting in heavenly places figuratively. *Science* exactly reverses this process;

[1] *St Paul and Protestantism*, p. 60.
[2] *Ibid.*, p. 70.

for *science*, the spiritual notion is the real one, the materialist notion is figurative.'[1]

Thus Paul's notion of spiritual death and resurrection was 'scientific' in this sense; the 'materialist' or physical resurrection of Christ is, for us (though it was not so for Paul), figurative.

Now the elements in popular religion which were exposing it to scientific attack, and which Arnold therefore wished to remove, were partly, as we have suggested, the petrified formulae of Calvinism, but more particularly the whole 'miraculous' element in Christianity itself. The 'proof' of Christianity had long been made to rest upon miracle and upon prophecy, instead of upon its own internal and verifiable truth. And now that both prophecy and miracle are being impugned by the *Zeitgeist*, many feel that 'the whole certainty of religion seems discredited, and the basis of conduct gone'.[2] It is mainly to such that Arnold addresses himself: it is not *religion* that is discredited, he tells them, it is only *Aberglaube*! Religion not only has natural truth, truth verifiable and 'scientific', but is needed now more and more, needed perhaps as it never was before. Let us not abandon it, then, merely because certain inessential extra-beliefs are now seen to be what they are. We must remind ourselves that in his diagnosis of the contemporary situation Arnold had uppermost in mind the following considerations: first, that the time-spirit had sapped the miraculous 'foundations' of Christianity; secondly, that the orthodox, instead of confronting this, were on the whole stiffening their adherence to the threatened beliefs; thirdly, that religion itself was endangered by being supposed to be inseparable from *Aberglaube*; lastly, that it could and must be saved from both obscurantists and sceptics by being restored to its genuine foundation in natural truth. Religion has in the past attached its emotion to certain supposed facts, and now that the facts are failing it, the 'liberals'—particularly on the Continent, but also here (witness the followers of Bradlaugh, for example)—are beginning to assume that religion itself is an

---

[1] *Ibid.*, p. 89 (my italics). [2] *Literature and Dogma*, p. 108.

exploded imposture. Arnold, addressing himself on the one hand to the liberals, tells them that the 'impostures' (not that they were ever really such) are not of the essence, and that religion stands firm upon a basis of experience when all that is unbelievable has fallen away; and on the other hand, addressing the orthodox, he insists that only by disengaging religion from miracle can it be saved from total destruction. I need not summarize his further argument in any detail here; it is enough to say, first, that he proceeds to give examples, taken from many recently examined by biblical scholars, of the misinterpretation of certain crucial prophecies; and secondly, that, on the subject of miracles, he holds that whether or no they *can* happen, in reality they *do not* happen, but that belief in them, in certain circumstances, always arises. 'The human mind, as its experience widens, is turning away from them. And for this reason: it sees, as its experience widens, how they arise.'[1] Prediction and miracle were attributed to Christianity 'as its supports, because of its grandeur, and because of the awe and admiration which it inspired'. The Catholics fancy that the Bible miracles *and* those of their own Church form a class apart from all other recorded miracles; the Protestants, while rejecting those of the Roman Church, believe the same of the Bible miracles. The Protestant notion is 'doomed to an earlier ruin than the Catholic', because it 'invites to a criticism by which it must finally itself perish'. 'The sanction of Christianity' then, 'if Christianity is not to be lost along with its miracles, must be found elsewhere.'

The value of the New Testament is not diminished by the discovery that the writers of it were subject to error: 'the book contains all that we know of a wonderful spirit, far above the heads of his reporters, still farther above the head of our popular theology, which has added its own misunderstanding of the reporters to the reporters' misunderstanding of Jesus'.[2] To extract the essential things from the New Testament, we require not so much profound scholarship, and certainly not so much scholastic subtlety, as wisdom and purity: wisdom, in the sense of ripeness; experience of men's

[1] *Ibid.*, p. 129.   [2] *Ibid.*, pp. 159-60.

ways of thinking, feeling and speaking; literary tact, above all; and purity, to feel without impediment the irresistible force of Christ's teaching and example. Instead, the New Testament has been made the basis of a great superstructure of subtle speculation, much of it based upon 'an immense literary misapprehension'. Instead of seeing that, around so extraordinary a figure as Jesus, many extra-beliefs must, in early ages, inevitably have clustered, men have taken the extra-beliefs to be the essential thing, and have lost sight of the true Jesus in the 'thaumaturgic personage' who has replaced him. Arnold freely grants that without the extra-beliefs Christianity would never have got established, and would still not commend itself to many of the faithful. This does not disturb him overmuch: better Christianity plus *Aberglaube* than no Christianity at all, and those who now enjoy a simple traditional faith he would not unsettle. The form in which Christianity first expressed and crystallized its saving truths was the only form in which, at that stage and in that mental climate, it could have expressed and preserved them. But mental climates change: this is 'development' (as Newman calls it), or widening of horizons, and the saving truths, if they are not to be lost, need restating in the language of each age. They need restating, today, in language which is in every respect true to the experience of today. It is not, let us repeat, with the holders of 'simple faith' that Arnold is concerned, it is with those (conceived by him to be a growing multitude, soon to include nearly everybody) who, rejecting creed and dogma as false science, and rejecting miracle as legend, are likely to reject Christianity itself along with them. 'Our one object', he writes, 'is to save the revelation in the Bible from being made *solidary*, as our Comtist friends say, with miracles.'[1] And it could only be saved, he believed, in an age when men are demanding proof and verification in every sphere, by placing the centre of gravity not in the 'materializing mythology' of traditional dogma, but in the aforesaid saving truths, which are invulnerable to any time-spirit, and can be proved by any who will enter experimentally upon the divine life, using the

[1] *Ibid.*, p. 249.

method and secret of Christ. 'If we love one another, God dwelleth in us': that is the way to speak of God to the modern multitude, and not to proffer the barren definitions of credal metaphysics, which they will certainly reject. The Apostles' Creed, recounting the 'points of the legend', he calls 'the popular science of Christianity'; the Nicene Creed, embodying the abstruse conceptions of a later culture, and further removed from the influence of Christ himself, he calls 'the learned science of Christianity'. And the Athanasian Creed, enshrining the results of a fierce metaphysical struggle, he calls 'learned science with a strong dash of violent and vindictive temper'. No, he says, 'the real essence of Scripture is a much simpler matter. It is, for the Old Testament: *To him that ordereth his conversation aright shall be shown the salvation of God!*—and, for the New Testament, *Follow Jesus*!' 'Religion has been made to stand on its apex instead of its base; righteousness is supported on ecclesiastical dogma, instead of ecclesiastical dogma being supported on righteousness.'[1]

We now begin to meet the conservative side of Arnold's thought; so far, he has been abreast of the forward-marching intellect: now, the backward-yearning affections come into play. Like George Eliot, he is very tender with all that has ever been held holy and true, or has become entwined with the best impulses of humanity. He is no stern agnostic corroding all certainties: still less is he the shallow rationalist who delights in 'showing up' religion. His attempt is 'an attempt conservative, and an attempt religious'. In one passage he even expresses hesitation in attacking any anthropomorphism or extra-belief, if it has served its purpose in sanctioning and aiding conduct; given righteousness, he almost says here, never mind what mythology supports it. But of course he does not commit himself to this line; to do so would have stultified his whole argument. Sooner or later the question will always arise about any extra-belief, 'is it sure?' can it be 'verified'? and it was precisely his concern that the assumptions of faith should be such that these questions could be quite honestly answered in the affirmative.

[1] *Ibid.*, pp. 289-91.

Arnold's conservatism comes out clearly in his praise of the Bible as a manual of righteousness. 'When our philosophical Liberal friends say', he writes,

> 'that by universal suffrage, public meetings, Church-disestablishment, marrying one's deceased wife's sister, secular schools, industrial development, man can very well live; and that if he studies the writings, say, of Mr Herbert Spencer into the bargain, he will be perfect, he will have "in modern and congenial language the truisms common to all systems of morality", and the Bible is become quite old-fashioned and superfluous for him';—[1]

what is Arnold's reply? That the Bible is the incomparable, the unique inspirer of conduct—of conduct which is three-fourths of life. It is so because it contains the 'poetry' of the Christian religion, that in religion which moves and penetrates and transforms. And from this matchless and truly divine fountain, he mournfully observes—anticipating the laments of some of our own contemporaries over the far worse situation of today—from this grand source of inspiration 'the masses of our society seem now to be cutting themselves off'. This is, he laments, 'the special moral feature of our times: the *masses* are losing the Bible and its religion'. And why is this? It is because the Bible has been 'made to depend upon a story, or set of asserted facts, which it is impossible to verify; and which hard-headed people, therefore, treat as either an imposture, or a fairy-tale that discredits all which is found in connexion with it'. This prospect—of losing the Bible as the basis of our civilization—Arnold, as educationalist, moralist, and apostle of culture, viewed with the deepest disquiet. There was yet time, perhaps, to retrieve the position, but only by abandoning most of the pseudo-science of the credal formulations, by filtering out the legendary accretions, and by concentrating on essential truths which can still bring life and immortality to light. Unlike some liberalizing iconoclasts, Arnold does *not* want to replace the Bible by Herbert Spencer, nor Christianity by the Religion of Humanity, nor the Church services by

[1] *Ibid.*, p. 311.

ethical lectures and readings from Confucius or the Upanishads or J. S. Mill. For him, Christianity and its Bible are the pre-eminent sources of regeneration, the supreme inspiration to live the life of the spirit. Even if this were not so, and other religions were equally potent to save, yet for us, who have grown up within the Christian civilization, and learnt from Christianity nearly all we know about the spiritual life, for us to be taught about it 'in some other guise, by some other instructor, would be almost impossible'.[1] No, we must stick to the Bible, and not seek—as some have sought in the twentieth century still more resolutely—to feed the hungry sheep on any *ersatz* or synthetic scripture compounded out of 'the truisms common to all systems of morality'. To do so is to lose the emotion which touches morality into religion. And for us, this emotion is best communicated by the poetry and mythology of the Bible, and the poetry and symbolism of the Church liturgy and ritual.

But wait! someone may here protest: what is this that Arnold is saying? First he tells us that most of our traditional beliefs are illusions, and that we must hold fast only what is scientifically demonstrable, and then he turns upon us and bids us cherish these illusions because of their poetic charm and their hallowed associations. Exactly! Arnold replies; keep them as *poetry*: keep them, that is to say, as something of inestimable value. To say that a thing is 'poetry' is not to diminish its importance: only the Philistines make the mistake of supposing that. 'The strongest part of our religion today is its unconscious poetry', he says in *The Study of Poetry*; a religion without poetry, a religion which is merely ethical, or merely theological, has no power to move the soul, and is no religion at all. Arnold, as everyone knows, conceived most loftily of poetry and its destiny: 'We should conceive of poetry worthily, and more highly than it has been the custom to conceive of it. ... More and more mankind will discover that we have to turn to poetry to interpret life for us, to console us, to sustain us. Without poetry, our science will appear incomplete; and most of what now passes with us for religion and philosophy will be

[1] *Last Essays on Church and Religion* (1903 ed.), p. 29.

replaced by poetry.'[1] And this from the man who has been telling us with almost wearisome iteration, throughout several longish books, to be suspicious of all but the primary findings of our moral consciousness? There is really no contradiction here. We must first appease the hard-headed modern multitude, sceptical, positive and rational, who will accept nothing but what is 'scientific'. Science? yes! religion is scientific, for it rests upon the solid foundation of our experience as moral beings. *Salvation through Righteousness*, and *Righteousness through Jesus Christ*: this basis, on which all our religion really rests, is subject to no assaults from science, for it is itself demonstrably true. The hard-headed must needs accept this, whereas they will no longer accept the old credal statements as 'facts'. But once they have been induced to acknowledge the basis of natural truth, then let them receive back the rich store of Christian mythology and symbolism, but receive it as poetry: receive it, that is, as something most precious, something without which no amount of natural truth will thoroughly move and transform them. 'It is a great error', he says,

> 'to think that whatever is thus perceived to be poetry ceases to be available in religion. The noblest races are those which know how to make the most serious use of poetry.'[2]

The right method of transforming popular religion, so as to make it true for our time—the method of Jesus himself—is not to introduce 'brand-new religious language', or to part with 'all the old and cherished images', but to preserve the old language and images, 'as far as possible conveying into them the soul of the new Christian ideal'. Arnold even takes the Roman Catholic Church to task for not seeing that her true strength, and her probable success in the future, lies in the completeness with which she has preserved the older forms of Christian worship: 'the eternity and universality, which is vainly claimed for Catholic dogma and the ultramontane system, might really be possible for Catholic worship'.[3] It thus becomes clearer how Arnold, holding the views that we

---
[1] *Essays in Criticism*, 2nd series (1915 ed.), p. 2.
[2] *Last Essays on Church and Religion*, p. 27.   [3] *Ibid.*, Preface, p. xxiv.

have seen, was yet able to come forward as the champion of the Church of England and its liturgy. 'We should avoid violent revolutions in the words and externals of religion', he says:

> 'Profound sentiments are connected with them; they are aimed at the highest good, however imperfectly apprehended. Their form often gives them beauty, the associations which cluster around them give them always pathos and solemnity. They are to be used as poetry.'

The layman, then, when 'rehearsing' the prayers and services of the Church, may rehearse many of them as 'the literal, beautiful rendering of what he himself feels and believes'; the rest, which cannot be so taken, he may rehearse as 'an approximative rendering of it;—as language *thrown out* by other men, in other times, at immense objects which deeply engaged their affections and awe, and which deeply engage his also; objects concerning which, moreover, adequate statement is impossible'.[1] But the Thirty-nine Articles? These, indeed, are 'plain prose': that is, 'they present the creeds as science, exact science; and this, at the present time of day, very many a man cannot accept'. Such men, therefore, cannot honestly take Orders, because to do so they must profess to accept these Articles. It is interesting to find that Arnold squarely faces this issue, though he advises those who subscribed years ago, 'when things had not moved to the point where they are now', and who have long been engaged in useful ministry, not to trouble themselves with scruples about their former subscription—not, in fact, to be Robert Elsmeres. Arnold hoped and wished that the terms of subscription could be greatly reduced and rendered acceptable, and believed (erroneously, as time has shown) that this would soon be possible.

Arnold's attachment to the Church of England was profound; it was connected with some of his deepest instincts. He defines the Church as 'a great national society for the promotion of goodness'—a definition which reminds us that he was the son of Thomas Arnold, who, like Coleridge, had

[1] *Ibid.*, p. 38.

regarded the Church as the whole nation in its spiritual aspect. The promotion of goodness through Christian ethics seemed to him so much the most important function of the Church, that in relation to this supreme end he could hold cheap even his own criticisms of its theology. Indeed, he only made them because he believed that, without such adjustments to the *Zeitgeist*, the promotion of goodness by the Church would be brought to a standstill. But readers of Arnold's literary criticism, remembering his plea for Academies, for fixed standards of excellence, for the grand manner and for high seriousness, will not be surprised to find that the idea of a Church Establishment, a religious institution on a national scale, appealed to him irresistibly: it was the grand name *with* the grand thing. If literature must be defended from provinciality and from eccentricity, and if culture must be defended against anarchy and against Philistine vulgarizations, then surely Religion—which is culture in its most exalted mood, the highest kind of seriousness—must be defended against the whims and notions of separatists, against Stiggins and Chadband, and the Rev. W. Cattle, and all the crudities of dissent, by being embodied in a great national institution which shall preserve continuity, and bear witness to the unity, beauty and historical development of the faith. Arnold's loathing for the 'dissidence of dissent', and for the whole ethos of middle-class nonconformity, with its hideous buildings, its harsh Hebraism and its crude sectarian outlook, reveals him in another guise as the same upholder of traditional standards, the man of Rugby and Oxford, who in his literary and social criticism pleads for Culture, the best that has been thought and said in the world, and appeals to Hellenism, the spirit of Greece, to teach us how to view things in their truth and beauty. As he saw things, Protestant Dissent was played out; like Archbishop Tillotson and Thomas Arnold, he wished to see the 'Puritans' reincorporated in the national establishment. He wrote *St. Paul and Protestantism* largely to show them that the theological grounds for separation had been rendered meaningless by the *Zeitgeist*, and to condemn the error of separation for the sake of certain notions, themselves as inadequate as those separated from. The Church, caring first and most for fostering piety and righteousness, has not its *raison d'être* in 'notions', and, as a historical institution, can permit and tolerate development, whereas the separatists, who have taken their stand on some one interpretation, cannot depart from their fixed 'truth', and are thus condemned to stagnation and sterility. Arnold held that Dissent, in his time, was becoming vaguely conscious of all this, and that, in looking for a fresh standing-ground, it was becoming merely political—an expression of class antagonism. He recognized, indeed, that the Church of England had become connected in the popular mind with wealth and privilege, and with 'all that *Lion and Unicorn* business which is too plentiful in our Prayer-Book'. He insisted, moreover, that a Church which is satisfied with things as they are, and is not striving to establish the Kingdom of God on earth—in the form of social justice and amelioration—is false to the spirit of Christianity and its founder. Nevertheless Protestant Dissent, in spite of its fine record, its historic witness for truth and freedom, was now 'touched by the finger of death'; its scriptural fundamentalism had been exploded by scholarship, and the time had come for its reabsorption in the national Church.

To some it may seem that Arnold's attachment to the Church was like his attachment to Oxford—the nostalgia of a sensitive modern intellectual for the home of lost causes and impossible loyalties, the yearning of a sick and divided soul for the freshness of the early world, for the calm of the early mountainous shore where the river of time takes its rise. But Arnold's distinction seems rather to be, that while exposing himself unfalteringly to the spiritual east winds of the nineteenth century, he should yet have retained so deep a sense of the beauty of holiness. It is this combination in him of the spirit of criticism with the spirit of poetry and religion which raises him above the level of the average Victorian agnostic of the type of Spencer, Lewes, Huxley, Stephen, Morley or Sidgwick. Not one of these could have written *Dover Beach* or *The Scholar Gypsy*! Because he was a critic and an educational reformer, Arnold wished to restate the creeds in modern terms, but because he was also a poet he saw that even greater than the need for restatement was the need to conserve, and preserve from destruction, all the beauty and the power of tradition. For this amongst many other reasons he has worn better than most Victorian liberals, and those religious books of his, now seldom read, books which are commonly to be sold at second-hand bookstalls for a shilling apiece, still contain matter of importance for all who are concerned today 'to preserve a spirit of sober piety and rational religion'.

Index

Antoninus, Marcus Aurelius, Mill on, 166, 182
Areopagitica, and Mill's *Liberty*, 164
Arnold, Matthew, 251-83; and his father, 51, 56, 64, 254, 258, 264, 267, 280, 281; and Newman, 73, 89, 254, 257, 260; and Carlyle, 113, 127, 254, 256, 257; and G. Eliot, 239, 252, 276
Arnold, Thomas, 51-72; and Coleridge, 2, 49, 53, 57, 61, 62, 64, 69, 108, 264, 280; and M. Arnold, 51, 56, 64, 254, 258, 264, 267, 280, 281; and the Oxford Movement, 60-3, 84-5, 100; and J. Hare, 65; and Newman, 60-3, 72, 84-5, 86, 96, 97, 100; Carlyle on, 69; and W. G. Ward, 84, 86, 96, 97, 100

Bacon, and Comte, 187
Bauer, G. L., and Strauss, 224
'Beauchamp, Philip', 134-5, 137
Belsham, T. (Unitarian minister), 209
Bentham, Jeremy, *Deontology*, 132-40, 170; and Coleridge, 1-2, 32, 49-50, 135, 141, 205; and religion, 32, 133-5; Newman on, 62; Carlyle on, 126; Sidgwick on, 132, 133, 140; and Mill, 1-2, 49-50, 132, 135, 136, 141, 144, 145-6, 154, 170, 173, 177, 205
Berkeley, G., 9
Bodichon, Mme, G. Eliot's letters to, 237, 238, 239
Boileau, 22
Bourl'honne, P., on G. Eliot, 228, 248, 250
Bowring, John, editor of Bentham's *Deontology*, 132; on his aims, 135; comments on Bentham, 136, 137, 138
Brabant, Dr, 218-19
Bradlaugh, 273
Bray, Charles, 209, 210; G. Eliot's letters to, 237-8, 244
Bridges, J. H., and Comte, 189
Bright, John, 254, 255
Brinton, Crane, on Parliament, 45
Buckle, *History of Civilization*, 157
Buddha, 130
Buller, Charles, on Mill, 142
Bunyan, Newman on, 84; Carlyle and, 114
Burke, 'noble living and noble dead', 49
Burns, 130
Butler, Samuel, *Hudibras* quoted, 17
Butler, Samuel, Erewhonian view of immortality, 183-4
Byron, 32

Caesar, 130
Cambridge Platonists, T. Arnold compared with, 54; M. Arnold compared with, 264, 266-7
Campbell, Thomas, Carlyle on, 108-9
Candide, 178
Carlile, Richard (publisher), 134
Carlyle, Margaret, 106-7
Carlyle, Thomas, 102-31; on Coleridge, 3, 108-13; and Coleridge, 102, 103, 108, 121, 126; and T. Arnold, 69; and Newman, 102, 103, 108; J. A. Froude on, 102-3, 125; R. H. Hutton on, 102, 124-125; and Goethe, 102, 116, 117, 130; 'Mark Rutherford' on, 103; remarks on Wordsworth applied to, 118; James Martineau on, 103, 130; F. D. Maurice on, 105-6; Sterling on, 105, 117; *Life of Sterling* quoted, 105, 110; letters to Sterling, 123-4; and Wordsworth, 109, 116, 121; and M. Arnold, 113, 127, 254, 256, 257; Mill learns from, 141, 157; on Mill, 141, 142-3, 151; and Mill's 'highly-instructed One or Few', 169; *entsagen* versus Mill's 'happiness', 171; and Mrs Taylor, 194; and Comte, 195; and G. Eliot, 217, 228, 238
Cecil, Lord David, on G. Eliot, 238
Chesterfield, Lord, 143
Chubb, Thomas, mentioned by Strauss, 223
Cobbe, Miss, and M. Arnold, 259
Cobden, and G. Eliot, 228
Colenso, Bishop, and M. Arnold, 258
Coleridge, Sir J. T., 51; T. Arnold's letters to, 53, 64
Coleridge, S. T., 1-50; J. S. Mill on, 1-2, 32, 49-50, 108, 135, 141, 205; and Bentham, 1-2, 49-50, 135, 141, 205; and T. Arnold, 2, 49, 53, 57, 61, 62, 64, 69, 108, 264, 280; and J. Hare, 2, 108; Newman on, 2-3, 61, 75, 108; Newman his disciple? 90-91; his 'Imagination' and Newman's 'Faith', 92; Newman continues his work, 96; and Sterling, 2, 108; F. D. Maurice on, 3-4, 31, 108; his influence on Maurice, 49; and Maurice, 54; and Carlyle, 3, 102, 103, 108-13, 121, 126; and Hume, 3; inverts Hume's teaching on Faith and Reason, 32, 90-1; and Hartley, 4, 5, 9; 'victory' over, 13-14, 15, 32; and Priestley, 4, 5. 44; and Southey, 5-6, 7; and Godwin, 5, 7-9, 44; and Locke, 'victory' over, 13-

284

INDEX

14, 15, 27, 32; and Kant, 34-5; and W. G. Ward, 99; influence on Mill, 141, 146, 149; Mill on *Dejection* Ode, 147; and G. Eliot, 239, 245
Combe, G. (phrenologist), and G. Eliot, 228
Comte, Auguste, 187-203; and Mill, 141, 146, 149-50, 154, 155, 156, 157, 187, 190, 191, 192, 195; and G. H. Lewes, 187, 188, 189-90, 246; and G. Eliot, 188, 207, 228; and Condorcet, 195; and De Maistre, 195.
Cowley, Coleridge on, 12, 27
Cromwell, 130
Cudworth, mentioned by G. Eliot, 229

Dante, and Carlyle, 130; and Comte, 195; and M. Arnold, 253
Darwin, Charles, 38; Mill's reading of, 176, 184-5; G. Eliot on, 238
Descartes, 27
De Quincey, Carlyle on, 109
Dickens, and G. Eliot, 228; and M. Arnold, 251
Disraeli, and M. Arnold, 256
Donne, 17
Dryden, 22
Duff, Sir M. Grant, M. Arnold's letter to, 265
Dumont, *Traité de Législation*, 146

Egerton, Lady, T. Arnold's letter to, 68
Eichhorn, *Letters on the New Testament*, 40; and Strauss, 223
Eliot, George, 204-50; and Comte, 188, 207, 228, 237; F. W. H. Myers on, 204, 238; and J. S. Mill, 205; and Strauss, 205, 207, 228, 237, 239; and Wordsworth, 205, 244-5; and C. Hennell, 207, 209, 211, 217, 218-20, 228; and Feuerbach, 207, 228, 230; and G. H. Lewes, 207, 228, 246; and the Misses Franklin, 208; and Miss Lewis, 208, 217; and Wilberforce, 208, 217; and Hannah More, 208, 217, 246; and Mrs Somerville, 209; and Carlyle, 217, 228, 238; letters to Sara Hennell, 218, 237, 239; and Cobden, 228; and Dickens, 228; and Mackay, 228-30; and H. Martineau, 228; and F. Newman, 228; and Prof. Owen, 228; and H. Spencer, 228; Bourl'honne on, 228, 248, 250; reference to Cudworth, 229; letters to Mme Bodichon, 237, 238, 239; letters to Bray, 237-8, 244; Lord D. Cecil on, 238; on Darwin, 238; and M. Arnold, 239, 252, 276; and Coleridge, 239, 245; and F. D. Maurice, 239; and Renan, 239; and Sidgwick, 239; letters to Mrs Ponsonby, 240; on Methodism, 242; on Savonarola, 243-4
Eliot, T. S., *Waste Land* quoted, 23
Emerson, R. W., 73
Euhemerus, and Strauss, 222, 224

Feuerbach, Ludwig, *Essence of Christianity*, 227-36; and G. Eliot, 207, 228, 230
Fontanès, M., M. Arnold's letter to, 257
Franklin, The Misses (G. Eliot's schoolteachers), 208
Frederick the Great, 130
Frend, W., 5
Fricker, Mrs., 7
Froude, J. A., on Newman, 84, 102; on Carlyle, 102-3, 125
Froude, R. Hurrell, 76, 78, 79, 86; W. G. Ward on his 'thoroughness', 97
Fry, Elizabeth, Newman on, 84

Gabler, and Strauss, 224
Geddes, Alexander, 39
Godwin, W., Coleridge's attitude to, 5, 7-9, 44; *Political Justice* and Pantisocracy, 6
Goethe, and Carlyle, 102, 116, 117, 130
Gray, Thomas, 27
Grote, George, and Bentham, 134

Hardy, Thomas, 'Immanent Will', 122, 193; on the search for God, 176
Hare, Julius, on Coleridge, 2, 108; and T. Arnold, 65
Hartley, David, 2; and Coleridge, 4, 5, 9; Coleridge's 'victory' over, 13-14, 15, 32; and Mill, 144, 145
Hazlitt, Carlyle, on 109
Hegel, and Strauss, 222, 225; and Feuerbach, 230-1; and Marx, 231
Hennell, Caroline, 209, 210
Hennell, Charles, *Inquiry Concerning the Origin of Christianity*, 207-20; and G. Eliot, 207, 209, 211, 217, 218-20, 228; and Strauss, 218-20, 221-2, 225.
Hennell, Mary, 209
Hennell, Sara, 209; G. Eliot's letters to, 218, 237, 239
Herbert, G., 17
Hildebrand, Newman on, 75
Hitler, and Carlyle, 130-1
Hobbes, 30, 140; and Mill, 152, 154
Hodges, Prof. H. A., 66
Hodgson, Prof. Leonard, on Biblical scholarship, 38
Holbach, *Système de la Nature*, 210
Holcroft, T., 5
Homer, 195
Hooker, Richard, quoted, 39; and T. Arnold, 54, 59; and R. H. Froude, 76

Hort, F. A. J., 3
Housman, A. E., 246
Howard, J., Newman on, 84; Mill on, 182
Hume, David, Atheism, 3; Faith and Reason, 32, 90-1; Carlyle on, 110-11; and Mill, 177, 185
Hutton, R. H., on Carlyle, 102, 124-5; on Mill, 142
Huxley, T. H., and M. Arnold, 282

Johnson, Dr, 22, 130
Jonson, Ben, 22
Joubert, and M. Arnold, 251

Kant, and Coleridge, 34-5; and W. G. Ward, 99; and Strauss, 220, 224
Keble, 51; Assize Sermon, 76
Keats, quoted to illustrate Imagination and Fancy, 18-19; Imagination, 23; 'What the imagination seizes as beauty', 25; 'proved upon the pulses', 32, 94; born same year as Carlyle, 102; on *Paradise Lost*, 104
Kempis, Thomas à, and Maggie Tulliver, 249
Kingsley, Charles, 3; and Newman, 86
Kosciusko, 5

Lamarck, cited by Comte, 193
Langland, Carlyle compared with, 129
Lawrence, D. H., quoted on the 'two ways of knowing', 27-8, 29, 30, 94; and Carlyle, 121; 161
Lecky, and Carlyle, 130
Lessing, *Tracts*, 40
Lewes, G. H., and Comte, 187, 188, 189-190, 246; and G. Eliot, 207, 228, 246; his essays in the *Westminster*, 246; and M. Arnold, 282
Lewis, Miss (G. Eliot's school-teacher), 208, 217
Locke, Coleridge's 'victory' over, 13-14, 15, 27, 32
Lowe, R., and M. Arnold, 256
Lowes, J. L., on Coleridge, 26
Loyola, Newman on, 75
Luther, Newman on, 75; and W. G. Ward, 99; compared with Carlyle, 125
Lyell, Sir C., 38

Macaulay, and Mill, 154 *n*., 157; and M. Arnold, 251
Mackay, R. W., 205; G. Eliot's review of his *Progress of the Intellect*, 228-30
Mahomet, 130
Maine, Sir H., Mill's reading of, 176
Maistre, J. de, and Comte, 195
Malthus, and Mill, 158-62

Martineau, Harriet, translation of Comte, 191-3; and G. Eliot, 228
Martineau, James, and Coleridge, 3, 103; on Carlyle, 103, 130
Marx, and Carlyle, 126; and Mill, 149, 156; and Comte, 187, 190; on Feuerbach, 231, 235-6
Maurice, F. D., on Coleridge, 3-4, 31, 108; Coleridge's influence on, 49; in succession from Hooker to Temple, 54; and the Oxford Tracts, 85; and J. Martineau, 103; on Carlyle, 105-6; influence on Mill, 146, 149; and G. Eliot, 239
Methodism, and the Oxford Movement, 74, 77; G. Eliot on, 242
Michelangelo, and M. Arnold, 253
Mill, James, 2; educates his son, 143; 'geometric' method, 154 and *n*.; and religion, 167-77; his Manichaeism, 183
Mill, John Stuart, 141-86; on Coleridge and Bentham, 1-2, 49-50, 135, 141, 205; and Coleridge, 1-2, 32, 49-50, 108, 135, 141, 146, 149, 205; and Bentham, 1-2, 49-50, 132, 135, 136, 141, 144, 145-6, 154, 170, 173, 177, 205; learns from Carlyle, 141, 157; Carlyle on, 141, 142-143, 151; compared with Carlyle, 169; and Carlyle's *entsagen*, 171; and Comte, 141, 146, 149-50, 154, 155, 156, 157, 187, 190, 191, 192, 195; R. H. Hutton on, 142; and Hartley, 144, 145; and Ricardo, 144; influence of Maurice on, 146; influence of Wordsworth on, 148-149; and G. Eliot, 205; and M. Arnold, 278
Milton, and Coleridge, 11; Coleridge's comparison of, with Cowley, 12; *Nativity* Ode, 17; Coleridge's comparison of, with Shakespeare, 21; example of 'Imagination' from, 22; place in Coleridge's view of poetic history, 23, 24, 27; Miltonics and Carlylese, 104
'Mirabeau', *see* Holbach
Mirabeau, and Carlyle, 130
Moore, Thomas, Carlyle on, 109
More, Hannah, on poverty, 133; and G. Eliot, 208, 217, 246
Morley, John, as disciple of Mill, 176; and Comte, 188; and M. Arnold, 282
Morrison, Dr, and M. Arnold, 259
Myers, F. W. H., on G. Eliot, 204, 238

Napoleon, 130
Newman, Francis, and G. Eliot, 228
Newman, J. H., 73-101; and Coleridge, 2-3, 61, 75, 90-1, 92, 96, 108; on Scott, 2, 61, 75; on Southey, 3, 75; on Wordsworth, 3, 61, 75; and T. Arnold, 60-3,

INDEX

72, 84-5, 86, 96, 97, 100; his Essay, *State of Religious Parties*, 62, 75; M. Arnold on, 73; and M. Arnold, 73, 89, 254, 257, 260; J. A. Froude on, 84, 102; and Carlyle, 102, 103, 108; and J. Martineau, 103
Newton, 'inspired guess', 37
Niebuhr, Barthold Georg, and T. Arnold, 65

Origen, quoted by Strauss, 223
Otway, quoted by Coleridge, 13
Owen, Prof., and G. Eliot, 228

Paley, 37; *Evidences*, 135
Palmerston, Lord, and M. Arnold, 263
Pantisocracy, 6-7, 44
Pascal, on Nature's God, 92, 119
Pater, Walter, and M. Arnold, 254
Paulus, 'a Christian Euhemerus' (Strauss), 224
Peacock, T. L., his Mr Foster compared with Bowring, 137
Pheidias, and M. Arnold, 253
Philo, and Strauss, 222
Plato, 6, 30; and Strauss, 222
Polybius, and Strauss, 222
Ponsonby, Mrs, G. Eliot's letters to, 240
Poole, Thomas, 6, 14
Priestley, Joseph, and Coleridge, 4, 5, 44, 209
Pusey, 39

Radcliffe, Mrs, 'a transforming eye', 24
Reimarus, 40; mentioned by Strauss, 223
Renan, *Vie de Jésus*, and G. Eliot, 239; and M. Arnold, 258
Ricardo, David, 2; and Mill, 144, 158
Richards, I. A., on Coleridge, 16-17
Robert Elsmere (Mrs Humphry Ward), 207-208, 227, 280
Rousseau, 130, 161; Mill on the 'paradoxes' of, 166; Mill on *naturam sequi*, 177
Rose, Hugh, on R. H. Froude, 86
Ruskin, and M. Arnold, 254
'Rutherford, Mark', on Carlyle, 103; on Wordsworth, 118

Saint-Simon, and Mill, 149, 150
Savonarola, G. Eliot on, 243-4
Schelling, and Strauss, 220, 224
Scott, Sir W., Newman on, 2, 61, 75
Semler, and Strauss, 224
Shakespeare, 11; quoted by Coleridge, *King Lear*, 13; *Venus and Adonis*, 16-17, 18; *Merchant of Venice* quoted, 18; Coleridge's comparison of, with Milton, 20-21, 27, 130, 259

Shelley, 32
Sidney, Sir Philip, quoted, 15
Sidgwick, Henry, on Bentham, 132, 133, 140; and G. Eliot, 239; and M. Arnold, 282
Smith, John, and M. Arnold, 267
Socrates, Mill on, 166, 171, 172, 182
Somerville, Mrs and G. Eliot, 209
Southey, R., and Coleridge, 5-6, 7; Newman on, 3, 75; Carlyle on, 109
Spencer, Herbert, and G. Eliot, 228; and M. Arnold, 277, 282
Spinoza, 9, 35
Stanley, A. P., *Life of Arnold* quoted, 53 ff; on the Oxford Movement, 90, 100
Stephen, Leslie, on Mill's *Logic*, 151; on Mill's departure from *laissez-faire*, 162; and M. Arnold, 282
Stevenson, R. L., and religious beliefs, 217
Sterling, John, and Coleridge, 2, 108; on Carlyle, 105, 117; Carlyle's *Life* of, quoted, 105, 110; Carlyle's letter to, 123-124; compares Carlyle with Luther, 124; and Mill, 149
Strachey, Lytton, on T. Arnold, 51-2
Strauss, D., *Life of Jesus*, 218, 220-7; and G. Eliot, 205, 207, 228, 237, 239; and C. Hennell, 218-20, 221-2, 225; and Hegel, 222, 225; and M. Arnold, 258

Taylor, Helen, on Mill's *Three Essays on Religion*, 176
Taylor, Mrs. (Mrs. J. S. Mill), 194
Temple, William, 54
Thelwall, J., 9
Thirlwall, Connop, 39
Tillotson, Archbishop, and M. Arnold, 281

Van Mildert, Bampton Lectures (1814), 39
Vater, and Strauss, 224
Vaux, Clotilde de, and Comte, 194-5, 201
Virgil, 259
Volney, *Ruins of Empires*, 210
Voltaire, Carlyle on, 110-11
Von Hügel, 'superhumanness of religion', 31
Von Humboldt, Mill's motto from (for *Liberty*), 163

Ward, Mrs Humphry, 208
Ward, Wilfrid, on W. G. Ward, 99
Ward, W. G., and T. Arnold, 84, 86, 96, 97, 100; and the Oxford Movement, 96-100; *Ideal of a Christian Church*, 98-9
Washington, George, Mill on, 182
Welsh, Jane (Mrs Carlyle), Carlyle's letters to, 109, 123, 128

Wesley, Charles, quoted (on Faith), 36
Wesley, John, Newman, on 84
Wette, De, and Strauss, 224
Whichcote, Benjamin, compared with T. Arnold, 53; and M. Arnold, 266-7
White, William Hale, *see* 'Rutherford, Mark'
Wilberforce, William, on poverty, 133; and G. Eliot, 208, 217
Wilson, Prof. J. Dover, on M. Arnold, 261
Wolf, Friedrich August, and T. Arnold, 65
Woolston, mentioned by Strauss, 223
Wordsworth, W., 3; *The Borderers*, 8-9; Coleridge's friendship with, 9-10; Coleridge's early response to, 11-12; and Coleridge's *Dejection*, 15; theory of metrical language, 21; Coleridge on his poetic aims, 21-22; examples of Imagination from, 23; political disillusionment, 24-5; 'wedded to the universe,' 25, 27; Coleridge's hopes for his philosophical poem, 30; Newman on, 3, 61, 75; and T. Arnold, 62; quoted on the Lake District, 69; Aldous Huxley on, 69; quoted, 70, 71, 72, 102; Carlyle on, 109; and Carlyle, 116, 121; 'Mark Rutherford' on, 118; effect on Mill, 148-9; Mill on his 'follow Nature', 177; and G. Eliot, 205, 244-5.

Selected titles: revised June 1966

harper ⚜ torchbooks

HUMANITIES AND SOCIAL SCIENCES

American Studies: General

CARL N. DEGLER, Ed.: Pivotal Interpretations of American History TB/1240, TB/1241
A. S. EISENSTADT, Ed.: The Craft of American History: Recent Essays in American Historical Writing Vol. I TB/1255; Vol. II TB/1256
MARCUS LEE HANSEN: The Atlantic Migration: 1607-1860. Edited by Arthur M. Schlesinger TB/1052
MARCUS LEE HANSEN: The Immigrant in American History TB/1120
JOHN HIGHAM, Ed.: The Reconstruction of American History △ TB/1068
ROBERT H. JACKSON: The Supreme Court in the American System of Government TB/1106
JOHN F. KENNEDY: A Nation of Immigrants. △ Illus. TB/1118
RALPH BARTON PERRY: Puritanism and Democracy TB/1138
ARNOLD ROSE: The Negro in America TB/3048

American Studies: Colonial

BERNARD BAILYN, Ed.: The Apologia of Robert Keayne: Self-Portrait of a Puritan Merchant TB/1201
BERNARD BAILYN: The New England Merchants in the Seventeenth Century TB/1149
JOSEPH CHARLES: The Origins of the American Party System TB/1049
LAWRENCE HENRY GIPSON: The Coming of the Revolution: 1763-1775. † Illus. TB/3007
PERRY MILLER: Errand Into the Wilderness TB/1139
PERRY MILLER & T. H. JOHNSON, Eds.: The Puritans: A Sourcebook Vol. I TB/1093; Vol. II TB/1094
EDMUND S. MORGAN, Ed.: The Diary of Michael Wigglesworth, 1653-1657: The Conscience of a Puritan TB/1228
EDMUND S. MORGAN: The Puritan Family TB/1227
RICHARD B. MORRIS: Government and Labor in Early America TB/1244
KENNETH B. MURDOCK: Literature and Theology in Colonial New England TB/99
WALLACE NOTESTEIN: The English People on the Eve of Colonization: 1603-1630. † Illus. TB/3006
LOUIS B. WRIGHT: The Cultural Life of the American Colonies: 1607-1763. † Illus. TB/3005

American Studies: From the Revolution to 1860

JOHN R. ALDEN: The American Revolution: 1775-1783. † Illus. TB/3011
MAX BELOFF, Ed.: The Debate on the American Revolution, 1761-1783: A Sourcebook △ TB/1225

RAY A. BILLINGTON: The Far Western Frontier: 1830-1860. † Illus. TB/3012
EDMUND BURKE: On the American Revolution. ‡ Edited by Elliott Robert Barkan TB/3068
WHITNEY R. CROSS: The Burned-Over District: The Social and Intellectual History of Enthusiastic Religion in Western New York, 1800-1850 TB/1242
GEORGE DANGERFIELD: The Awakening of American Nationalism: 1815-1828. † Illus. TB/3061
CLEMENT EATON: The Growth of Southern Civilization: 1790-1860. † Illus. TB/3040
LOUIS FILLER: The Crusade Against Slavery: 1830-1860. † Illus. TB/3029
FELIX GILBERT: The Beginnings of American Foreign Policy: To the Farewell Address TB/1200
FRANCIS GRIERSON: The Valley of Shadows: The Coming of the Civil War in Lincoln's Midwest: A Contemporary Account TB/1246
JAMES MADISON: The Forging of American Federalism. Edited by Saul K. Padover TB/1226
BERNARD MAYO: Myths and Men: Patrick Henry, George Washington, Thomas Jefferson TB/1108
JOHN C. MILLER: Alexander Hamilton and the Growth of the New Nation TB/3057
RICHARD B. MORRIS, Ed.: The Era of the American Revolution TB/1180
R. B. NYE: The Cultural Life of the New Nation: 1776-1801. † Illus. TB/3026
FRANCIS S. PHILBRICK: The Rise of the West, 1754-1830. † Illus. TB/3067
TIMOTHY L. SMITH: Revivalism and Social Reform: American Protestantism on the Eve of the Civil War TB/1229
A. F. TYLER: Freedom's Ferment TB/1074
GLYNDON G. VAN DEUSEN: The Jacksonian Era: 1828-1848. † Illus. TB/3028
LOUIS B. WRIGHT: Culture on the Moving Frontier TB/1053

American Studies: The Civil War to 1900

THOMAS C. COCHRAN & WILLIAM MILLER: The Age of Enterprise: A Social History of Industrial America TB/1054
W. A. DUNNING: Reconstruction, Political and Economic: 1865-1877 TB/1073
HAROLD U. FAULKNER: Politics, Reform and Expansion: 1890-1900. † Illus. TB/3020
ROBERT GREEN MCCLOSKEY: American Conservatism in the Age of Enterprise: 1865-1910 TB/1137
ARTHUR MANN: Yankee Reformers in the Urban Age: Social Reform in Boston, 1880-1900 TB/1247
CHARLES H. SHINN: Mining Camps: A Study in American Frontier Government. ‡ Ed. by R. W. Paul TB/3062
VERNON LANE WHARTON: The Negro in Mississippi: 1865-1890 TB/1178

† The New American Nation Series, edited by Henry Steele Commager and Richard B. Morris.
‡ American Perspectives series, edited by Bernard Wishy and William E. Leuchtenburg.
* The Rise of Modern Europe series, edited by William L. Langer.
¶ Researches in the Social, Cultural, and Behavioral Sciences, edited by Benjamin Nelson.
§ The Library of Religion and Culture, edited by Benjamin Nelson.
Σ Harper Modern Science Series, edited by James R. Newman.
◦ Not for sale in Canada.
△ Not for sale in the U. K.

1

American Studies: 1900 to the Present

A. RUSSELL BUCHANAN: The United States and World War II. † *Illus.* Vol. II TB/3044; Vol. II TB/3045
FOSTER RHEA DULLES: America's Rise to World Power: 1898-1954. † *Illus.* TB/3021
JOHN D. HICKS: Republican Ascendancy: 1921-1933. † *Illus.* TB/3041
SIDNEY HOOK: Reason, Social Myths, and Democracy TB/1237
WILLIAM E. LEUCHTENBURG: Franklin D. Roosevelt and the New Deal: 1932-1940. † *Illus.* TB/3025
ARTHUR S. LINK: Woodrow Wilson and the Progressive Era: 1910-1917. † *Illus.* TB/3023
GEORGE E. MOWRY: The Era of Theodore Roosevelt and the Birth of Modern America: 1900-1912. † TB/3022
RUSSEL B. NYE: Midwestern Progressive Politics: 1870-1958 TB/1202
JACOB RIIS: The Making of an American. ‡ Edited by Roy Lubove TB/3070
PHILIP SELZNICK: TVA and the Grass Roots: A Study in the Sociology of Formal Organization TB/1230
IDA M. TARBELL: The History of the Standard Oil Company: Briefer Version.‡ Edited by David M. Chalmers TB/3071
GEORGE B. TINDALL, Ed.: A Populist Reader ‡ TB/3069

Anthropology

JACQUES BARZUN: Race: A Study in Superstition. Revised Edition TB/1172
JOSEPH B. CASAGRANDE, Ed.: In the Company of Man: Portraits of Anthropological Informants TB/3047
W. E. LE GROS CLARK: The Antecedents of Man: Intro. to Evolution of the Primates.° △ *Illus.* TB/559
CORA DU BOIS: The People of Alor. *New Preface by the author. Illus.* Vol. I TB/1042; Vol. II TB/1043
DAVID LANDY: Tropical Childhood: Cultural Transmission and Learning in a Puerto Rican Village TB/1235
L. S. B. LEAKEY: Adam's Ancestors: The Evolution of Man and His Culture. △ *Illus.* TB/1019
ROBERT H. LOWIE: Primitive Society. Introduction by Fred Eggan TB/1056
EDWARD BURNETT TYLOR: The Origins of Culture. Part I of "Primitive Culture." § Intro. by Paul Radin TB/33
EDWARD BURNETT TYLOR: Religion in Primitive Culture. Part II of "Primitive Culture." § Intro. by Paul Radin TB/34
W. LLOYD WARNER: A Black Civilization: A Study of an Australian Tribe. ¶ *Illus.* TB/3056

Art and Art History

WALTER LOWRIE: Art in the Early Church. *Revised Edition.* 452 illus. TB/124
EMILE MÂLE: The Gothic Image: Religious Art in France of the Thirteenth Century. § △ 190 illus. TB/44
MILLARD MEISS: Painting in Florence and Siena after the Black Death. 169 illus. TB/1148
ERICH NEUMANN: The Archetypal World of Henry Moore. △ 107 illus. TB/2020
DORA & ERWIN PANOFSKY: Pandora's Box: The Changing Aspects of a Mythical Symbol TB/2021
ERWIN PANOFSKY: Studies in Iconology: Humanistic Themes in the Art of the Renaissance △ TB/1077
ALEXANDRE PIANKOFF: The Shrines of Tut-Ankh-Amon. Edited by N. Rambova. 117 illus. TB/2011
JEAN SEZNEC: The Survival of the Pagan Gods △ TB/2004
OTTO VON SIMSON: The Gothic Cathedral △ TB/2018
HEINRICH ZIMMER: Myths and Symbols in Indian Art and Civilization. 70 illustrations TB/2005

Business, Economics & Economic History

REINHARD BENDIX: Work and Authority in Industry TB/3035
GILBERT BURCK & EDITORS OF FORTUNE: The Computer Age: And Its Potential for Management TB/1179
THOMAS C. COCHRAN: The American Business System: A Historical Perspective, 1900-1955 TB/1080
ROBERT DAHL & CHARLES E. LINDBLOM: Politics, Economics, and Welfare TB/3037
PETER F. DRUCKER: The New Society: The Anatomy of Industrial Order △ TB/1082
EDITORS OF FORTUNE: America in the Sixties: The Economy and the Society TB/1015
ROBERT L. HEILBRONER: The Great Ascent: The Struggle for Economic Development in Our Time TB/3030
FRANK H. KNIGHT: The Economic Organization TB/1214
FRANK H. KNIGHT: Risk, Uncertainty and Profit TB/1215
ABBA P. LERNER: Everybody's Business TB/3051
PAUL MANTOUX: The Industrial Revolution in the Eighteenth Century ° △ TB/1079
HERBERT SIMON: The Shape of Automation: For Men and Management TB/1245
PERRIN STRYKER: The Character of the Executive: Eleven Studies in Managerial Qualities TB/1041

Contemporary Culture

JACQUES BARZUN: The House of Intellect △ TB/1051
CLARK KERR: The Uses of the University TB/1264
JOHN U. NEF: Cultural Foundations of Industrial Civilization △ TB/1024
NATHAN M. PUSEY: The Age of the Scholar: Observations on Education in a Troubled Decade TB/1157
PAUL VALÉRY: The Outlook for Intelligence △ TB/2016

Historiography & Philosophy of History

JACOB BURCKHARDT: On History and Historians. △ Intro. by H. R. Trevor-Roper TB/1216
J. H. HEXTER: Reappraisals in History: New Views on History & Society in Early Modern Europe △ TB/1100
H. STUART HUGHES: History as Art and as Science: Twin Vistas on the Past TB/1207
GEORGE H. NADEL, Ed.: Studies in the Philosophy of History: Essays from History and Theory TB/1208
KARL R. POPPER: The Open Society and Its Enemies △
  Vol. I: The Spell of Plato TB/1101
  Vol. II: The High Tide of Prophecy: Hegel, Marx and the Aftermath TB/1102
KARL R. POPPER: The Poverty of Historicism ° △ TB/1126
G. J. RENIER: History: Its Purpose and Method △ TB/1209
W. H. WALSH: Philosophy of History △ TB/1020

History: General

L. CARRINGTON GOODRICH: A Short History of the Chinese People. △ *Illus.* TB/3015
DAN N. JACOBS & HANS H. BAERWALD: Chinese Communism: Selected Documents TB/3031
BERNARD LEWIS: The Arabs in History △ TB/1029

History: Ancient

A. ANDREWES: The Greek Tyrants △ TB/1103
ADOLF ERMAN, Ed.: The Ancient Egyptians TB/1233
MICHAEL GRANT: Ancient History ° △ TB/1190
SAMUEL NOAH KRAMER: Sumerian Mythology TB/1055
NAPHTALI LEWIS & MEYER REINHOLD, Eds.: Roman Civilization. Sourcebook I: The Republic TB/1231
NAPHTALI LEWIS & MEYER REINHOLD, Eds.: Roman Civilization. Sourcebook II: The Empire TB/1232

History: Medieval

P. BOISSONNADE: Life and Work in Medieval Europe △ TB/1141
HELEN CAM: England before Elizabeth △ TB/1026
NORMAN COHN: The Pursuit of the Millennium △ TB/1037

G. G. COULTON: Medieval Village, Manor, and Monastery
TB/1022
CHRISTOPHER DAWSON, Ed.: Mission to Asia △ TB/315
HEINRICH FICHTENAU: The Carolingian Empire: *The Age of Charlemagne* △ TB/1142
F. L. GANSHOF: Feudalism △ TB/1058
DENO GEANAKOPLOS: Byzantine East and Latin West △
TB/1265
W. O. HASSALL, Ed.: Medieval England: *As Viewed by Contemporaries* △ TB/1205
DENYS HAY: The Medieval Centuries ○ △ TB/1192
J. M. HUSSEY: The Byzantine World TB/1057
FERDINAND LOT: The End of the Ancient World and the Beginnings of the Middle Ages TB/1044
G. MOLLAT: The Popes at Avignon: 1305-1378 △ TB/308
CHARLES PETIT-DUTAILLIS: The Feudal Monarchy in France and England ○ △ TB/1165
HENRI PIRENNE: Early Democracies in the Low Countries TB/1110
STEVEN RUNCIMAN: A History of the Crusades. △
Volume I: *The First Crusade and the Foundation of the Kingdom of Jerusalem. Illus.* TB/1143
Volume II: *The Kingdom of Jerusalem and the Frankish East, 1100-1187. Illus.* TB/1243
FERDINAND SCHEVILL: Siena: *The History of a Medieval Commune.* Intro. by William M. Bowsky TB/1164
HENRY OSBORN TAYLOR: The Classical Heritage of the Middle Ages TB/1117
F. VAN DER MEER: Augustine the Bishop: *Church and Society at the Dawn of the Middle Ages* △ TB/304
J. M. WALLACE-HADRILL: The Barbarian West: *The Early Middle Ages, A.D. 400-1000* △ TB/1061

History: Renaissance & Reformation

JACOB BURCKHARDT: The Civilization of the Renaissance in Italy. △ *Illus.* Vol. I TB/40; Vol. II TB/41
JOHN CALVIN & JACOPO SADOLETO: A Reformation Debate. △ Edited by John C. Olin TB/1239
FEDERICO CHABOD: Machiavelli and the Renaissance △
TB/1193
EDWARD P. CHEYNEY: The Dawn of a New Era, 1250-1453. * *Illus.* TB/3002
G. CONSTANT: The Reformation in England: *The English Schism, Henry VIII, 1509-1547* △ TB/314
WALLACE K. FERGUSON et al.: Facets of the Renaissance
TB/1098
WALLACE K. FERGUSON et al.: The Renaissance: *Six Essays. Illus.* TB/1084
JOHN NEVILLE FIGGIS: The Divine Right of Kings. *Introduction by G. R. Elton* TB/1191
JOHN NEVILLE FIGGIS: Political Thought from Gerson to Grotius: 1414-1625: *Seven Studies* TB/1032
MYRON P. GILMORE: The World of Humanism, 1453-1517.* *Illus.* TB/3003
FRANCESCO GUICCIARDINI: Maxims and Reflections of a Renaissance Statesman (Ricordi) TB/1160
J. H. HEXTER: More's Utopia: *The Biography of an Idea.* New Epilogue by the Author TB/1195
HAJO HOLBORN: Ulrich von Hutten and the German Reformation TB/1238
JOHAN HUIZINGA: Erasmus and the Age of Reformation. △ *Illus.* TB/19
JOEL HURSTFIELD, Ed.: The Reformation Crisis △ TB/1267
ULRICH VON HUTTEN et al.: On the Eve of the Reformation: *"Letters of Obscure Men"* TB/1124
PAUL O. KRISTELLER: Renaissance Thought: *The Classic, Scholastic, and Humanist Strains* TB/1048
PAUL O. KRISTELLER: Renaissance Thought II: *Papers on Humanism and the Arts* TB/1163
NICCOLÒ MACHIAVELLI: History of Florence and of the Affairs of Italy TB/1027
ALFRED VON MARTIN: Sociology of the Renaissance. *Introduction by Wallace K. Ferguson* △ TB/1099
GARRETT MATTINGLY et al.: Renaissance Profiles. △ Edited by J. H. Plumb TB/1162
J. E. NEALE: The Age of Catherine de Medici ○ △ TB/1085
ERWIN PANOFSKY: Studies in Iconology: *Humanistic Themes in the Art of the Renaissance* △ TB/1077
J. H. PARRY: The Establishment of the European Hegemony: 1415-1715 △ TB/1045
J. H. PLUMB: The Italian Renaissance: *A Concise Survey of Its History and Culture* △ TB/1161
A. F. POLLARD: Henry VIII. ○ △ *Introduction by A. G. Dickens* TB/1249
A. F. POLLARD: Wolsey. ○ △ *Introduction by A. G. Dickens* TB/1248
CECIL ROTH: The Jews in the Renaissance. *Illus.* TB/834
A. L. ROWSE: The Expansion of Elizabethan England. ○ △ *Illus.* TB/1220
GORDON RUPP: Luther's Progress to the Diet of Worms ○ △
TB/120
FERDINAND SCHEVILL: The Medici. *Illus.* TB/1010
FERDINAND SCHEVILL: Medieval and Renaissance Florence. *Illus.* Volume I: *Medieval Florence* TB/1090
Volume II: *The Coming of Humanism and the Age of the Medici* TB/1091
G. M. TREVELYAN: England in the Age of Wycliffe, 1368-1520 ○ △ TB/1112
VESPASIANO: Renaissance Princes, Popes, and Prelates: *The Vespasiano Memoirs: Lives of Illustrious Men of the XVth Century* TB/1111

History: Modern European

FREDERICK B. ARTZ: Reaction and Revolution, 1815-1832. * *Illus.* TB/3034
MAX BELOFF: The Age of Absolutism, 1660-1815 △
TB/1062
ROBERT C. BINKLEY: Realism and Nationalism, 1852-1871. * *Illus.* TB/3038
ASA BRIGGS: The Making of Modern England, 1784-1867: *The Age of Improvement* ○ △ TB/1203
CRANE BRINTON: A Decade of Revolution, 1789-1799. * *Illus.* TB/3018
D. W. BROGAN: The Development of Modern France. ○ △
Volume I: *From the Fall of the Empire to the Dreyfus Affair* TB/1184
Volume II: *The Shadow of War, World War I, Between the Two Wars. New Introduction by the Author* TB/1185
J. BRONOWSKI & BRUCE MAZLISH: The Western Intellectual Tradition: *From Leonardo to Hegel* TB/3001
GEOFFREY BRUUN: Europe and the French Imperium, 1799-1814. * *Illus.* TB/3033
ALAN BULLOCK: Hitler, A Study in Tyranny ○ △ TB/1123
E. H. CARR: The Twenty Years' Crisis, 1919-1939 ○ △
TB/1122
GORDON A. CRAIG: From Bismarck to Adenauer: *Aspects of German Statecraft. Revised Edition* TB/1171
WALTER L. DORN: Competition for Empire, 1740-1763. * *Illus.* TB/3032
FRANKLIN L. FORD: Robe and Sword: *The Regrouping of the French Aristocracy after Louis XIV* TB/1217
CARL J. FRIEDRICH: The Age of the Baroque, 1610-1660. * *Illus.* TB/3004
RENÉ FUELOEP-MILLER: The Mind and Face of Bolshevism TB/1188
M. DOROTHY GEORGE: London Life in the Eighteenth Century * TB/1182
LEO GERSHOY: From Despotism to Revolution, 1763-1789. * *Illus.* TB/3017
C. C. GILLISPIE: Genesis and Geology: *The Decades before Darwin* § TB/51
ALBERT GOODWIN: The French Revolution △ TB/1064
ALBERT GUÉRARD: France in the Classical Age: *The Life and Death of an Ideal* △ TB/1183
CARLTON J. H. HAYES: A Generation of Materialism, 1871-1900. * *Illus.* TB/3039
J. H. HEXTER: Reappraisals in History: *New Views on History & Society in Early Modern Europe* △ TB/1100
STANLEY HOFFMANN et al.: In Search of France TB/1219

3

A. R. HUMPHREYS: The Augustan World: *Society and Letters in 18th Century England* ° △ TB/1105
DAN N. JACOBS, Ed.: The New Communist Manifesto & Related Documents. Third edition, revised TB/1078
HANS KOHN: The Mind of Germany △ TB/1204
HANS KOHN, Ed.: The Mind of Modern Russia: *Historical and Political Thought of Russia's Great Age* TB/1065
FRANK E. MANUEL: The Prophets of Paris: *Turgot, Condorcet, Saint-Simon, Fourier, and Comte* TB/1218
KINGSLEY MARTIN: French Liberal Thought in the Eighteenth Century TB/1114
L. B. NAMIER: Personalities and Powers △ TB/1186
L. B. NAMIER: Vanished Supremacies: *Essays on European History, 1812-1918* ° △ TB/1088
JOHN U. NEF: Western Civilization Since the Renaissance: *Peace, War, Industry, and the Arts* TB/1113
FREDERICK L. NUSSBAUM: The Triumph of Science and Reason, 1660-1685. * Illus. TB/3009
JOHN PLAMENATZ: German Marxism and Russian Communism ° △ TB/1189
RAYMOND W. POSTGATE, Ed.: Revolution from 1789 to 1906: *Selected Documents* TB/1063
PENFIELD ROBERTS: The Quest for Security, 1715-1740. * Illus. TB/3016
PRISCILLA ROBERTSON: Revolutions of 1848: *A Social History* TB/1025
LOUIS, DUC DE SAINT-SIMON: Versailles, The Court, and Louis XIV △ TB/1250
A. J. P. TAYLOR: From Napoleon to Lenin: *Historical Essays* ° △ TB/1268
A. J. P. TAYLOR: The Habsburg Monarchy, 1809-1918 ° △ TB/1187
G. M. TREVELYAN: British History in the Nineteenth Century and After: 1782-1919 △ TB/1251
H. R. TREVOR-ROPER: Historical Essays ° △ TB/1269
JOHN B. WOLF: The Emergence of the Great Powers, 1685-1715. * Illus. TB/3010
JOHN B. WOLF: France: 1814-1919: *The Rise of a Liberal-Democratic Society* TB/3019

Intellectual History & History of Ideas

HERSCHEL BAKER: The Image of Man TB/1047
R. R. BOLGAR: The Classical Heritage and Its Beneficiaries △ TB/1125
J. BRONOWSKI & BRUCE MAZLISH: The Western Intellectual Tradition: *From Leonardo to Hegel* △ TB/3001
NORMAN COHN: Pursuit of the Millennium △ TB/1037
C. C. GILLISPIE: Genesis and Geology: *The Decades before Darwin* § TB/51
ARTHUR O. LOVEJOY: The Great Chain of Being: *A Study of the History of an Idea* TB/1009
FRANK E. MANUEL: The Prophets of Paris: *Turgot, Condorcet, Saint-Simon, Fourier, and Comte* TB/1218
RALPH BARTON PERRY: The Thought and Character of William James: *Briefer Version* TB/1156
BRUNO SNELL: The Discovery of the Mind: *The Greek Origins of European Thought* △ TB/1018
PAUL VALÉRY: The Outlook for Intelligence △ TB/2016
PHILIP P. WIENER: Evolution and the Founders of Pragmatism. △ Foreword by John Dewey TB/1212

Literature, Poetry, The Novel & Criticism

JACQUES BARZUN: The House of Intellect △ TB/1051
W. J. BATE: From Classic to Romantic: *Premises of Taste in Eighteenth Century England* TB/1036
JAMES BOSWELL: The Life of Dr. Johnson & The Journal of a Tour to the Hebrides with Samuel Johnson LL.D.: *Selections* ° △ TB/1254
ERNST R. CURTIUS: European Literature and the Latin Middle Ages △ TB/2015
ALFRED HARBAGE: As They Liked It: *A Study of Shakespeare's Moral Artistry* TB/1035

A. R. HUMPHREYS: The Augustan World: *Society in 18th Century England* ° △ TB/1105
ALDOUS HUXLEY: Antic Hay & The Giaconda Smile. ° △ Introduction by Martin Green TB/3503
ALDOUS HUXLEY: Brave New World & Brave New World Revisited. ° △ Introduction by Martin Green TB/3501
HENRY JAMES: The Tragic Muse TB/1017
ARNOLD KETTLE: An Introduction to the English Novel. △
Volume I: *Defoe to George Eliot* TB/1011
Volume II: *Henry James to the Present* TB/1012
RICHMOND LATTIMORE: The Poetry of Greek Tragedy △ TB/1257
J. B. LEISHMAN: The Monarch of Wit: *An Analytical and Comparative Study of the Poetry of John Donne* ° △ TB/1258
J. B. LEISHMAN: Themes and Variations in Shakespeare's Sonnets ° △ TB/1259
SAMUEL PEPYS: The Diary of Samuel Pepys. ° *Edited by O. F. Morshead. Illus. by Ernest Shepard* TB/1007
ST.-JOHN PERSE: Seamarks TB/2002
V. DE S. PINTO: Crisis in English Poetry, 1880-1940 ° △ TB/1260
GEORGE SANTAYANA: Interpretations of Poetry and Religion § TB/9
C. K. STEAD: The New Poetic ° △ TB/1263
HEINRICH STRAUMANN: American Literature in the Twentieth Century. △ *Third Edition, Revised* TB/1168
PAGET TOYNBEE: Dante Alighieri: *His Life and Works. Edited with Intro. by Charles S. Singleton* TB/1206
DOROTHY VAN GHENT: The English Novel TB/1050
E. B. WHITE: One Man's Meat. TB/3505
BASIL WILLEY: Nineteenth Century Studies: *Coleridge to Matthew Arnold* ° △ TB/1261
BASIL WILLEY: More Nineteenth Century Studies: *A Group of Honest Doubters* ° △ TB/1262
RAYMOND WILLIAMS: Culture and Society, 1780-1950 ° △ TB/1252
RAYMOND WILLIAMS: The Long Revolution ° △ TB/1253
MORTON DAUWEN ZABEL, Editor: Literary Opinion in America Vol. I TB/3013; Vol. II TB/3014

Myth, Symbol & Folklore

JOSEPH CAMPBELL, Editor: Pagan and Christian Mysteries. Illus. TB/2013
MIRCEA ELIADE: Cosmos and History: *The Myth of the Eternal Return* § △ TB/2050
MIRCEA ELIADE: Rites and Symbols of Initiation: *The Mysteries of Birth and Rebirth* △ TB/1236
DORA & ERWIN PANOFSKY: Pandora's Box: *The Changing Aspects of a Mythical Symbol.* △ *Revised Edition. Illus.* TB/2021
HELLMUT WILHELM: Change: *Eight Lectures on the I Ching* △ TB/2019

Philosophy

G. E. M. ANSCOMBE: An Introduction to Wittgenstein's Tractatus. *Second edition, Revised* ° △ TB/1210
HENRI BERGSON: Time and Free Will ° △ TB/1021
H. J. BLACKHAM: Six Existentialist Thinkers ° △ TB/1002
CRANE BRINTON: Nietzsche TB/1197
ERNST CASSIRER: The Individual and the Cosmos in Renaissance Philosophy △ TB/1097
FREDERICK COPLESTON: Medieval Philosophy ° △ TB/376
F. M. CORNFORD: Principium Sapientiae: *A Study of the Origins of Greek Philosophical Thought* △ TB/1213
F. M. CORNFORD: From Religion to Philosophy § TB/20
WILFRID DESAN: The Tragic Finale: *An Essay on the Philosophy of Jean-Paul Sartre* TB/1030
A. P. D'ENTRÈVES: Natural Law △ TB/1223
PAUL FRIEDLÄNDER: Plato: *An Introduction* △ TB/2017
W. K. C. GUTHRIE: The Greek Philosophers: *From Thales to Aristotle* ° △ TB/1008

4

F. H. HEINEMANN: Existentialism and the Modern Predicament § TB/28
EDMUND HUSSERL: Phenomenology and the Crisis of Philosophy TB/1170
IMMANUEL KANT: The Doctrine of Virtue, *being Part II of the* Metaphysic of Morals TB/110
IMMANUEL KANT: Groundwork of the Metaphysic of Morals. *Trans. & analyzed by H. J. Paton* TB/1159
IMMANUEL KANT: Lectures on Ethics § △ TB/105
IMMANUEL KANT: Religion Within the Limits of Reason Alone. § *Intro. by T. M. Greene & J. Silber* TB/67
QUENTIN LAUER: Phenomenology TB/1169
GABRIEL MARCEL: Being and Having △ TB/310
GEORGE A. MORGAN: What Nietzsche Means △ TB/1198
MICHAEL POLANYI: Personal Knowledge △ TB/1158
WILLARD VAN ORMAN QUINE: Elementary Logic: *Revised Edition* TB/577
WILLARD VAN ORMAN QUINE: From a Logical Point of View: *Logico-Philosophical Essays* TB/566
BERTRAND RUSSELL et al.: The Philosophy of Bertrand Russell Vol. I TB/1095; Vol. II TB/1096
L. S. STEBBING: A Modern Introduction to Logic △ TB/538
ALFRED NORTH WHITEHEAD: Process and Reality: *An Essay in Cosmology* △ TB/1033
PHILIP P. WIENER: Evolution and the Founders of Pragmatism. *Foreword by John Dewey* TB/1212
WILHELM WINDELBAND: A History of Philosophy
Vol. I: *Greek, Roman, Medieval* TB/38
Vol. II: *Renaissance, Enlightenment, Modern* TB/39
LUDWIG WITTGENSTEIN: The Blue and Brown Books ° TB/1211

Political Science & Government

JEREMY BENTHAM: The Handbook of Political Fallacies. *Introduction by Crane Brinton* TB/1069
KENNETH E. BOULDING: Conflict and Defense TB/3024
CRANE BRINTON: English Political Thought in the Nineteenth Century TB/1071
ROBERT DAHL & CHARLES E. LINDBLOM: Politics, Economics, and Welfare TB/3037
F. L. GANSHOF: Feudalism △ TB/1058
G. P. GOOCH: English Democratic Ideas in Seventeenth Century TB/1006
SIDNEY HOOK: Reason, Social Myths and Democracy △ TB/1237
DAN N. JACOBS, Ed.: The New Communist Manifesto & Related Documents. *Third edition, Revised* TB/1078
DAN N. JACOBS & HANS BAERWALD, Eds.: Chinese Communism: *Selected Documents* TB/3031
KINGSLEY MARTIN: French Liberal Thought in the Eighteenth Century △ TB/1114
ROBERTO MICHELS: First Lectures in Political Sociology. *Edited by Alfred de Grazia* ¶ ° TB/1224
BARRINGTON MOORE, JR.: Political Power and Social Theory: *Seven Studies* ¶ TB/1221
BARRINGTON MOORE, JR.: Soviet Politics—The Dilemma of Power ¶ TB/1222
BARRINGTON MOORE, JR.: Terror and Progress—USSR ¶ TB/1266
JOHN B. MORRALL: Political Thought in Medieval Times △ TB/1076
KARL R. POPPER: The Open Society and Its Enemies △
Vol. I: *The Spell of Plato* TB/1101
Vol. II: *The High Tide of Prophecy: Hegel, Marx, and the Aftermath* TB/1102
JOSEPH A. SCHUMPETER: Capitalism, Socialism and Democracy ¶ TB/3008

Psychology

ALFRED ADLER: The Individual Psychology of Alfred Adler △ TB/1154
HERBERT FINGARETTE: The Self in Transformation ¶ TB/1177
SIGMUND FREUD: On Creativity and the Unconscious § △ TB/45

WILLIAM JAMES: Psychology: *Briefer Course* TB/1034
C. G. JUNG: Psychological Reflections △ TB/2001
C. G. JUNG: Symbols of Transformation △
Vol. I: TB/2009; Vol. II TB/2010
JOHN T. MC NEILL: A History of the Cure of Souls TB/126
KARL MENNINGER: Theory of Psychoanalytic Technique TB/1144
ERICH NEUMANN: Amor and Psyche △ TB/2012
ERICH NEUMANN: The Origins and History of Consciousness △ Vol. I *Illus.* TB/2007; Vol. II TB/2008
JEAN PIAGET, BÄRBEL INHELDER, & ALINA SZEMINSKA: The Child's Conception of Geometry ° △ TB/1146
JOHN H. SCHAAR: Escape from Authority: *The Perspectives of Erich Fromm* TB/1155

Sociology

JACQUES BARZUN: Race: *A Study in Superstition* TB/1172
BERNARD BERELSON, Ed.: The Behavioral Sciences Today TB/1127
ALLISON DAVIS & JOHN DOLLARD: Children of Bondage ¶ TB/3049
ST. CLAIR DRAKE & HORACE R. CAYTON: Black Metropolis
Vol. I TB/1086; Vol. II TB/1087
ALVIN W. GOULDNER: Wildcat Strike ¶ TB/1176
R. M. MACIVER: Social Causation TB/1153
ROBERT K. MERTON, LEONARD BROOM, LEONARD S. COTTRELL, JR., Editors: Sociology Today: *Problems and Prospects* ¶ Vol. I TB/1173; Vol. II TB/1174
TALCOTT PARSONS & EDWARD A. SHILS, Editors: Toward a General Theory of Action TB/1083
JOHN H. ROHRER & MUNRO S. EDMONSON, Eds.: The Eighth Generation Grows Up TB/3050
ARNOLD ROSE: The Negro in America TB/3048
PHILIP SELZNICK: TVA and the Grass Roots TB/1230
GEORG SIMMEL et al.: Essays on Sociology, Philosophy, and Aesthetics. ¶ *Edited by Kurt H. Wolff* TB/1234
HERBERT SIMON: The Shape of Automation △ TB/1245
PITIRIM A. SOROKIN: Contemporary Sociological Theories: *Through the First Quarter of the 20th Century* TB/3046
MAURICE R. STEIN: The Eclipse of Community: *An Interpretation of American Studies* TB/1128
W. LLOYD WARNER & Associates: Democracy in Jonesville: *A Study in Quality and Inequality* TB/1129
W. LLOYD WARNER: Social Class in America: *The Evaluation of Status* TB/1013

RELIGION

Ancient & Classical

J. H. BREASTED: Development of Religion and Thought in Ancient Egypt TB/57
HENRI FRANKFORT: Ancient Egyptian Religion TB/77
G. RACHEL LEVY: Religious Conceptions of the Stone Age and their Influence upon European Thought. △ *Illus. Introduction by Henri Frankfort* TB/106
MARTIN P. NILSSON: Greek Folk Religion TB/78
H. J. ROSE: Religion in Greece and Rome △ TB/55

Biblical Thought & Literature

W. F. ALBRIGHT: The Biblical Period from Abraham to Ezra TB/102
C. K. BARRETT, Ed.: The New Testament Background: *Selected Documents* △ TB/86
C. H. DODD: The Authority of the Bible △ TB/43
M. S. ENSLIN: Christian Beginnings △ TB/5
M. S. ENSLIN: The Literature of the Christian Movement △ TB/6
JOHN GRAY: Archaeology and the Old Testament World. △ *Illus.* TB/127
JAMES MUILENBURG: The Way of Israel △ TB/133
H. H. ROWLEY: The Growth of the Old Testament △ TB/107

D. WINTON THOMAS, Ed.: Documents from Old Testament Times △ TB/85

The Judaic Tradition

LEO BAECK: Judaism and Christianity JP/23
SALO W. BARON: Modern Nationalism and Religion JP/18
MARTIN BUBER: Eclipse of God △ TB/12
MARTIN BUBER: For the Sake of Heaven TB/801
MARTIN BUBER: The Knowledge of Man △ TB/135
MARTIN BUBER: Moses △ TB/837
MARTIN BUBER: The Origin and Meaning of Hasidism △ TB/835
MARTIN BUBER: Pointing the Way △ TB/103
MARTIN BUBER: The Prophetic Faith TB/73
MARTIN BUBER: Two Types of Faith ° △ TB/75
ERNST LUDWIG EHRLICH: A Concise History of Israel: From the Earliest Times to the Destruction of the Temple in A.D. 70 ° △ TB/128
MAURICE S. FRIEDMAN: Martin Buber △ TB/64
GENESIS: The NJV Translation TB/836
SOLOMON GRAYZEL: A History of the Contemporary Jews TB/816
WILL HERBERG: Judaism and Modern Man TB/810
ABRAHAM J. HESCHEL: God in Search of Man JP/7
ISAAC HUSIK: A History of Medieval Jewish Philosophy JP/3
FLAVIUS JOSEPHUS: The Great Roman-Jewish War, with The Life of Josephus TB/74
JACOB R. MARCUS The Jew in the Medieval World TB/814
MAX L. MARGOLIS & ALEXANDER MARX: A History of the Jewish People TB/806
T. J. MEEK: Hebrew Origins TB/69
C. G. MONTEFIORE & H. LOEWE, Eds.: A Rabbinic Anthology JP/32
JAMES PARKES: The Conflict of the Church and the Synagogue: The Jews and Early Christianity JP/21
PHILO, SAADYA GAON, & JEHUDA HALEVI: Three Jewish Philosophers TB/813
HERMAN L. STRACK: Introduction to the Talmud and Midrash TB/808
JOSHUA TRACHTENBERG: The Devil and the Jews: The Medieval Conception of the Jew and its Relation to Modern Anti-Semitism JP/22

Christianity: General

ROLAND H. BAINTON: Christendom: A Short History of Christianity and its Impact on Western Civilization. △ Illus. Vol. I TB/131; Vol. II TB/132

Christianity: Origins & Early Development

AUGUSTINE: An Augustine Synthesis. △ Edited by Erich Przywara TB/335
ADOLF DEISSMANN: Paul: A Study in Social and Religious History TB/15
EDWARD GIBBON: The Triumph of Christendom in the Roman Empire (Chaps. XV-XX of "Decline and Fall," J. B. Bury edition). § △ Illus. TB/46
MAURICE GOGUEL: Jesus and the Origins of Christianity ° △ Vol. I TB/65; Vol. II TB/66
EDGAR J. GOODSPEED: A Life of Jesus TB/1
ROBERT M. GRANT: Gnosticism and Early Christianity △ TB/136
ADOLF HARNACK: The Mission and Expansion of Christianity in the First Three Centuries TB/92
R. K. HARRISON: The Dead Sea Scrolls ° △ TB/84
EDWIN HATCH: The Influence of Greek Ideas on Christianity § △ TB/18
ARTHUR DARBY NOCK: Early Gentile Christianity and Its Hellenistic Background TB/111
ARTHUR DARBY NOCK: St. Paul ° △ TB/104
ORIGEN: On First Principles △ TB/310
JAMES PARKES: The Conflict of the Church and the Synagogue JP/21
SULPICIUS SEVERUS et al.: The Western Fathers: Being the Lives of Martin of Tours, Ambrose, Augustine of Hippo, Honoratus of Arles and Germanus of Auxerre. △ Edited and translated by F. R. Hoare TB/309
JOHANNES WEISS: Earliest Christianity Vol. I TB/53; Vol. II TB/54

Christianity: The Middle Ages and The Reformation

JOHN CALVIN & JACOPO SADOLETO: A Reformation Debate. Edited by John C. Olin TB/1239
G. CONSTANT: The Reformation in England: The English Schism, Henry VIII, 1509-1547 △ TB/314
CHRISTOPHER DAWSON, Ed.: Mission to Asia: Narratives and Letters of the Franciscan Missionaries in Mongolia and China in the 13th and 14th Centuries △ TB/315
JOHANNES ECKHART: Meister Eckhart: A Modern Translation by R. B. Blakney TB/8
DESIDERIUS ERASMUS: Christian Humanism and the Reformation TB/1166
ÉTIENNE GILSON: Dante and Philosophy △ TB/1089
WILLIAM HALLER: The Rise of Puritanism △ TB/22
HAJO HOLBORN: Ulrich von Hutten and the German Reformation TB/1238
JOHAN HUIZINGA: Erasmus and the Age of Reformation. △ Illus. TB/19
A. C. MC GIFFERT: Protestant Thought Before Kant. △ Preface by Jaroslav Pelikan TB/93
JOHN T. MCNEILL: Makers of the Christian Tradition: From Alfred the Great to Schleiermacher △ TB/121
G. MOLLAT: The Popes at Avignon, 1305-1378 △ TB/308
GORDON RUPP: Luther's Progress to the Diet of Worms ° △ TB/120

Christianity: The Protestant Tradition

KARL BARTH: Church Dogmatics: A Selection △ TB/95
KARL BARTH: Dogmatics in Outline △ TB/56
KARL BARTH: The Word of God and the Word of Man TB/13
RUDOLF BULTMANN et al.: Translating Theology into the Modern Age: Historical, Systematic and Pastoral Reflections on Theology and the Church in the Contemporary Situation. Volume 2 of Journal for Theology and the Church, edited by Robert W. Funk in association with Gerhard Ebeling TB/252
WINTHROP HUDSON: The Great Tradition of the American Churches TB/98
SOREN KIERKEGAARD: Edifying Discourses TB/32
SOREN KIERKEGAARD: The Journals of Kierkegaard ° △ TB/52
SOREN KIERKEGAARD: The Point of View for My Work as an Author: A Report to History. § Preface by Benjamin Nelson TB/88
SOREN KIERKEGAARD: The Present Age § △ TB/94
SOREN KIERKEGAARD: Purity of Heart △ TB/4
SOREN KIERKEGAARD: Repetition: An Essay in Experimental Psychology. △ Translated with Introduction & Notes by Walter Lowrie TB/117
SOREN KIERKEGAARD: Works of Love △ TB/122
WALTER LOWRIE: Kierkegaard: A Life Vol. I TB/89; Vol. II TB/90
JOHN MACQUARRIE: The Scope of Demythologizing Bultmann and his Critics △ TB/134
PERRY MILLER & T. H. JOHNSON, Editors: The Puritans: A Sourcebook Vol. I TB/1093; Vol. II TB/1094
JAMES M. ROBINSON et al.: The Bultmann School of Biblical Interpretation: New Directions? Volume 1 of Journal of Theology and the Church, edited by Robert W. Funk in association with Gerhard Ebeling TB/251
F. SCHLEIERMACHER: The Christian Faith. Introduction by Richard R. Niebuhr Vol. I TB/108; Vol. II TB/109

F. SCHLEIERMACHER: On Religion: *Speeches to Its Cultured Despisers*. Intro. by Rudolf Otto TB/36
PAUL TILLICH: Dynamics of Faith △ TB/42
EVELYN UNDERHILL: Worship △ TB/10
G. VAN DER LEEUW: Religion in Essence and Manifestation: *A Study in Phenomenology*. △ *Appendices by Hans H. Penner* Vol. I TB/100; Vol. II TB/101

Christianity: The Roman and Eastern Traditions

DOM CUTHBERT BUTLER: Western Mysticism § ○ △ TB/312
A. ROBERT CAPONIGRI, Ed.: Modern Catholic Thinkers I: *God and Man* △ TB/306
A. ROBERT CAPONIGRI, Ed.: Modern Catholic Thinkers II: *The Church and the Political Order* △ TB/307
THOMAS CORBISHLEY, S. J.: Roman Catholicism TB/112
CHRISTOPHER DAWSON: The Historic Reality of Christian Culture TB/305
G. P. FEDOTOV: The Russian Religious Mind: *Kievan Christianity, the 10th to the 13th Centuries* TB/70
G. P. FEDOTOV, Ed.: A Treasury of Russian Spirituality TB/303
ÉTIENNE GILSON: The Spirit of Thomism TB/313
DAVID KNOWLES: The English Mystical Tradition TB/302
GABRIEL MARCEL: Being and Having TB/310
GABRIEL MARCEL: Homo Viator TB/397
GUSTAVE WEIGEL, S. J.: Catholic Theology in Dialogue TB/301

Oriental Religions: Far Eastern, Near Eastern

TOR ANDRAE: Mohammed § △ TB/62
EDWARD CONZE: Buddhism ○ △ TB/58
EDWARD CONZE et al., Editors: Buddhist Texts Through the Ages △ TB/113
ANANDA COOMARASWAMY: Buddha and the Gospel of Buddhism. △ *Illus.* TB/119
H. G. CREEL: Confucius and the Chinese Way TB/63
FRANKLIN EDGERTON, Trans. & Ed.: The Bhagavad Gita TB/115
SWAMI NIKHILANANDA, Trans. & Ed.: The Upanishads: *A One-Volume Abridgment* △ TB/114
HELLMUT WILHELM: Change: *Eight Lectures on the I Ching* △ TB/2019

Philosophy of Religion

NICOLAS BERDYAEV: The Beginning and the End § △ TB/14
NICOLAS BERDYAEV: Christian Existentialism △ TB/130
NICOLAS BERDYAEV: The Destiny of Man △ TB/61
RUDOLF BULTMANN: History and Eschatology ○ TB/91
RUDOLF BULTMANN AND FIVE CRITICS: Kerygma and Myth: *A Theological Debate* △ TB/80
RUDOLF BULTMANN and KARL KUNDSIN: Form Criticism: *Two Essays on New Testament Research* △ TB/96
MIRCEA ELIADE: The Sacred and the Profane △ TB/81
LUDWIG FEUERBACH: The Essence of Christianity. § *Introduction by Karl Barth. Foreword by H. Richard Niebuhr* TB/11
ÉTIENNE GILSON: The Spirit of Thomism TB/313
ADOLF HARNACK: What is Christianity? § △ *Introduction by Rudolf Bultmann* TB/17
FRIEDRICH HEGEL: On Christianity TB/79
KARL HEIM: Christian Faith and Natural Science △ TB/16
IMMANUEL KANT: Religion Within the Limits of Reason Alone. § *Intro. by T. M. Greene & J. Silber* TB/67
K. E. KIRK: The Vision of God: *The Christian Doctrine of the Summum Bonum* △ TB/137
JOHN MACQUARRIE: An Existentialist Theology: *A Comparison of Heidegger and Bultmann*. ○ △ *Preface by Rudolf Bultmann* TB/125
PAUL RAMSEY, Ed.: Faith and Ethics: *The Theology of H. Richard Niebuhr* TB/129
PIERRE TEILHARD DE CHARDIN: The Divine Milieu ○ △ TB/384
PIERRE TEILHARD DE CHARDIN: The Phenomenon of Man ○ △ TB/383

Religion, Culture & Society

JOSEPH L. BLAU, Ed.: Cornerstones of Religious Freedom in America: *Selected Basic Documents, Court Decisions and Public Statements* TB/118
C. C. GILLISPIE: Genesis and Geology: *The Decades before Darwin* § TB/51
KYLE HASELDEN: The Racial Problem in Christian Perspective TB/116
WALTER KAUFMANN, Ed.: Religion from Tolstoy to Camus. *Enlarged Edition* TB/123
JOHN T. MCNEILL: A History of the Cure of Souls TB/126
KENNETH B. MURDOCK: Literature and Theology in Colonial New England TB/99
H. RICHARD NIEBUHR: Christ and Culture △ TB/3
H. RICHARD NIEBUHR: The Kingdom of God in America TB/49
RALPH BARTON PERRY: Puritanism and Democracy TB/1138
PAUL PFUETZE: Self, Society, Existence: *Human Nature and Dialogue in the Thought of George Herbert Mead and Martin Buber* TB/1059
WALTER RAUSCHENBUSCH: Christianity and the Social Crisis. ‡ *Edited by Robert D. Cross* TB/3059
KURT SAMUELSSON: Religion and Economic Action: *A Critique of Max Weber's* The Protestant Ethic and the Spirit of Capitalism ¶ ○ △ TB/1131
TIMOTHY L. SMITH: Revivalism and Social Reform: *American Protestantism on the Eve of the Civil War* △ TB/1229
ERNST TROELTSCH: The Social Teaching of the Christian Churches ○ △ Vol. I TB/71; Vol. II TB/72

NATURAL SCIENCES AND MATHEMATICS

Biological Sciences

CHARLOTTE AUERBACH: The Science of Genetics Σ △ TB/568
MARSTON BATES: The Natural History of Mosquitoes. *Illus.* TB/578
A. BELLAIRS: Reptiles: *Life History, Evolution, and Structure*. △ *Illus.* TB/520
LUDWIG VON BERTALANFFY: Modern Theories of Development: *An Introduction to Theoretical Biology* TB/554
LUDWIG VON BERTALANFFY: Problems of Life △ TB/521
HAROLD F. BLUM: Time's Arrow and Evolution TB/555
JOHN TYLER BONNER: The Ideas of Biology Σ △ TB/570
A. J. CAIN: Animal Species and their Evolution △ TB/519
WALTER B. CANNON: Bodily Changes in Pain, Hunger, Fear and Rage. *Illus.* TB/562
W. E. LE GROS CLARK: The Antecedents of Man ○ △ TB/559
W. H. DOWDESWELL: Animal Ecology. △ *Illus.* TB/543
W. H. DOWDESWELL: The Mechanism of Evolution △ TB/527
R. W. GERARD: Unresting Cells. *Illus.* TB/541
DAVID LACK: Darwin's Finches. △ *Illus.* TB/544
ADOLF PORTMANN: Animals as Social Beings ○ △ TB/572
O. W. RICHARDS: The Social Insects. △ *Illus.* TB/542
P. M. SHEPPARD: Natural Selection and Heredity △ TB/528
EDMUND W. SINNOTT: Cell and Psyche: *The Biology of Purpose* TB/546
C. H. WADDINGTON: How Animals Develop. △ *Illus.* TB/553
C. H. WADDINGTON: The Nature of Life △ TB/580

Chemistry

J. R. PARTINGTON: A Short History of Chemistry △ TB/522

Communication Theory

J. R. PIERCE: Symbols, Signals and Noise: *The Nature and Process of Communication* △ TB/574

7

Geography

R. E. COKER: This Great and Wide Sea: *An Introduction to Oceanography and Marine Biology*. Illus. TB/551
F. K. HARE: The Restless Atmosphere △ TB/560

History of Science

MARIE BOAS: The Scientific Renaissance, 1450-1630 ○ △ TB/583
W. DAMPIER, Ed.: Readings in the Literature of Science. Illus. TB/512
A. HUNTER DUPREE: Science in the Federal Government: *A History of Policies and Activities to 1940* △ TB/573
ALEXANDRE KOYRÉ: From the Closed World to the Infinite Universe: *Copernicus, Kepler, Galileo, Newton, etc.* △ TB/31
A. G. VAN MELSEN: From Atomos to Atom: *A History of the Concept Atom* TB/517
O. NEUGEBAUER: The Exact Sciences in Antiquity TB/552
HANS THIRRING: Energy for Man △ TB/556
LANCELOT LAW WHYTE: Essay on Atomism △ TB/565

Mathematics

E. W. BETH: The Foundations of Mathematics △ TB/581
H. DAVENPORT: The Higher Arithmetic △ TB/526
H. G. FORDER: Geometry: *An Introduction* △ TB/548
S. KÖRNER: The Philosophy of Mathematics △ TB/547
D. E. LITTLEWOOD: Skeleton Key of Mathematics: *A Simple Account of Complex Algebraic Problems* △ TB/525
GEORGE E. OWEN: Fundamentals of Scientific Mathematics TB/569
WILLARD VAN ORMAN QUINE: Mathematical Logic TB/558
O. G. SUTTON: Mathematics in Action. ○ △ Illus. TB/518
FREDERICK WAISMANN: Introduction to Mathematical Thinking. *Foreword by Karl Menger* TB/511

Philosophy of Science

R. B. BRAITHWAITE: Scientific Explanation TB/515
J. BRONOWSKI: Science and Human Values. *Revised and Enlarged Edition* △ TB/505
ALBERT EINSTEIN et al.: Albert Einstein: Philosopher-Scientist. *Edited by Paul A. Schilpp* Vol. I TB/502 Vol. II TB/503
WERNER HEISENBERG: Physics and Philosophy: *The Revolution in Modern Science* △ TB/549
JOHN MAYNARD KEYNES: A Treatise on Probability. ○ △ *Introduction by N. R. Hanson* TB/557
KARL R. POPPER: The Logic of Scientific Discovery △ TB/576
STEPHEN TOULMIN: Foresight and Understanding: *An Enquiry into the Aims of Science.* △ *Foreword by Jacques Barzun* TB/564
STEPHEN TOULMIN: The Philosophy of Science △ TB/513
G. J. WHITROW: The Natural Philosophy of Time ○ △ TB/563

Physics and Cosmology

JOHN E. ALLEN: Aerodynamics: *A Space Age Survey* △ TB/582
STEPHEN TOULMIN & JUNE GOODFIELD: The Fabric of the Heavens: *The Development of Astronomy and Dynamics.* △ Illus. TB/579
DAVID BOHM: Causality and Chance in Modern Physics. △ *Foreword by Louis de Broglie* TB/536
P. W. BRIDGMAN: The Nature of Thermodynamics TB/537
P. W. BRIDGMAN: A Sophisticate's Primer of Relativity △ TB/575
A. C. CROMBIE, Ed.: Turning Point in Physics TB/535
C. V. DURELL: Readable Relativity △ TB/530
ARTHUR EDDINGTON: Space, Time and Gravitation: *An Outline of the General Relativity Theory* TB/510
GEORGE GAMOW: Biography of Physics Σ △ TB/567
MAX JAMMER: Concepts of Force: *A Study in the Foundation of Dynamics* TB/550
MAX JAMMER: Concepts of Mass in Classical and Modern Physics TB/571
MAX JAMMER: Concepts of Space: *The History of Theories of Space in Physics. Foreword by Albert Einstein* TB/533
G. J. WHITROW: The Structure and Evolution of the Universe: *An Introduction to Cosmology.* △ Illus. TB/504

Code to Torchbook Libraries:
TB/1+   : The Cloister Library
TB/301+   : The Cathedral Library
TB/501+   : The Science Library
TB/801+   : The Temple Library
TB/1001+   : The Academy Library
TB/2001+   : The Bollingen Library
TB/3001+   : The University Library
JP/1+   : The Jewish Publication Society Series